State Sovereignty
and International Criminal Law

Morten Bergsmo and LING Yan (editors)

2012
Torkel Opsahl Academic EPublisher
Beijing

ISBN 978-82-93081-35-7

*Dedicated to the memory of Professor LI Haopei
and his service to international law*

PUBLICATION SERIES PREFACE

The Torkel Opsahl Academic EPublisher is pleased to release *State Sovereignty and International Criminal Law* in its *Publication Series*. The book deals with a topic which champions of the international criminal justice movement should strive to appreciate also from the perspective of States that have reservations about the extensive reach of contemporary war crimes justice. The chapters were originally prepared in the context of the *FICHL LI Haopei Lecture Series*. The anthology is published in separate Chinese and English versions. R. Frazier Lowell, NIE Jingjing, SONG Tianying and XUE Ru have assisted with translations.

FAN Yuwen has provided invaluable and noble assistance with the Chinese version. We also thank Dr. YI Ping, ZHANG Xin and ZHANG Yueyao for their assistance.

Morten Bergsmo
Editor-in-Chief

Kiki A. Japutra
Executive Editor

FOREWORD BY CHRISTIAN TOMUSCHAT

This anthology is important for several reasons. First, it brings together a diversity of quality contributions on difficult current topics such as the reach of universal criminal jurisdiction for serious international crimes, immunity of State officials in respect of such crimes, and the consequences of the criminalisation of aggression in the context of the Rome Statute of the International Criminal Court. These are three clusters of controversy subject to intense discussions in international courts, between governments, and among academics. The present book contributes to those discussions.

Secondly, the theme of the anthology is *State Sovereignty and International Criminal Law*. This formulation speaks less to those who are already persuaded of the value of international criminal justice, than to those States and actors who have reservations about how fast and far it has developed. By engaging the laden concept of 'state sovereignty', the book reaches out to everyone interested in international criminal law, inviting an inclusive and responsible dialogue on the need to balance the development of international criminal law with legitimate state interests. The editors suggest that time has come to "consolidate the significant gains in the development of international criminal law since 1993" rather "than further development at the risk of over-extension". Coming from two Chinese and European professors in international criminal law – both of whom have been involved in the field since 1993 – this suggestion calls for further reflection. Indeed, the time has come to take stock and reassess what has been achieved twenty years after the establishment of the International Criminal Tribunal for the former Yugoslavia and ten years after the coming into force of the Rome Statute of the International Criminal Court. The widespread feeling of satisfaction with the institutionalisation of international criminal justice should not blind our eyes for the necessity of carefully pondering the strengths and the shortcomings of this new wing of the constitution of the international community.

The chapters of this book were all prepared in the context of the LI Haopei Lecture Series of the Forum for International Criminal and Humanitarian Law. This Series seeks to foster dialogue among international lawyers in China, Europe and elsewhere. The quality and topicality of this anthology suggests that the Series is succeeding. Its great merit is to provide Chinese scholars with a voice that will be heard everywhere in the legal world. Unfortunately, for many decades, China was *de facto* excluded from debates about topics of paramount importance for humankind although, as the largest nation on the globe, its views and arguments are indispensable when universal standards of conduct are being elaborated. It may be hoped that contacts as those established by the Forum within the framework of its Lecture Series will continue and expand their reach, facilitating dialogue and co-operation between international lawyers in China and Europe as well as more widely.

Christian Tomuschat
Emeritus Professor, Humboldt University
Former Member, International Law Commission

TABLE OF CONTENTS

1

On State Sovereignty and Individual Criminal Responsibility for Core International Crimes in International Law

Morten Bergsmo[*] and LING Yan[**]

In his 2011 study *On China*, Dr. Henry A. Kissinger describes how – in the wake of the end of the Soviet Union – a "new political dispensation in the West" emerged from 1990 onwards, whereby a "new concept insisted that the world was entering a 'post-sovereign' era"[1], characterised, it was thought at the time, by the rule of some aspects of international law over traditional State sovereignty. He witnessed how a "mood of triumphalism" began to descend on Washington in 1990–1991,[2] in response to the political changes taking place in the former Soviet Union and Eastern Europe. It was in that climate that civil society and other actors called for the establishment of the International Criminal Tribunal for the former

---

[*] **Morten Bergsmo** is Visiting Professor, Peking University Law School; Visiting Fellow, Stanford University; Researcher, University of Oslo; and ICC Consultant and Co-ordinator of the ICC Legal Tools Project. He was formerly Visiting Professor, Georgetown University Law Center (2010–2012); Fernand Braudel Senior Fellow, European University Institute (2011 Spring); Visiting Scholar, U.C. Berkeley (2010 Spring); Senior Researcher, PRIO (2006–2009); Special Adviser to the Office of the Director of Public Prosecution of Norway (2007–2008); Senior Legal Adviser and Chief of the Legal Advisory Section, ICC Office of the Prosecutor (2002–2005); Co-ordinator of the establishment of the ICC Office of the Prosecutor (2002–2003); Legal Adviser, ICTY (1994–2002); and Legal Adviser, U.N. Commission of Experts for the former Yugoslavia established pursuant to Security Council resolution 780 (1992) (1993–1994). He represented the ICTY to the U.N. negotiation process to establish the ICC (1996–2002).

[**] **LING Yan** is Professor at the Faculty of International Law at China University of Political Science and Law (2004–), Director of its Research Center for International Criminal Law and Humanitarian Law (www.rcicl.org/english/index.asp), and Deputy Director of its Institute of Air and Space Law. She has worked as a legal officer for the ICTR (1998–2004). She is Co-Director of the *FICHL LI Haopei Lecture Series*.

[1] Henry Kissinger, *On China*, Allen Lane, London, 2011, pp. 454–455.

[2] *Ibid.*, p. 436.

Yugoslavia ('ICTY') to adjudicate serious violations of international humanitarian law in the former Yugoslavia, the one European State where political tension and violence descended into armed conflicts in the early 1990s. Enveloped in its prevailing rhetoric at the time, the establishment of the Tribunal was agreed by consensus in the United Nations Security Council in May 1993, with lukewarm support from some members of the Council, including France and the United Kingdom, but to the general acclaim of human rights civil society and international lawyers worldwide.

The renaissance of contemporary international criminal justice cannot be extricated from this historical context, partially characterised as it was by "post-sovereign" rhetoric and aspiration. Although United Nations Security Council Resolution 827 (1993)[3] establishing the ICTY was adopted 15-0, a variety of interests must have motivated States when they constructed the legal bases of the ICTY and, the following year, the Rwanda Tribunal ('ICTR'). For most European States, supporting the establishment of the Tribunals was almost a matter of equal treatment under the Nuremberg legacy: Just as Germany after World War II had to live with the International Military Tribunal at Nuremberg, so the republics of the former Yugoslavia had to live with the ICTY. Others may have gone along out of mere exasperation at the inefficiency of traditional means to prevent and respond to atrocities: We might as well try an international tribunal and see if it will work better than the measures of the past. Others again accepted the establishment of the ICTY only when promised that the work to set up a permanent international criminal court would be accelerated, in part as a response to the argument of the late Slobodan Milošević that the ICTY represented selective justice, targeted against the Serbs.[4] Moreover, an analysis of the explanations of vote after Resolution 827 (1993) was adopted shows that several Security Council members actually had significant reservations although they voted in favour, suggesting that intense diplomacy had preceded the vote.

Regardless of the diversity of interests motivating capitals at the time of the vote, this form of international judicial intervention by resort

---

[3] For a persistent URL of the text, see http://www.legal-tools.org/doc/0bff83/.

[4] Mr. Thorvald Stoltenberg (then Co-Chairman of the Steering Committee of the International Conference for the former Yugoslavia and Special Representative of the U.N. Secretary-General for the former Yugoslavia) has recounted to the author Morten Bergsmo that this question was raised in capitals at the time.

to Security Council action under Chapter VII of the United Nations Charter would have been perceived differently in different States. In a trium-
phant Washington, many may have perceived the ICTY and ICTR as affirmations of "those principles which inevitably affect the way Americans
view and react to events in other countries", reflecting a "simple faith in
the enduring value of those principles and their universal applicability".[5]
Conveniently, the party to the ex-Yugoslav conflicts suspected of having
committed most violations was an ally of Russia, the former and at that
time introverted enemy of the United States. It was meant to be a relatively inexpensive 'post-sovereign' intervention, in a situation where the
Security Council and its permanent members could control both the overall scope and duration of the Tribunal's work.

For many Europeans, on the other hand, the Security Council's judicial intervention confirmed the binding nature of the Nuremberg Principles on which their post-World War II order had been constructed. It was
an affirmation that binding international law is indeed the basis of restora-
tion and maintenance of international peace and security. It was a welcome reiteration of the modern European article of faith that only by con-
straining the nation State through a thick web of international law can the
unprecedented evil generated by European States through two world wars
be prevented from recurring. The Tribunals – and later the International
Criminal Court ('ICC') – reflected the secular salvation that European
States embraced following the end of World War II, as a protection
against their inherent capacity for wrongdoing.

For many Africans the establishment of the ICTR showed that the
United Nations was willing to respond judicially in equal measure to
mass-atrocity against African civilians as to European victimisation in the
former Yugoslavia. Many more persons had been killed in Rwanda in
1994 than in the immediately preceding armed conflicts in the former
Yugoslavia. The ICTR became a positive measure of equal treatment after
the earlier establishment of the ICTY.

The establishment of the Rwanda and ex-Yugoslavia Tribunals
would have been perceived in quite a different light in some capitals outside the African and Western groups of States. For example, in the largest
nation, China, the exercise of foreign jurisdiction over her territory is al-

---

[5]   Former U.S. President George H.W. Bush, as quoted by Henry A. Kissinger, 2011, p.
       417, *supra* note 1.

most universally associated with the catastrophic outcome of the 1839 Opium War and more than one hundred years of intervention and instability. In the words of Dr. Kissinger, "the traumatic event of China's history was the collapse of central authority in China in the nineteenth century, which tempted the outside world into invasion, quasi-colonialism, or colonial competition and produced genocidal levels of casualties in civil wars, as in the Taiping Rebellion".[6] It would lack historical awareness to expect Chinese to welcome imposed external criminal jurisdiction as compatible with the national interest.

Importantly, Chinese and European citizens and officials may therefore have negative and positive biases respectively towards contemporary international judicial intervention for equally valid and tragic historical reasons. 'Post-sovereignty' – to borrow from Dr. Kissinger – may mean peace and order to some, and war and suffering to others. It is not easy for those engaged in either paradigm to always appreciate the differences of approach and their background. Understanding the other side on our own terms only, may well lead to misunderstanding and unnecessary disagreement.

This anthology seeks to foster a better mutual understanding among Chinese, European and other international lawyers of the relationship between State sovereignty and international criminal law. Not only do the two co-exist, but they cannot exist without each other. Criminal justice presupposes sovereign States. Punishment is an evil imposed by the community through the State to prevent another evil – the crime – thereby seeking to protect the community. This requires the existence of a State, that it has a criminal law and criminal justice institutions, and that the State acts through these institutions in the form of investigation, prosecution, adjudication and administration of sentence. International criminal justice depends equally on States, to establish and accept the jurisdiction in question, fund the institution, give it access to information required to build criminal cases, to arrest and transfer suspects, and to serve sentences.

State sovereignty and international criminal justice are in other words two faces of one coin. But they are minted to speak a different language, to different constituencies, and this can lead to conceptual tension. The chapters of this book illustrate this tension in learned and real ways.

---

[6]   *Ibid.*, p. 423.

The book emphasises three main areas of tension: (1) It considers in some detail the immunity of State officials incriminated by evidence of atrocities from the exercise of foreign or international criminal jurisdiction. To which extent can immunity be invoked to shield State officials from criminal responsibility for suspected core international crimes? (2) With the closing down of the *ad hoc* international criminal tribunals as they complete their work, attention is unavoidably shifting to the exercise of national jurisdiction over core international crimes, including by States not directly affected by the said crimes. The scope of so-called universal jurisdiction for such crimes remains relevant to perceptions of State sovereignty. (3) Could the amendments to the Statute of the ICC at its 2010 Review Conference with regard to the crime of aggression – preparing the ground for its future investigation, prosecution and adjudication by the ICC – exacerbate tensions between the interests of State sovereignty and accountability?

The book succeeds in bringing together a diversity of qualified perspectives on these issues, from government lawyers, judges in international jurisdictions, law professors of different backgrounds, and from other non-State actors.

In Chapter 3 below – entitled *Brief Analysis of a Few Controversial Issues in Contemporary International Criminal Law* – Dr. ZHOU Lulu considers how international criminal law has entered a new stage of development with the establishment of the ICC. Against the expanding case law of the international criminal jurisdictions during the past ten years and the changing international situation, certain important theories of international criminal law are being re-evaluated. The chapter discusses each of the three above-mentioned controversial issues in contemporary international criminal law: the crime of aggression, universal jurisdiction, and criminal immunity for State officials in foreign countries. After careful analysis, Dr. ZHOU concludes that (1) the amendments on the crime of aggression adopted by the 2010 ICC Review Conference could challenge international security and stability; (2) absolute universal jurisdiction is only applicable to the crime of piracy, and it has no solid legal basis and is harmful to international relations if applied arbitrarily; and (3) the immunity of State officials in foreign states is different from that before international criminal courts. Under current international law, she concludes, State officials still enjoy criminal immunity in foreign States.

In Chapter 4 – *Has Non-Immunity for Heads of State Become a Rule of Customary International Law?* – Judge LIU Daqun discusses sovereign immunity for heads of State under customary international law. He explains how sovereign immunity is a well-established rule of international law, and argues that with significant doubts over the extent of State practice and *opinio juris* in this regard, it cannot yet be said that non-immunity for heads of State has become a rule under customary international law. Such immunity is complex, involving issues linked to international criminal tribunals and domestic courts, the contracting parties to the ICC Statute and non-States Parties, the nature of the alleged crimes, international judicial co-operation, and the role of the Security Council of the United Nations. He argues that a referral from the Security Council is the most effective way for the ICC to have jurisdiction over non-States Parties, since its resolution adopted pursuant to Chapter VII could remove the immunity of the head of a non-contracting State to the ICC Statute. It depends on its political will whether the Security Council could or would like to adopt a resolution requesting all States to co-operate with the ICC to arrest and transfer fugitives or removing the immunity of the head of State.

In Chapter 5 – *Immunity for State Officials from Foreign Jurisdiction for International Crimes* – Professor JIA Bingbing explains how immunity for State officials is part of State immunity, and that there is disagreement in practice and theory over the granting of State immunity in cases of international crimes. He shows how current practice still places State immunity on a higher level to other rules of international law that found national jurisdiction, as opposed to international jurisdiction, and ventures to explain how this may be due to the unchanged foundation of the international order based in the United Nations Charter. He writes that any denial of State immunity of foreign officials by a national court, without a basis in international law, "will challenge the fundamental principles of that order, and, on its own, will not likely generate new rules of customary law".

In Chapter 6 – *International Criminal Court: A Judicial Guarantee for International Peace and Security?* – GUO Yang discusses the development of a legal framework for the crime of aggression in the context of the ICC Statute. After more than sixty years of efforts since the end of World War II, the international community adopted a definition of the crime of aggression and the conditions under which the ICC could exercise its jurisdiction over the crime. He describes how these amendments of the ICC Statute are acclaimed by some scholars and States as a milestone for the development of international criminal law. He argues that this may serve as warning shots for aggressive States and "could contribute to strengthening international peace and security". However, he explains, the amendments are also criticised by some as insufficient in that they do not satisfy the principle of specialty, so they cannot serve the purpose of prevention and punishment of the crime. He argues that the conditions provided by the amendments pose further challenges to the current international peace and security regime. By analysing the adopted definition and conditions for the exercise of jurisdiction, he explores whether the definition actually covers only traditional wars between States, which, he says, could be viewed as a cautious reinforcement of the current regime of international peace and security within the United Nations system. He concludes that granting the ICC the capacity to legally review the use of force by States will not make the world less safe than it is today.

Judge Erkki Kourula lucidly opens Chapter 7 – *Universal Jurisdiction for Core International Crimes* – by suggesting that "[u]niversal jurisdiction is a valuable tool in the fight against impunity", while acknowledging that "there still exists a divergence of views on its purpose, definition, usefulness and indeed its exercise in practice". He proceeds to discuss some of the challenges that have emerged in recent years as far as the application of universal jurisdiction is concerned in the prosecution of core international crimes, from the perspective of the differing approaches taken in national jurisdictions and in the European Union and the African Union more widely, the differing political perspectives, to the role of international courts and tribunals in the overall fight against impunity for such crimes. He addresses issues such as the lack of a uniform position on universal jurisdiction between States in general, the question of converging jurisdictions and subsidiarity, immunities of State officials, and the overall feasibility of prosecutions based on universal jurisdiction. He concludes by observing that further work to ensure the effective implementation of the principle of universal jurisdiction for core international crimes "will be welcome", given that its application in practice remains controversial. At present, he writes, "thanks to the universality principle together with the International Criminal Court and other institutions of international criminal justice, the international community will continue fighting impunity in a genuine spirit of humanity".

In Chapter 8 – *The Connotation of Universal Jurisdiction and its Application in the Criminal Law of China* – Professor MA Chengyuan gives a detailed exposé on the status of universal jurisdiction in the Chinese legal system. He explains how universal jurisdiction, as the complement of territorial and nationality jurisdiction, usually refers to the criminal jurisdiction which a State exercises over a crime committed abroad by a foreigner. Like the previous author, he acknowledges that, though universal jurisdiction is well-established in both theory and practice, there have been controversies among scholars of different States as to its connotation and categories. He opines that universal jurisdiction is the criminal jurisdiction that a State can exercise over a crime committed abroad by a foreigner not against this State or its citizens in accordance with international law or domestic criminal law. Importantly, he divides universal jurisdiction into three categories based on different legal sources: (1) universal jurisdiction based on customary international law, (2) universal jurisdiction based on international treaty, and (3) universal jurisdiction based on domestic law. Each has its characteristics. The universal jurisdiction stipulated by Article 9 of the Criminal Law of China is based on international treaty. As such, he argues, it can neither apply to crimes in customary international law, nor to crimes committed abroad by foreigners not provided in international criminal conventions. Insofar as China has not transformed most of the crimes stipulated by these conventions into its Criminal Law, he claims that she has violated the principle of *pacta sunt servanda* and the obligations arising from these conventions. Furthermore, he concludes, as there are no such crimes in the Criminal law of China, to prosecute these crimes in accordance with international conventions will violate the principles of *nullum crimen sine lege* and *nulla poena sine lege*, as well as the principle of prohibition of analogy.

In Chapter 9 – *Universal Jurisdiction Before the United Nations General Assembly: Seeking Common Understanding under International Law* – Professor ZHU Lijiang gives a detailed account of the discussions in the United Nations General Assembly on universal jurisdiction in recent years. The process was largely advanced by the Group of African States. By the end of 2011, 74 States had made statements on universal jurisdiction before the Sixth Committee of the General Assembly, and 61 States had submitted their reports on relevant legislative and judicial practice to the United Nations Secretary-General. Professor ZHU explains how these statements and reports reflect *opinio juris* and State practice in the formation of rules under customary international law in relation to universal jurisdiction. The statements focus on the following issues: the definition of universal jurisdiction (including the necessity of covering civil universal jurisdiction, the nature of jurisdiction of an international criminal court or tribunal, and the relationship of universal jurisdiction with the principle of *aut dedere aut judicare*); the rationale of universal jurisdiction under international law; the categories of crimes falling within the scope of universal jurisdiction; the preconditions to the exercise of universal jurisdiction (including the requirement of presence of suspects in the territory of the forum State; subsidiarity *vis-à-vis* the criminal jurisdiction of the State where the crimes were committed, the State whose national is the suspect or victim, and an international criminal court or tribunal; respect for the fundamental principles in Article 2 of the Charter of the United Nations; and the immunity of foreign officials from criminal jurisdiction of foreign courts); the necessity of establishing an international regulatory body on universal jurisdiction; and the necessity of moving the discussion on universal jurisdiction to the International Law Commission. Having examined the relevant statements and reports, Professor ZHU opines that under present customary international law it can only be safely asserted that universal jurisdiction has been firmly established as a right of sovereign States and that it has its own rationale under international law. However, he argues, its definition, the crimes falling within its scope, and the preconditions to its exercise "remain unclear under the present customary international law". His analysis suggests that this is the common understanding that has been achieved among the 74 States that had made statements in the General Assembly by August 2012. He cautions prudence in dealing with issues involving universal jurisdiction, not "confusing *lex ferenda* with *lex lata*". The development of the law depends on *opinio juris* and practices of States. Against that background, he expresses the hope that more States will make statements on universal jurisdiction before the Sixth Committee and submit descriptions of their practices to the Secretary-General of the United Nations.

In the final Chapter 10 – *The International Criminal Court and Immunities under International Law for States Not Party to the Court's Statute* – Professor Claus Kreß describes how the international law of immunities is in fashion, having been at the heart of two recent judgments of the International Court of Justice, being the subject of two recent resolutions adopted by the *Institut de Droit International* as well as a topic to which the International Law Commission is currently addressing its attention. This necessarily generates a considerable amount of scholarly writing. He discusses two closely related questions in proceedings before the International Criminal Court. The first question is "whether international law immunities of States not party to the Statute of the ICC prevent the latter from exercising its jurisdiction over an incumbent Head of State, Head of Government, Foreign Minister and certain other holders of high-ranking office of such a State. Only if this first question is answered in the negative does the second question arise, which is whether such international law of immunities precludes the ICC from requesting a State Party to arrest and surrender a suspect who falls into one the above-listed categories and who is sought by an arrest warrant issued by the Court". Professor Kreß points out that both questions are highly relevant insofar as ICC Pre-Trial Chamber I decided on 4 March 2009 that the Court is not prevented by Sudan's immunity under international law from exercising its jurisdiction over the incumbent President of this non-party State, Al Bashir. More than two years later, a differently composed Pre-Trial Chamber I specified in two decisions that the Court is also not precluded from requesting the States Parties of Chad and Malawi to arrest Al Bashir during his visit to their country and to surrender him to the Court. Shortly thereafter, on 9 January 2012, the African Union Commission expressed its serious concern and disagreement with the decisions of the Chamber. Professor Kreß acknowledges that:

> [...] at times, the maintenance of the international legal order, on the one hand, and the stability of inter-State relations, on the other hand, may prove to be conflicting goals. Clearly, the international criminal proceedings against *Al Bashir* adversely affect the stability of the relations of all those States which support those proceedings, with the State of Sudan, as long as *Al Bashir* stays in power. At the same time, however, those criminal proceedings aim at the maintenance and at the strengthening of the *noyau dur* of the international legal order.

He concludes by recognising that "international criminal law *stricto sensu* comes at a price with respect to the stability of inter-State relations", but that "this price is worth paying, provided that the scope of application of substantive international criminal law *stricto sensu* will not be diluted, but remains confined to the conduct that constitutes a fundamental assault to the *noyau dur* of the international legal order".

The nine chapters described above were prepared in the context of the *FICHL LI Haopei Lecture Series.*[7] In Chapter 2 – *The Life and Contributions of Professor LI Haopei* – Ambassador WANG Houli gives us a glimpse into the life of service to international law of the late LI Haopei (1906–1997), one of the leading international lawyers of China who ended his long career as a Judge of the ICTY in The Hague. Professor LI Haopei embodies lifelong service to international law through government, teaching, research and translation, diplomacy, and international judicial institutions. To him there could have been little doubt that both sides of the tension between State sovereignty and international criminal justice are fundamentally important. It is for those of us who seek to serve in Professor LI's legacy, to further diffuse this tension, by that helping to consolidate the significant gains in the development of international criminal law since 1993 when he took up his work in The Hague as an ICTY Judge. Such consolidation – rather than further development at the risk of over-extension – may now be called for. To use a metaphor he may have appreciated: The ancient pines that adorn the courtyards of Confucius' Mansion in Qufu not only have crowns that have attracted enthusiasm for generations, but they have weathered storms because their root systems extend horizontally several times wider than the width of the canopy. Similarly, the stem and roots of international criminal law and justice draw nourishment from the soil of State sovereignty. This should not be ignored as the champions of the international criminal justice movement seek to extend and branch out the reach of substantive and personal jurisdiction for core international crimes.

---

[7] For information, see http://www.fichl.org/li-haopei-lecture-series/ with sub-pages that contain information on the purpose and organisation of the Series, as well as the life and service to international law of the late Professor LI Haopei.

2

The Life and Contributions
of Professor LI Haopei[*]

WANG Houli[**]

I am very happy to have been invited to contribute some words to the anthology *State Sovereignty and International Criminal Law* published in honour of the late Professor LI Haopei's service to international law. I feel that offering these words is not only an honour but also my duty.

Professor LI Haopei and I had enjoyed a rich relationship, and were very close to one another. In the beginning, Professor LI was my teacher when I was at the Dongwu University Law School in Shanghai. After that, we became colleagues in the Department of Treaty and Law at the Ministry of Foreign Affairs. And next, he became my neighbour in the Guang Huali dormitory at the Ministry of Foreign Affairs. Finally, he was my comrade at the May Seventh Cadre School of the Ministry of Foreign Affairs. I am very familiar not only with Professor LI, but also with his wife and his family members. Professor LI has left a deep impression on me, and I have learned a lot through my experiences with him.

Professor LI graduated from the Shanghai Dongwu University Law School in 1928, after which he studied abroad in England, and when he returned to China in 1939 he served as the dean and as a professor in the Law Department at the University of Wuhan. He was then appointed by Zhejiang University to found the Law School of Zhejiang University. He also served as a professor and the dean of the school. After the People's Republic of China was established in 1949, he served as a committee

---

[*] This chapter is adapted from a text prepared as a speech in the *FICHL LI Haopei Lecture Series*. It has been translated by R. Frazier Lowell.

[**] **WANG Houli**, Legal Adviser to the Ministry of Foreign Affairs, China. Formerly, President of the China Society of International Law; Ambassador to Libya and First Secretary at the Chinese Embassy in the former Soviet Union; and Director-General of the Department of Treaty and Law, Ministry of Foreign Affairs.

member in the Legislative Affairs Office of the State Council, a senior researcher at the Institute of International Relations, and a professor at the China Foreign Affairs University. Throughout his service, he has trained many qualified legal experts in China, and has made quite a contribution to the building of our legal system.

In order to improve the quality of work done by the Department of Treaty and Law, the Ministry of Foreign Affairs transferred Professor LI to the Ministry of Foreign Affairs from his position at the Foreign Affairs University to serve as a legal advisor, assigning him to a position in the Department of Treaty and Law. At that time there was a Legal Advisory Office at the Department of Treaty and Law, and those serving were made up of the most well known experts in law and diplomacy. The duties and functions of a legal advisor is to provide advice and take part in discussions tackling major difficult issues that may arise when dealing with certain diplomatic legal cases, and to conduct research and write reports regarding major practical international legal problems. Most of the time Professor LI and I had spent working together was at the Department of Treaty and Law at the Ministry of Foreign Affairs.

Professor LI is an authoritative figure in the realm of Chinese legal studies, and is also exceptionally well known on the international level as well. He had rich experience in legal studies, was well versed in many subjects, was familiar with the scholarship both of China and that of abroad, and had quite wide horizons. He was well versed in such realms as civil law, criminal law, international law, private international law, and comparative law. His research was wide in scope and deep in nature, and practically covered all the areas of legal studies. He was not only extremely familiar with law both inside and outside of China, but he also had a strong command of many foreign languages: English, French, German, Russian and Latin, and possibly even Japanese.

He had published many books related to private international law, nationality law, and the law of treaties, all of which have been chosen as teaching materials and reference materials by university law departments. He had also translated foreign works into Chinese, such as the Napoleonic Code, German Criminal Code, Martin Wolff's *Private International Law*, Alfred Verdross' *International Law*, the Soviet Law of Evidence, and the Judgment of the International Military Tribunal for the Trial of German Major War Criminals. Through these efforts, Professor LI introduced foreign law and different schools of thought to China.

While working at the Department of Treaty and Law at the Ministry of Foreign Affairs, he provided valuable suggestions and views in regards to important and difficult international law cases, which proved to be indispensable in correctly managing these cases. After undertaking careful and meticulous research, he would take the initiative in providing valuable suggestions regarding whether or not China should become a signatory in certain international conventions. On occasion, he had taken part in international diplomatic conferences discussing international law as a delegation member representing the Chinese government, and at these meetings had raised his own constructive and legally sound viewpoints.

At different times, Professor LI had written and published high quality articles that have provided unique insight.

I asked him in 1985 to give four months of lectures for the entire department officers. His book entitled *Introduction to the Law of Treaties* is not only an excellent guide for the Department of Treaty and Law at the Ministry of Foreign Affairs towards a better understanding of the law of treaties, it has also been recognised as a classic work on Chinese international law, has been awarded first prize by the National Book Foundation, and has been recommended as a must-read for graduate students of law.

Professor LI was appointed as an editorial board member and chief editor for the Private International Law section in the *Encyclopedia Sinica, Volume of Law* .

In 1985, Professor LI Haopei was elected as a member of the Institute of International Law.

Professor LI had a voracious appetite for learning. In his office, he had huge volumes of books on his enormous bookshelf and on both sides of his desk. He checked out more books than any other member of the Ministry of Foreign Affairs Library and the Department of Treaty and Law Reference Room. We would often see him struggling to carry huge stacks of books back to his office.

Professor LI held high expectations of himself and his students in the classroom, was very meticulous with details, only made statements that could be backed up with solid evidence, and understood legal matters very well. When I would go to his office to ask for consultation in regards to specific legal cases or for advice about a certain academic question, he would always immediately put to one side the work that he was busy with, politely ask me to sit, and in a warm and modest way, would slowly and patiently respond to each of my questions, giving me a detailed explanation. Sometimes, he would decide to come to my office afterword, and would pass off to me a written document that either added further explanation to the case or question which I had brought to him, or provided his legal basis or citation of the source from which he derived his explanation. This sort of serious and responsible attitude, as well as his rigorous attitude toward learning, often moved me very deeply. I believe that anyone who works in law should definitely learn from and adhere to Professor LI's serious attitude towards scholarship.

I would like to take a moment to point out some of Professor LI's personal qualities that were seen through the work that he did, which were: Integrity, a strong conscience and a belief in a job well done. The way that we traditionally handle cases at the Department of Treaty and Law, is that when we come across major and difficult legal cases involving foreign relations, the leader of the department will call all of the legal advisors together to discuss the matter. Those who take part in the meeting will earnestly work to understand the spirit of the policy, work out the main points in the case, and express one's own opinion from the aspects of politics, diplomacy, and law. Under normal circumstances, everyone's opinion, including that of Professor LI, will be essentially the same, or similarly be expressed from different angles. But sometimes Professor LI would express a distinct opinion with a solid argument that was very different from others expressed, and he would persistently adhere to his argument. Even if in the end his suggestion was not adopted, I would still very much value his input, and would gain even more respect for his personal character. He would approach each case completely from his own understanding and from a strict legal perspective, and even if his opinion was different from that of the group, or even from that of the leader in charge, he would still refuse to change his stance and simply echo the opinions of the others. I believe, regardless of whether his suggestion was adopted or not, that this kind of spirit, character, and style should be recognised and encouraged by others. After all, the purpose and job of advisors is to raise one's own sound and reasonable arguments. Different viewpoints, even if they are the viewpoints of the minority, sometimes prove to be more important and more valuable towards the correct management of the case.

Professor LI worked at the Department of Treaty and Law at the Ministry of Foreign Affairs for exactly 30 years, from 1963 to 1993. I began working at the Department of Treaty and Law before him, and left the Department in 1989 to work abroad, working with the Professor for a total of 26 years. I have benefited greatly from my time spent working with him, and he has left a great impression on me. He is my senior who I have the utmost respect for, a man with exemplary conduct and a noble character, and was a kind, affable, outstanding scholar of law.

Professor LI was very serious and responsible in his work, was very meticulous when it came to details, and even when he was assigned to physical labour with the Cadre School, he would work hard and enjoy the physical exercise at the same time. In November of 1969, during the Cultural Revolution, cadres from the Ministry of Foreign Affairs were sent together in big groups with those of the other central offices located in Beijing to take part in rural labour. At that time, the Department of Treaty and Law had been eliminated, with the entire staff being sent to take part in manual labour, regardless of age, and including elderly expert consultants. Professor LI and I were sent at the same time, first to Hunan province, after which we were transferred to the Shanggao County Ministry of Foreign Affairs May Seventh Cadre School in Jiangxi Province. At the Cadre School in Jiangxi, Professor LI and I were assigned to the vegetable team, with the primary responsibility of planting vegetables and managing the fields. Because Professor LI was over the age of 60 at the time, he took care of the lighter physical labour, pulling and digging up weeds in the vegetable patches, and while waiting for the cabbage to ripen, he would remove by hand insects and pests from outside and inside the leaves. Even though it was light physical labour, it was still very trialling for Professor LI, bending his back under the burning sun, in addition to wearing thick glasses to help with his near-sightedness. But even so, he paid as meticulous of attention to detail as ever when picking out the insects, carefully pulling out each furry insect with a small pair of tongs and placing them in a small water bottle. The small vegetable bugs in the vegetable patches that he worked in were rarely able to escape these tongs.

For every task that Professor LI Haopei put his mind to, that he thought was suitable for him, he was always able to carefully see through to the end. In addition to his daily reading and writing, he would also make sure to take time for exercise. In 1986, when he was giving a presentation to the students of the Department of Law at his alma mater in Suzhou, he made a point to emphasise: "On the one hand, you must take time for exercise in order to enhance your physical fitness, and on the other hand you must seize every moment to engage yourself in learning". This was also his motto in life. When I was working with him at the Department of Treaty and Law at the Ministry of Foreign Affairs, whenever it came time for work-break exercises, everyone would see a white-haired elderly man on the roof-porch outside the office hallway concentrating intently on his Tai Chi. This elderly man was Professor LI.

He would always walk to and from work. From his home in Guang Huali he would walk to the Ministry of Foreign Affairs located in Dongsi. At a fast pace, this would take about 45 minutes, and he would make this walk in all four seasons, and even through the wind and rain. Knowing that he was quite elderly, I contacted the secretary for administrative services, and asked that they assign a driver to take Professor LI and the former director SHAO Tianren to and from work. Professor LI accepted the ride to work, but when he entered the office building he would not take the elevator, instead preferring to work his way up the adjacent staircase with the help of the handrail, and without stopping for rest would make his way up six stories to his office, sometimes with a big briefcase loaded with heavy books in the other hand.

In 1993, Professor LI was elected to serve as a judge in the U.N. *ad hoc* International Criminal Tribunal for the former Yugoslavia. At the time he was 87, which possibly is the highest aged judge that any international court has ever selected to oversee his or her first case. Even at this venerable age, his physical condition, energy for work, and mental capacity were no less than those younger than him, except for the fact that he was a little hard at hearing. His broad and profound legal knowledge, rich work experience, serious attitude toward work, amazing capacity for foreign languages, and his great modesty and integrity of character, won him the respect and admiration of his colleagues at the court.

We would like to thank Norwegian scholar, Professor Morten Bergsmo, for organising this series of lectures and seminars, which is entitled LI Haopei in commemoration of the contributions Professor LI has made toward the development of international law and international criminal justice, and through this series of seminars we would also like to encourage the development and dissemination of international law throughout the world. I hope that today's young students of law will inherit and carry forward LI Haopei's strict scholarly spirit and upright character, and become outstanding experts of law at the national and also international level.

3

Brief Analysis of a Few Controversial Issues in Contemporary International Criminal Law[*]

ZHOU Lulu[**]

Ten years ago, with the establishment of the International Criminal Court, international criminal law entered a new stage of development. For ten years, with the experience of international criminal trials growing richer every day and with the changing international situation, certain important theories of international criminal law are being re-evaluated. This paper aims primarily at discussing three controversial issues in contemporary international criminal law: the crime of aggression, universal jurisdiction, and criminal immunity for state officials in foreign countries.

[*]   Translated by R. Franzier Lowell, revised by ZHOU Lulu. The author notes that this article only represents her personal view and does not represent the position or opinion of the Department or Ministry she serves.

[**] **ZHOU Lulu** is Director of the Treaty Division of the Department of Treaty and Law, Ministry of Foreign Affairs of China. She graduated from China University of Political Science and Law in 1997. She obtained a Master's degree from Hong Kong University in 2004 and a Ph.D. from Renmin University in 2007. She has represented the Chinese Government or been a member of Chinese delegations on many bilateral or multilateral occasions, such as the negotiation between China and Peru regarding the *Agreement on Mutual Legal Assistance in Criminal Affairs*, the consultation of the U.N. framework on the *Convention on Protection of all Persons from Enforced Disappearance*. ZHOU has written, co-authored, edited or co-translated several books (including *Research on the Fundamental Principles of Contemporary International Criminal Law*, *The International Criminal Court: A Commentary on the Rome Statute*, and *International Criminal Court*). She has also published several articles (including *Inspiration of the New Development of EU Extradition System*, *Research on the Provisions Regarding the Relationship between ICC and UN Security Council*, *The Obligations Erga Omnes and its impact on International Criminal Law*, *The Legal Impact of the Amendment of Crime of Aggression – from the Angle of the Conditions of the ICC to Exercise Its Jurisdiction*).

3.1. The Crime of Aggression

On 11 June 2010, States Parties of the Rome Statute of the International Criminal Court (hereinafter referred to as the 'Rome Statute') attending the Review Conference adopted by consensus[1] the sixth resolution on the amendments to the crime of aggression. These amendments laid out the definition, conditions for exercising jurisdiction, and elements of the crime of aggression, as well as an understanding of the amendments.

After the amendments regarding the crime of aggression were adopted, some scholars experienced a feeling of encouragement, thinking that this had not only realised the long-cherished hope of the international community to establish a common definition for the crime of aggression, but also protected the independence of the International Criminal Court, and established a foundation on which the Court may exercise jurisdiction over crimes of aggression in the future. However, issues of dispute that arose during the negotiation process cannot be resolved simply because the amendments were adopted. It still needs in-depth analysis to determine whether the amendments will actually serve as a reasonable and effective basis for future trials, and play a role in pursuing those accountable for crimes of aggression, with the goal of maintaining world peace. The potential impact of the amendments on contemporary international politics and the international legal system should not be ignored.

The history of establishing and defining the crime of aggression can be traced back to the formulation of the Treaty of Versailles in 1919. After World War I, representatives of the five victorious nations met at the Palace of Versailles outside Paris to draft the terms of the German Peace Treaty (the 'Treaty of Versailles'), trying to establish an orderly post-war framework as well as hold the criminals initiating wars accountable.[2] But

---

[1] France did not associate herself with the consensus, and did not oppose the adoption of the amendments.

[2] A committee to investigate who had started the war and also to enforce punishment of these culprits – the committee which was under the leadership of a ten-member council made up of members of the five nations that had come together to draft the Treaty of Versailles – stated the following: "All those residing in enemy states, regardless of the seniority of rank, and including the national leadership, as long as they have violated the laws of war or those of customary practice, or have violated humanitarian law, all must be held criminally responsible". The committee divided all types of criminal actions into two basic categories: (1) instigating world war and working in co-ordination with acts of war; (2) violating the laws of war or those of customary

for various reasons,[3] the efforts to hold those who had committed international crimes accountable were in vain.

After World War II, the Nuremberg Tribunal and the International Military Tribunal for the Far East were established to hold war criminals in Germany and Japan accountable for their crimes. Both Tribunals included 'crimes against peace' in the crimes under their jurisdiction. This was the prototype or formal origin of the crime of aggression. However, the Nuremberg Charter and the Far East Military Tribunal Charter only simply ruled that planning, initiating or carrying out war of aggression constitutes a crime against peace. The two Charters failed to stipulate in detail either the components of wars of aggression or the elements of crimes against peace.[4] In spite of this, the Nuremberg Tribunal determined that Karl Dönitz committed crimes against peace;[5] and the Far East Tribunal found 25 individuals guilty of crimes against peace.[6]

---

practice, or having violated humanitarian law. See Bassiouni, *International Criminal Law*, 1999, vol. 2, p. 316.

[3] This includes the fact that the German Emperor had fled to Holland and was given asylum by that country.

[4] In 1945 countries including the U.S., England, France and the former Soviet Union concluded the Agreement for the Prosecution and Punishment of the Major War Criminals of the European Axis (also referred to as the 'Charter of the Nuremberg Tribunal'), establishing the Nuremberg International Military Tribunal, holding individuals criminally responsible for crimes against peace, war crimes, and crimes against humanity. Crimes against peace referred to "planning, preparation, initiation or waging of a war of aggression, or a war in violation of international treaties, agreements or assurances, or participation in a common plan or conspiracy for the accomplishment of any of the foregoing" (see Article 6, Section 8 of the Nuremberg Charter). In 1946, countries such as China, the U.S., and the former Soviet Union completed the Far East Military Tribunal Charter in order to punish Japanese criminals for their war crimes, defining crimes against peace and in Article 5, Section 1 incorporating the same description given in the above-mentioned Nuremberg Charter.

[5] See selections from Karl Dönitz's pleading of innocence, available at http://warstudy.com/history/world_war/german_navy_strategy/034.xml, last accessed on 13 October 2012.

[6] On 12 November 1948, the Far East Tribunal announced the decision with regards to 25 Class-A war criminals, stating that they are responsible for crimes against peace, war crimes and crimes against humanity, and sentenced seven individuals to death by hanging, 16 individuals to life imprisonment, and two individuals to limited prison sentences. See "Zhanfan Yongyuan shi Zhanfan, Fananzhe Bibai" (War Criminals will always be War Criminals, Those who Try to Reverse the Verdict are Doomed to

The United Nations has committed to end all forms of aggressive war ever since its establishment. In 1946, the United Nations General Assembly adopted Resolution 95(1), unanimously confirming the principles of international law outlined in the Nuremberg Charter. In 1950, the International Law Commission codified the Principles of the Nuremberg Tribunal based on Resolution 95(1), stating in the sixth principle that crimes against peace "are punishable as crimes under international law", using the same definition contained in the Nuremberg Charter.

Following this, the international community continued its ongoing efforts to establish a clear definition of crimes of aggression. But since this was all taking place during the Cold War, the process was slow. After many years of hard work, the U.N. General Assembly adopted Resolution 3314 on 14 December 1974, which included a definition of 'aggression', and also listed certain manifestations of crimes of aggression. But U.N. General Assembly resolutions are not legally binding, and so the given definitions were unable to serve as a legal basis for determining crimes of aggression. After this, international legal academia, including the International Law Commission, continued to search for a possible definition of crimes of aggression with the U.N. General Assembly's Resolution as a starting point. But there was no substantial progress.

In 1998, the Diplomatic Conference to discuss the establishment of the Statute of the International Criminal Court took place in Rome, where crimes of aggression and other crimes such as war crimes, genocide, and crimes against humanity were included in the jurisdiction of the Statue. However, because of irreconcilable differences among the parties on the definition of crimes of aggression as well as the conditions for the Court to have jurisdiction over such crimes, the Conference had no choice but to leave the articles concerning crimes of aggression to be decided at a later date. The Conference only decided that in principle, after the articles in question were established, the Court would be able to exercise jurisdiction over crimes of aggression.[7]

After the Rome Statute entered into force in 2002, a Special Working Group on the Crime of Aggression was established, and became a main mechanism for a new round of negotiations on crimes of aggression.

Failure), available at http://www.china.com.cn/chinese/zhuanti/rbzf/897592.htm, last accessed on 13 October 2012.

[7] See the Rome Statute, Article 5(2).

Parties became involved in heated debates revolving around such issues as the definition of crimes of aggression, elements of such crimes, conditions for jurisdiction, and the issue of how such articles should enter into force. The amendments pertaining to the crime of aggression as stated in Resolution 6 were finally adopted at the 2010 ICC Review Conference held in Uganda.

3.1.1. The Definition of Crime of Aggression

During the discussions in the crime of aggression Special Working Group, two main opinions were raised regarding how crime of aggression should be defined. The first opinion was that there should be a specific definition of crime of aggression, and specific aggressive actions should be listed. This would mainly adhere to the Definition of Aggression attached to the U.N. General Assembly Resolution 3314 (XXIX). The other opinion was that a generic definition of crimes of aggression should be established based on Article 6, Section 1 of the Nuremberg Charter on crimes against peace, which stated:

> [...] in order to realize the purpose of this statute and in accordance with the UN Security Council's previous determination of act of aggression, the crime of aggression refers to the following: planning, preparation, initiation or waging of a war of aggression.[8]

Through years of negotiations, the parties have essentially reached a consensus to consider both approaches to definition together. Before determining the criminal responsibility of an individual carrying out crimes of aggression, it must first be decided whether or not there existed an act of aggression by a state.

The current definition provided by the amendments on the crime of aggression reflects three characteristics of such crime, namely: (1) specific contextual element for crimes of aggression, (2) leader's crime, and (3) threshold requirements.

1. *Contextual element for the crime of aggression.* Crimes of aggression are not carried out by one or more individuals, and individual criminal activity must occur against the backdrop of the invasion by a nation or group. To put it another way, crime of aggression by the

---

[8] See Special Working Group on the Crime of Aggression discussion paper, 3 June 2005, Princeton Meeting.

individual must happen within the context of acts of aggression. This is also the chief characteristic distinguishing crime of aggression from other core crimes. In fact, the main reason why it is so difficult to establish the definition of the 'crime of aggression' is that this crime closely relates to justice of war, and also with international peacekeeping missions.[9] Maintaining peace and determining aggressive behaviour is an extremely difficult task of a political nature. Different nations and ethnic groups may understand and comprehend the same behaviour or situation differently, based on their own historical and cultural background or value system, possibly coming to opposite conclusions on the nature of the behaviour in question. For example, actions seen as separatism by one country may be seen by another country as a struggle for human rights;[10] actions in opposition to foreign oppression, which are part of a struggle for national liberation, may be seen by another nation as terrorism that needs to be suppressed.[11] In the process of discussing the crime of aggression, some countries have proposed the inclusion of such variations as economic invasion and cultural invasion,[12] but these proposals have not been included because of insurmountable differences of opinion amongst the parties involved. Despite the fact that the possible forms of acts of aggression are virtually infinite, it is still essential to determine the existence of an act of aggression as a precondition to pursuing individual responsibility for crimes of aggression. Obtaining the competence to determining the existence of acts of aggression is like holding the key that can initiate a proceeding against an aggressor.

2. *A crime by leaders.* Acts of aggression and wars of aggression are both acts of states, which both require national military forces, equipment and sources in order to be carried out. This means that

---

[9] See Carsten Stahn, "The 'End', the 'Beginning of the End' or the 'End of the Beginning'? Introducing Debates and Voices on the Definition of 'Aggression'", in *Leiden Journal of International Law*, 2010, vol. 23, pp. 875–876.

[10] For example, the so-called 'struggle for independence' by the Chechen nationalists; in the eyes of its regional authority, it may be considered as activities of separatism by the central government of Russia.

[11] The conflict between Palestine and Israel is a classic example.

[12] MA Chengyuan, "Guoji Xingfa Lun" (International Criminal Law Theory), in *China University of Political Science and Law Publishing House*, 2008, p. 285.

having the opportunity to plan, prepare for, initiate or wage a war of aggression, and thus take part in the above-mentioned activities, does not reside in the common individual, but in a leader who is of a certain higher rank, and who has the capability, credentials and opportunity to control, command or influence the state's decision or military forces. This is what the amendments on the crime of aggression refer to as an individual "in a position effectively to exercise control or to direct the political or military action of a state". Emphasis is placed on the fact that the crime of aggression is a crime that it is specifically committed by a leader and it is done so in order to apply different treatment to those who participate in, as a mere material fact, acts of aggression and those who play a leading role in acts of aggression. In practice, many low ranking soldiers will take part in specific acts of aggression by simply following military orders, but they know nothing about the intention, scale and goals of the overall act of aggression. Therefore, differentiation between the particular individual who participates in acts of aggression and those who are responsible for launching the aggressive action is not only a technical legal issue, but rather relates to the judicial policy of how crimes of aggression should be effectively punished and prevented.

3. *Threshold requirements.* There are certain threshold requirements contained in the definition of the crime of aggression, that is, only when the act of aggression "by its character, gravity and scale, constitutes a manifest violation of the Charter of the United Nations", will the crime of aggression apply. This threshold requirement originates from the fact that customary international law only considers serious acts of aggression like 'aggressive war' to be crimes of aggression or crimes against peace. This fact can be verified by referring to such documents as the Nuremberg Charter, the Far East Military Tribunal Charter, U.N. General Assembly Resolution 95(I), the Nuremberg principles of international law, as well as the 1970 Declaration of Friendly Relations.[13] These documents clearly point out that "aggressive war is a crime against peace". Section 5, Article 2 of U.N. General Assembly Resolution 3314 confirms this position, differentiating between war of aggression and act of ag-

---

[13] Principle 1(2) of the Friendly Relations Declaration of 1970.

gression, stipulating that "a war of aggression is a crime against international peace, aggression gives rise to international responsibility". Existing international law does not provide a clear standard of justification on how to define whether a war of aggression has taken place. In practice we can only make this distinction according to the limited criteria for judging the legitimacy of war usually found in customary international law, which shows that only wars of self-defence or wars undertaken under collective security mechanism outlined in the U.N. Charter are legitimate wars.[14] The trend to differentiate between 'war of aggression' and 'act of aggression' is adjusted in the Draft Code of Crimes against the Peace and Security of Mankind.[15] The International Law Commission explained in detail why it tried to eliminate the differentiation between aggressive war and aggressive actions in the first reading comments on the Draft Code.[16] This viewpoint of the Commission was partially accepted during the discussions held by the Special Working Group for crimes of aggression with minor modification. The Special Working Group did not differentiate between aggressive war and aggressive actions, but instead divided aggressive actions into different categories, creating a threshold requirement for aggressive acts that may constitute crimes of aggression, which is what the current

---

[14] Using force in self-defence or with the authorisation of the Security Council under the collective security system are two legitimate reasons for use of force under the U.N. Charter (Article 51 of the U.N. Charter).

[15] Draft of 1991, Articles 15 and 16.

[16] The International Law Commission noted a distinction between war of aggression and act of aggression, and summarised in its report that:

> [...] some members felt that the notion of a war of aggression indicated the level of magnitude required for the conduct to result in individual criminal responsibility [...] however, other members rejected this distinction as artificial or spurious for the following reasons: the concept of war is a relative concept; wars of aggression inevitably include acts of aggression; the distinction between the seriousness and the legal consequences of the two was misleading and unsustainable in practice; [...] the emphasis on wars of aggression was misplaced since declarations of war no longer existed in international relations [...].

See International Law Commission, "Report of the Commission to the General Assembly on the work of its forty-seventh session", in *Yearbook of the International Law Commission*, 1995, vol. II, part II, *para*. 63.

amendment has described as "by its character, gravity and scale, constitutes a manifest violation of the Charter of the United Nations". The Special Working Group's approach to this matter can to some extent be seen as a confirmation of customary international law.

The author believes that the amendment specifying threshold requirements for crimes of aggression is, on the one hand, rational to some degree because it not only conforms to the distinction between 'unlawful offences' and 'international crime', but also keeps in mind the reality that international judicial institutions, with no enforcement forces and limited resources, have to concentrate their efforts on the most serious crimes and criminals. But on the other hand, these threshold requirements leave great discretion to prosecutors and judges which could lead to abuse, and at the same time does not fulfil the principle of peaceful settlement of international disputes under international law that requires all states to do everything possible to refrain from use of force, regardless of how minor scale it may be.

3.1.2. Precondition for the Court to Exercise Jurisdiction over Crimes of Aggression

This issue is essentially of the same nature as that of identifying the instigator of an act of aggression, and also that of the relationship between the Court and the Security Council. This is the most difficult issue to overcome during discussions on the crime of aggression.

According to the Rome Statute, there are three triggering mechanisms of the Court's jurisdiction: referral by a State Party, by the Security Council and *proprio motu* initiation of investigation. During negotiations in the Working Group and the Review Conference, the issue of preconditions primarily focused on that of referrals by State Parties and *proprio motu* initiation. The international community has seen two widely differing viewpoints on this issue.

One view states that Article 39 of the U.N. Charter clearly grants the U.N. Security Council the competence to decide whether or not aggression or aggressive acts have occurred. Therefore, the Security Council has the competence to determine the existence of a threat to the peace, breach of the peace or act of aggression; and it is the only institution that has the competence to determine acts of aggression. Maintaining the independence of the International Criminal Court cannot prevail over the collective security system or derogate from or jeopardise the competence of the Security Council to maintain peace and security. To these ends, only on the condition that the Security Council has determined an act of aggression can the Court have jurisdiction over crimes of aggression. Failing that, the Court may not obtain jurisdiction over such crimes. Those who hold this opinion are primarily the five permanent members of the Security Council.

Another viewpoint suggests that the Security Council is a political institution, and if its affirmation that crimes of aggression have taken place is a precondition for the Court to exercise its jurisdiction, this will result in the work of the Court becoming impaired by politics, making it impossible to guarantee the independence of the judiciary. Those who hold this opinion consider that, although the U.N. Charter assigns responsibility for maintaining peace and security to the Security Council, it has not specified that it is the only institution that has the competence to determine the existence of an act of aggression, and institutions such as the International Court of Justice and the U.N. General Assembly may also discuss affairs involving aggression. Those who hold this viewpoint are primarily countries from Latin America and Africa.

At a later stage of the ICC Review Conference in 2010, the Chair presented a room paper with a green light proposal, which gave more flexibility to the Security Council to determine acts of aggression as a condition for the Court to exercise its jurisdiction.[17] According to this proposal, where there is a State Party referral or *proprio motu* initiation of investigation, and no determination of an act of aggression has been made by the Security Council, the Court can exercise its jurisdiction when the Security Council has requested the Prosecutor to proceed with the investigation. It is up to the Security Council to give the green light to the Prosecutor. This option did not obtain unanimous support. Those favouring that the Security Council should not be able to serve as a filter – represented by Argentina, Brazil and Switzerland – submitted a further proposal, according to which, and under the same scenario, the Court could exercise

---

[17]   2010 Conference Room Paper submitted by the Chair of the Review Conference, see Stefan Barriga and Claus Kreß (eds.), *Crime of Aggression Library: the Travaux Preparatoires of the Crime of Aggression*, Cambridge University Press, 2012, p. 730, para. 4.

its jurisdiction when the Pre-trial Chamber has authorised the commencement of an investigation.[18] This proposal was later developed into a
red light proposal by the President of the Conference.[19]

In the end, the ICC Review Conference adopted the current text for
exercising jurisdiction over crimes of aggression on the basis of the 'red
light proposal', which states that conditions for jurisdiction are specifically separated into two categories: The first is that, in regards to cases
(situations) referred to the Court by the Security Council, the Court may
exercise jurisdiction over anything that involves crimes of aggression,
regardless of whether the involved countries are States Parties to the
Court, or whether they have accepted the jurisdiction of the Court. The
second is for referral by States Parties or *proprio motu* initiation of investigations when the prosecutor has to identify whether the Security Council
has determined an act of aggression. If the Council has done so, the
prosecutor may continue with an investigation; if the Council fails to do
so within a period of six months – unless the Pre-Trial Chamber of the
Court gives authorisation and the Council has not suspended the investigation – the prosecutor may continue investigating the crime of aggression.[20]

With the above-mentioned preconditions for the Court's exercise of
jurisdiction, France did not associate herself with the consensus when the
amendments were adopted by consensus. And China, the U.S. and Russia

---

[18] *Ibid.*, p. 741.

[19] In the 2010 President's second paper, there are two alternatives on the exercise of
jurisdiction over the crime of aggression (state referral and *proprio motu* initiation):

Alternative 1: in the absence of such a determination, the Prosecutor may not proceed
with the investigation in respect of a crime of aggression [unless the Security Council
has, in a resolution adopted under Chapter VII of the Charter of the United Nations,
requested the Prosecutor to proceed with the investigation].

Alternative 2: where not such determination is made within six months after the date
of notification, the Prosecutor may proceed with the investigation in respect of a
crime of aggression, provided that Pre-Trial Division has authorised the commencement of the investigation in respect of a crime of aggression in accordance with the
procedure contained in Article 15 [and the Security Council does not decide other-
wise]. See Stefan Barriga and Claus Kreß (eds.), *Crime of Aggression Library: the
Travaux Preparatoires of the Crime of Aggression*, Cambridge University Press,
2012, p. 782.

[20] See Resolution 6, RC/Res. 6, attachment no. 1, adopted by the Review Conference on
11 June 2010.

stated their position, expressing their disagreement or dissatisfaction with the amendments from different angles. The author believes that, while the preconditions may seem to have maintained the independence of the Court, in actuality, they greatly impact the international legal and political system, adding more destabilising factors to international peace and security. This is because of the following reasons.

Firstly, the issue of preconditions involves the interpretation of Article 39 of the Charter of the United Nations. The author is of the view that since the Charter empowers the Security Council and no other institution with the competence to maintain peace and security, naturally the task of determining acts of aggression – which is closely related to peace and security – has been assigned to the Council. The fact that it is difficult for the Council to make decisions on aggression is a very complicated issue involving international politics. Sometimes those decisions involve nations that have a huge impact on international or regional stability. The foundation of the Charter of the United Nations is the collective security mechanism, and the veto possessed by the permanent members of the Security Council is an inseparable part of this system. It could be said that, even though the U.N. cannot possibly prevent all wars, it can still play a role in preventing large-scale wars that threaten world peace and security from happening.[21] In situations where the Security Council cannot come to a decision by consensus and the ICC is empowered with the authority to determine acts of aggressions, the concurrent competences will derogate from the role of the Security Council and the post-World War II international security system established pursuant to the United Nations Charter. It will cast doubt on the real effectiveness of the amendments on the crime of aggression on the maintenance of peace and security by punishing criminals of crimes of aggression.

Secondly, although the Security Council is a political organ, it does not necessarily neglect to exercise its power to determine the existence of aggression. In history, the Security Council had adopted some resolutions on aggression, condemning the aggressive acts of some countries. For example, from 1973 to 1987, the Security Council adopted resolutions condemning 'aggressive acts' or 'act of aggression' by South Africa against

---

[21]   The veto that the five permanent members of the Security Council possess produces strategic contention and balancing. Since World War II, there has not been a world war or a large-scale regional war involving many nations.

Zambia and neighbouring countries like Angola or Namibia.[22] In 1977, the Security Council adopted Resolution 405, which "strongly condemns the act of armed aggression penetrated against the Republic of Benin on 16 January 1977".[23] In 1985, the Security Council, by adopting Resolution 573, drew:

> [...] attention to the serious effect which aggression carried out by Israeli and all acts contrary to the Charter [...], condemns vigorously the act of armed aggression perpetrated by Israel against Tunisian territory in flagrant violation of the Charter of United Nations, international law and norms or conduct [...].[24]

Iraq is an example often cited during the discussion on the crime of aggression to prove the Security Council's political nature and inability to determine the existence of an act of aggression. On 2 August 1992, Iraq invaded Kuwait and the Security Council adopted several resolutions condemning the invasion without using the term of aggression.[25] However, in this author's view, the sanction measures taken against Iraq in those resolutions were even more severe than those in previous resolutions using the term aggression against South Africa and Israel. At the same time, in Resolution 667 (1990), the Security Council considers "the act of Iraq to order the closure or consular mission in Kuwait and withdraw privileges and immunities of these missions and personals [...] constitute aggressive acts and flagrant violation of international law [...]".[26]

After comparing the above-mentioned instances, it seems to this author that the Security Council is very cautious in selecting its wording like 'aggressive', 'aggression', 'invasion' or others, and it relies on compre-

---

22 In Security Council Resolution 326 (1973), "the Security Council is [...] convinced recent provocative and aggressive acts perpetrated by the illegal regime against Zambia aggravate the situation [...]". In Security Council Resolution 387 (1976), "the Security Council [is] gravely concerned at the act of aggression committed by South Africa against the People's Republic of Angola and the violation of its sovereignty and territorial integrity". Other similar condemnation can be found in Security Council Resolutions 546 (1984), 571 (1985), 568 (1985), and 572 (1985).

23 Security Council Resolution 405 (1977).

24 Security Council Resolution 573 (1985).

25 From Security Council resolutions 660 (1990) to 666 (1990).

26 Security Council Resolution 667 (1990).

hensive assessments, including factual details, intention and effect of act, degree of intrusion, *et cetera*, before it reaches its conclusion.

Thirdly, some delegations argue that they do not deny the Security Council's competence to determine acts of aggression, but that this is not the Council's exclusive competence, but that both the General Assembly and the International Court of Justice have concurrent competence. It must be pointed out that both the General Assembly and International Court of Justice are very different from ICC. The International Court of Justice is a judicial body within the United Nations framework and can only exercise its jurisdiction with the consent and acceptance of the state concerned. On the other hand, the ICC is an independent institution outside United Nations system with the aim of pursuing individual responsibility. The ICC may exercise its jurisdiction even without the consent of the state concerned. Moreover, the prosecution system of the ICC follows the Tokyo Tribunal style and not that of Nuremberg in that the prosecution is decided by a single prosecutor rather than by a prosecution committee with several prosecutors, the latter being less likely to be abused.[27] To date, some influential powers or regional powers such as the USA, Russia, China, India, Egypt and Israel have not participated in the ICC. With only one trial completed after ten years and even more doubt expressed by some African countries,[28] the ICC has not proven its effectiveness as expected. Comparing with the General Assembly, it has adopted resolutions involving aggression[29] by 193 member states of the U.N. Those resolutions entail a political and moral impact other than the likely negative effects on the states or individuals concerned. Moreover, the General Assembly's role in determining aggression, if there is any, is very restrictive since it has to terminate once the Security Council intervenes.

---

[27] In the International Military Tribunal for the Far East, the U.S., the U.K., USSR and China all assigned a prosecutor, each prosecutor had a vote, and would be the chair of the prosecution committee in turn. According to such a system, all prosecution decisions are made by the majority agreement of prosecutors. See JIAN Songji, "The Retroactive Power for ICC to Exercise its Jurisdiction over Crime of Aggression", in *Study of Law,* 2008, vol. 9, p. 70.

[28] For more discussions on this, see David Hoile, *The International Criminal Court: Europe's Guantanamo Bay?*, African Research Centre, 2010.

[29] See General Assembly Resolution 377(v). See also General Assembly Resolution 2074 (xx), 17 December 1965.

The Security Council's role in the determination of aggression is not comparable to that of the General Assembly.

Fourthly, allowing the International Criminal Court to identify aggressive behaviour will create new institutional defects. The current amendments on the crime of aggression give the Court the competence to determine acts of aggression. This gives the impression that the independence of the Court has been maintained, but it must be pointed out that when the Court and the Security Council both have competence to determine acts of aggression, it is possible that they would come to different conclusions. Under these circumstances, the amendments on the crime of aggression are unable to co-ordinate the opposing standpoints of the Court and the Security Council. The Security Council may find that a state has committed acts of aggression and therefore decide to impose sanctions, and the Court as an independent judicial institution may on the other hand determine that an act of aggression has not taken place (even though this is not very likely to occur). This may result in disapproval or challenge from states towards the Security Council. And according to Article 103 of the Charter of the United Nations the duty under the Charter takes priority, which means that ICC States Parties have to ignore the Court's determination rather than respect it. However, if the Court rules that a state has committed acts of aggression and the Security Council has not made a similar determination, or if Security Council, in accordance with the Rome Statute, simply orders the Court to suspend the investigation in question, this will not only weaken the authority of the Court, but inhibit any punitive measures taken against the state that has been found to have committed an act of aggression by the Court. Until then, not only will the international community be faced with the disorder brought on by the lack of clear right-or-wrong standards, the fragmentation of international law will be exacerbated which may stimulate states to more go their own ways. In the long term, this will be harmful to preventing acts of aggression and maintaining international legal order.

3.2. Universal Jurisdiction

3.2.1. Background of the Question

In recent years, the international community has discussed intensely the topic of universal jurisdiction. Since the end of the last century when the United Kingdom arrested former President Augusto Pinochet of Chile based on an extradition request from Spain,[30] western nations and human rights organisations have been advocating universal jurisdiction for human rights cases, stating that the serious encroachment of human rights is a crime that is a threat to the international community, that those who violate human rights are the common enemy of the people, and that every nation, as a representative of the international community, has the right to prosecute and try such cases. On this basis, these advocates have rejected the traditional principle of sovereign immunity.

In practice some countries that have applied 'universal jurisdiction' in a biased way have met with strong objections or opposition from the affected countries, resulting in diplomatic disputes. Meanwhile, individuals from nations who seek to apply universal jurisdiction frequently and actively may themselves become involved in accusations one day. For example, officials such as former U.S. President Bush, former British Prime Minister Blair, and former Israeli Prime Minister Sharon have been subjected to calls for criminal investigation in Europe by human rights organisations. But under pressure from the U.S.,[31] some European countries have taken measures to adjust policy on universal jurisdiction[32] so as

---

[30] Pinochet was originally a Chilean Army Chief of Staff. In 1973, he became president through a military coup. In 1990, he peacefully transferred power to Irwin, the winner of the 1989 presidential election, and was appointed as a life-long senator. In 1998, Pinochet travelled to a hospital in United Kingdom using his diplomatic passport. At this time, a Spanish judge issued an international order of arrest, seeking punishment for murder and encroachment of the human rights of Spaniards during Pinochet's term in office. The English authorities decided to detain Pinochet. Chile raised a complaint about the issue. The British courts went through several proceedings to determine whether Pinochet had immunity, and whether he should be extradited to Spain. In the end, the British House of Lords and the Court of Appeal ruled that Pinochet does not have immunity, and that the crimes he was alleged to have committed were sufficient basis for his extradition. The British Ministry of the Interior refused Spain's request on the basis of Pinochet's poor health, and allowed Pinochet to return to Chile.

[31] Former U.S. Secretary of Defence Rumsfeld expressed that, if Belgium did not abolish the order that contained clauses referring to "the right of universal jurisdiction", NATO headquarters in Brussels would be moved elsewhere. See http://china.findlaw.cn/bianhu/xingfazhishi/xsgxq/pubianguanxiaquan/1028.html, last accessed on 13 October 2012.

[32] In March 2003, Belgium modified a 1993 order and allowed investigative institutions to use arguments such as that the criminal act did not take place in Belgium or that the suspect is not a citizen of or in Belgium, in order to refuse to try certain cases relating

---

to avoid accusation of allies. These conflicting scenarios further exposed the double standard of universal jurisdiction. It must therefore be considered carefully.

In October 2009, the sixty-fourth session of the U.N. General Assembly Sixth Committee started its first debate on the principle of universal jurisdiction through a proposal raised by the representative of Rwanda on behalf of the African Group.[33] Due to the diversity of opinion no consensus could be reached. This reflects the fact that nations have different views on the legal position and application of universal jurisdiction. The fact that some nations advocate the application of universal jurisdiction for certain controversial cases has generated serious concerns for other nations.

The session of the U.N. General Assembly Sixth Committee adopted a resolution requiring that the U.N. Secretary-General invite each member state to provide information and opinions about the scope and application of the principle of universal jurisdiction, including applicable international accords, domestic laws and information obtained through the practice of legislation. This is meant to help build consensus through the exchange of ideas and information, and to strengthen the rule of international law and to reach the necessary balance of stability and order in international relations.

In 2010, the U.N. Secretary-General invited each nation to express its opinions on universal jurisdiction, and by July he published a report summarising these ideas. A total of 44 nations provided information and opinions, the results of which highlighted the fact that there are still major differences amongst states as to what universal jurisdiction entails. Reviewing the oral discussions held by the General Assembly over the years, the U.K. and France are supporters of the universal jurisdiction, but inclined to take some self-refraining measures. For example, in the U.K., it should be the prosecutor who decides to initiate proceedings involving universal jurisdiction; and in France the suspect must be within French territory in order for a case to be brought forward. In the U.S., even though there are crimes that can be tried under universal jurisdiction such

---

to war crimes, crimes against humanity, and homicide. By doing this, Belgium modified the 1993 order that claimed universal jurisdiction.

[33] See document A/64/452, "The scope and application of the principle of universal jurisdiction".

as genocide, torture and other crimes specified in anti-terror treaties, the country did not clearly support universal jurisdiction. It did, however, emphasise the importance of states to share their experiences with each other. Russia is against the excessive application of universal jurisdiction. African and Latin American countries express that they agree with universal jurisdiction, but request that it be applied in a restricted manner.

Universal jurisdiction is an important unresolved question that the International Court of Justice faces. In 2002, the ICJ intentionally avoided expressing its opinions on universal jurisdiction in the *Arrest Warrant* case (*The Democratic Republic of Congo v. Belgium*). Some judges nevertheless attempted to express their views on whether universal jurisdiction is in conformity with current international law. In the case of the *Republic of Congo v. France*, which is before the Court when this is being written, one of the controversial points concerns universal jurisdiction. The cases of *Belgium v. Senegal* and *Germany v. Italy* are also closely entwined with questions of universal jurisdiction and immunity. The issue of "either extradite or prosecute" which is on the agenda of the International Law Commission also touches on universal jurisdiction. Both the International Court of Justice and the International Law Commission show great caution when dealing with universal jurisdiction.

3.2.2.   Review and Analysis

The prevailing view is that the concept of universal jurisdiction originates in the consideration of jurisdiction in international law regarding the crime of piracy.[34] With the end of World War II and the occurrence of certain major international crimes thereafter, some countries and scholars widened the scope of application for universal jurisdiction to other serious crimes, for example war crimes and crimes against humanity. However,

---

[34] Customary international law dictates that universal jurisdiction may be applied to pirates on the basis that (1) the nature of the actions that pirates partake in can be seen to indicate that these individuals have abandoned their original national citizenship, and have therefore become stateless individuals; (2) actions of piracy have a certain level of mobility, therefore pirates can only be punished when the international community co-ordinates its actions; and (3) historically, each nation requires a full offensive against the crime of piracy. See ZHENG Lei, "Lun Haidaozui Pubian Guanxiaquan Jizhi de Juxianxing yu Biange" (Limits and Changes in Institutions Charged with Universal Jurisdiction for the Crime of Piracy), in *Zhongguo Haishangfa Niankan* (China Maritime Law Yearly), June 2009, vol. 20, issues 1 and 2.

the *Eichmann* case[35] and the *Pinochet* case are both seen as cases where universal jurisdiction has been applied.[36] In 2001, a meeting at Princeton University proposed some principles for universal jurisdiction, pointing out that universal jurisdiction is applicable to "piracy, the crime of slavery, war crimes, and crimes against peace, crimes against humanity, genocide, and torture".[37]

Nations, scholars and NGOs that advocate universal jurisdiction rely on the following theoretical bases. The first is the principle of sovereignty. The Permanent Court of International Justice affirmed the sovereign principle in the *Lotus* case, saying that sovereign states may act in any way they wish so long as they do not contravene an explicit prohibition.[38] The application of this principle – an outgrowth of the Lotus case – established the theoretical foundation of extraterritorial jurisdiction. The second is that there exists the 'obligation *erga omnes*' or the 'common interests of mankind',[39] therefore there is a necessity to exercise jurisdiction over cases that infringe on the common interests of the international community. The third is the necessity towards countering criminal activity, to ensure that criminal activity does not go unpunished and avoid allowing criminals to ride above the law.

---

[35] Adolf Eichmann was a general for Nazi Germany during World War II. In 1942, he was assigned the task of carrying out the final plan for massacring the Jewish people. After he was captured by the U.S. military, he managed to escape to Argentina. In 1961, Mossad operatives learned of his location, captured him, and secretly transported him to Israel.

[36] *"Pubian Guanxiaquan yu Guojia Zhuquan de Guanxi (4)"* (The Relationship between Universal Jurisdiction and National Sovereignty, 4), available at http://china.findlaw. cn/bianhu/zhuanti/pubianguanxiaquan/55609_4.html, last accessed on 13 October 2012.

[37] See the attachments to the note submitted by Canada and Holland in 2001 to the U.N. General Assembly that mention the principles proposed by the meeting at Princeton University (A/56/667).

[38] LIU Ye, *"Guojifa shang de 'Hehua Hao' Yuanze"* (The Lotus Principle and International Law), http://bjgy.chinacourt.org/public/detail.php?id=94739, last accessed on 15 October 2012.

[39] The concept of the 'common interests of mankind' originates from '*obligation erga omnes*'. In 1970 the International Court of Justice ruled in the *Barcelona Traction* case that the obligations a country has toward the international society is different from the obligations a country has toward another country, because the international community involves important common interests.

The majority believes that universal jurisdiction is applied, or claimed to be applied, by a state where the most serious crime is committed and when there is no connection of interests ('link point') between the forum state and place of crime, nationality or residence of the suspect or the victims or national interest. But when considering and applying related theories, we find that the international community in fact does not have a common understanding of when 'universal jurisdiction' is applicable, the most obvious evidence of which is that there exist two forms of universal jurisdiction: 'relative universal jurisdiction' and 'absolute universal jurisdiction'. The former requires that the suspect is found within the territory of the forum state in order for universal jurisdiction to be exercised, so it requires some connection, namely the location where the suspect is found. The latter does not require any connection. Clearly, there is a significant difference between the conditions of applicability of these two forms of 'universal jurisdiction' and the target to which it may be applied.

Can 'universal jurisdiction' actually be without limits? The author believes that in international law only the crime of piracy is applicable to a limitless, absolute form of universal jurisdiction ('universal jurisdiction *in absentia*') that is free of conditions such as link points. The establishment of universal jurisdiction should be limited to situations clearly allowed by international law, and should also be limited by international law. To put it in another way, absolute universal jurisdiction is permissible, in international law, to be exercised only over crimes of piracy, and should not be universally exercised over other crimes. Absolute universal jurisdiction, once exercised without limitation, will provoke nations to misuse their jurisdictions, and will stimulate political abuse of such jurisdiction, causing instability in international relations. Even for the three above-mentioned theoretical bases of universal jurisdiction, when analysed together with (absolute) universal jurisdiction, there will always be imperfections in theory and practice.

3.2.2.1. What About Using the 'Principle of Sovereignty' as the Theoretical Basis of Universal Jurisdiction?

According to principles of sovereignty in international law, a nation has jurisdiction over crimes committed within its territory, which refers to 'the principle of territory'. Besides this, under certain circumstances, a nation also has jurisdiction based on the nationality of the suspect ('positive principle of territory'), the nationality of the victim ('negative principle of territory') or the nation's security or other important interests ('protective principle of territory'). Bearing in mind that the sovereignty of each nation is equal, every nation may decide to exercise jurisdiction based on the principles of territory or the individual or national interests. Therefore in cases involving link points with various nations, there will unavoidably be conflicting jurisdictions among different nations. Under these circumstances, any nation who exercises its jurisdiction purely out of its own will, regardless of the opinions and propositions of other nations, may offend the sovereignty of other nations. This is in breach of the principle of equality of sovereign nations, and may cause conflicts between nations.

In fact, the principle established by *Lotus* case has already been revised and modified. In the *Arrest Warrant* case, the International Court of Justice analysed the domestic law of Holland, Germany and France and concluded that these countries do not have laws allowing for jurisdiction over suspects that are not found within their territory.[40] In fact, the times have changed in several respects since the *Lotus* case was tried.

First, International communication is getting more and more integrated, and globalisation has made communication between countries more intricate and complex. These days the activities of one nation will affect other nations on many levels, and concepts like global governance and co-ordination are now more ingrained among people. Arbitrary exercise of sovereignty will cause the infraction of the sovereignty of other nations.

Secondly, international criminal law permits specific judicial institutions to exercise jurisdiction over criminal activity outside of a nation's territory, but it does not empower any nation with that kind of jurisdiction. According to the principle of sovereign equality, a nation may determine and carry out jurisdiction only when it does not violate the sovereignty of other nations. Therefore, the establishment and exercise of jurisdiction by one nation should only be allowed when there is an appropriate link between the case and the forum state, and should be restricted in a reasonable way.

---

[40] Judgment of 14 February 2002, *Arrest Warrant* case of 11 April 2000 (*Democratic Republic of Congo v. Belgium*), available at http://www.legal-tools.org/doc/c6bb20/.

3.2.2.2. What About Taking the 'Principle of Obligation *Erga Omnes*' (the Common Interest of Humanity) as the Theoretical Basis of Universal Jurisdiction?

This theory seems to be very convincing, but there is some uncertainty involved that needs to be pointed out. First of all, what are the connotations and denotations of 'the common interest of humanity'? The International Court of Justice has in the *Barcelona Traction* case put forward the concept of 'obligations *erga omnes*'[41] and to some degree strengthened the legal basis for 'the common interest of humanity'. In 1970, U.N. General Assembly Resolution 2749 – the Declaration of Principles Governing the Seabed and Ocean Floor – was adopted by 108 states, providing that the deep seabed should be preserved for peaceful purposes and is the 'common heritage of mankind'.[42] In 1982, this 'common heritage of mankind' concept was said to relate to "the seabed and ocean floor and subsoil thereof, beyond the limits of national jurisdiction" under Article 136 of the United Nations Convention on the Law of the Sea ('UNCLOS').[43] However, these concepts and the ways in which they are referred to have neither clearly defined what is included in the 'common interests of mankind' nor established who is qualified to represent all of mankind in exercising jurisdiction. Therefore, if a country claims to represent all of mankind in exercising jurisdiction over other countries and their citizens, regardless of how morally-sound the argument may be, it still lacks legal basis.[44] In practice, arbitrarily claiming to represent the interests of the entire international community or of all of humanity in bringing other nations to trial will only cause legislative disorder and the prevalence of hegemonic actions.

The only consensus that the international community has reached is that any nation may represent all of humanity in exercising jurisdiction over acts of piracy that occur on the high seas. This is also the only crime

---

[41] Judgment of 5 February 1970, *Barcelona Traction, Light and Power Company, Limited* (*Belgium v. Spain*), available at http://www.legal-tools.org/doc/75e8c5/.

[42] UNGA Resolution 2749 (XXV), para. 1, U.N. Doc. A/RES/25/2749 (12 December 1970).

[43] United Nations Convention on the Law of the Sea Art. 1, para. 1, 10 December 1982, in *UNTS*, vol. 1833, p. 397.

[44] Luc Reydams, "The Rise and Fall of Universal Jurisdiction", http://papers.ssrn.com/so13/papers.cfm?abstract-id=1553734, last accessed on 12 September 2012.

that is permitted clearly in international law. Article 105 of the United Nations Convention on the Law of the Sea of 1982 states:

> On the high seas, or in any other place outside the jurisdiction of any State, every State may seize a pirate ship or aircraft, or a ship or aircraft taken by piracy and under the control of pirates, and arrest the persons and seize the property on board. The courts of the State that carried out the seizure may decide upon the penalties to be imposed [...].

This provision of universal jurisdiction, which is aimed at piracy, also reflects customary international law and rules. It is worth taking note that universal jurisdiction over piracy emphasises that it takes place "on the high seas or any other place that is *outside* the jurisdiction of any State". This point shows that the international community is very cautious when it comes to matters of universal jurisdiction, and works to avoid contradictions in the jurisdictional exercise of states.

3.2.2.3. What About the Theory of Combating Criminal Activity and Ensuring that Crimes Never Go Unpunished Being the Theoretical Basis of Universal Jurisdiction?

Jurisdiction is an important and integral part of sovereign states. Exercising jurisdiction is equivalent to exercising sovereignty. For a state, to exercise jurisdiction over a criminal act or an individual, is to take punitive measures on behaviours that are deemed to be wrong or harmful to the public order or security or interests of the people of that state. Punishment is in essence reflecting the relationship between a sovereign state and the victimised party. Therefore, whether or not a state exercises jurisdiction is in reality closely related to how the state makes judgments of morality, its social conscience and desire to contribute to the public good, and also its overall social culture. A behaviour that constitutes a crime in one state – such as euthanasia, homosexuality and polygamy – may not necessarily be considered a crime in the eyes of another state. Specifically because of this, a state should not casually attempt to extend its jurisdiction over certain activities or incidents taking place in other states or towards citizens of other countries.

When examining treaties concerning the punishment of current transnational or international crimes – including those concerning individual criminal responsibility for crimes in fields such as human rights and humanitarianism – we find that the jurisdiction established by the related treaties complements the traditional jurisdictional rights of each nation. The purpose is that when it is necessary – when the state in which the criminal suspect is located or when the state in which the criminal acts were committed or the state in which the suspect is a citizen believes that there is a necessity to punish such criminal activity – the punishment of the crime is made possible through the co-operation of the country in which the suspect is located. The exercise of this kind of jurisdiction requires many conditions to be met, including the following.

1. It is only exercised over specific crimes defined in international treaties, and can only be exercised towards parties of the treaty. In other words, being a party to a treaty is *prima facie* evidence of that state agreeing that the activities indicated in the treaty are criminal, and to combat the crimes through co-operation with other parties.

2. Under the condition that the suspect is appearing in the state's territory and that state refuses to extradite to other states, which means to strictly follow the principle of 'either extradite or prosecute'.

3. Following the complementarity rule, it means to respect the priority of the principle of territorial jurisdiction and national jurisdiction. When a concerned state finds a suspect located within its borders, it should immediately notify the country in which the crime was committed or the country in which the suspect is a citizen, and do everything possible to facilitate the extradition of the suspect to that state. When it is necessary, it may discuss conditions for extradition with such states.

4. There should be no exception of jurisdictional immunity, and the rules of immunity under international law should not be violated. According to international law, jurisdictional immunities are granted to heads of state or government and other officials. Reviewing provisions of treaties related to combating transnational crimes, there is no clear rule that deprives the immunity of foreign officials.[45]

---

[45] There are stipulations in the Statute of the International Criminal Court that suggest that having official status is unrelated to the application of the above-stated law. But the jurisdiction of the International Criminal Court as an international judicial agency is different from that of individual sovereign nations. The jurisdiction of the International Criminal Court is not that of universal jurisdiction. Since its jurisdiction is aimed towards the crimes stipulated in specific treaties, its jurisdiction comes from

3.2.3. Case Analysis

We must be cautious when dealing with universal jurisdiction and prevent its misuse that will cause disorder in the judicial system. There have in practice already been many cases of abusive application of universal jurisdiction. The examples of such misuse show that universal jurisdiction is always of secondary importance to political considerations, and is used to shield those with certain political ambitions.

1. The first case of inappropriate use of universal jurisdiction can be found in the process of combating piracy, which is already unanimously accepted to be target of universal jurisdiction. In recent years, pirates originating in Somalia have become a serious problem, but no state shows willingness to solve the problem by exercising universal jurisdiction in their domestic courts. The Canadian and Dutch navies have released pirates after capturing them.[46] This, once again, illustrates the weakness of using a concern to 'ensure crimes do not go unpunished' as a principle and basis of universal jurisdiction.

2. The second case is the misuse of universal jurisdiction by Belgium. Belgium issued an order of arrest against the foreign minister of Congo, which then decided to take Belgium to the International Court of Justice. Belgium lost the case, with the Court ruling that this was an offence of the immunity enjoyed by the foreign minister of Congo. In addition to this, as mentioned above, under pressure from the U.S. and Israel, Belgium had no choice but to revise its domestic law and add certain limitations to its exercise of universal jurisdiction. The United Kingdom also restricted its domestic courts' ability to exercise universal jurisdiction against her allies. This proves that the overriding objective of universal jurisdiction is not purely justice-oriented. Its application is always fraught with political motivation and may be misused through politics.[47]

---

the transferring of sovereignty from the involved nations, and is not held automatically by the Court.

[46] "Somali Haidao bei Zhua hou you bei Shifang" (Somali pirates released after capture), available at http://news.sohu.com/20090420/n263487071.shtml, last accessed on 13 October 2012.

[47] Belgian officials admit that its universal jurisdiction law (which allows for universal jurisdiction) may be misused, and may become a tool to accomplish the political goals

3.3. Criminal Immunity of State Officials Abroad

A principle often mentioned in recent years in the field of international criminal law, which seems to be recognised by the Rome Statute, is the principle of 'irrelevance of official capacity'. This is somewhat connected to the question of the criminal immunity of state officials abroad, but the two are not exactly the same.

3.3.1. The Institution of Immunity in International Law

The institution of immunity in international law includes state immunity, diplomatic and consular immunities, and immunity of special missions. There are both connections and differences among these different immunities. Diplomatic immunities and immunities of special mission are comparatively clear because they have already been laid out rather completely in international treaties,[48] so this chapter will not analyse them further. When it comes to state immunity and the immunity of officials, the primary basis is customary international law. This is also a controversial issue.

State immunity refers to a state being free from the administrative or legislative jurisdiction of other countries. There are two primary schools of thought that provide the theoretical basis for this: One is the 'principle of sovereign equality', which mandates that sovereigns are equal and as such have no jurisdiction over one another. The second is the 'principle of comity' of states, which entails refraining from exercising judicial powers over other states in order to encourage respectful international relations. In practice, the former has been more readily accepted.[49]

---

of those in power, see "Wanguo Guanxiaquan Fa Guande tai Kuan? Fang Bilishi Zhuhua Dashi" (Is the Universal Jurisdiction Law Applied to Loosely? Interview with the Belgian Ambassador to China), available at http://news.sohu.com/39/89/news211148939.shtml, last accessed on 13 October 2012.

[48] This is primarily referring to the Vienna Convention on Diplomatic Relations of 1961, the Vienna Convention on Consular Relations of 1963, and the United Nations Convention on Special Missions of 1969. The scope, rights and obligations of the above conventions are relatively clear.

[49] ZHANG Xiaosheng, "Guojifa shang de Tequan yu Huomian Zhidu Bijiao" (Comparison of the Regimes of Privilege and Immunity in International Law), available at http://www.rmlt.com.cn/qikan/2011-03-25/18918.html, last accessed on 13 October 2012.

In practice, state immunity has meant that the court of one state cannot try cases in which a foreign state is called to be the defendant. As for the concept of a state, in addition to referring to the state itself, it can also include the state's government and institutions, as well as officials and other representatives who represent the state in dealing with certain matters.[50] For quite a long time after the principle of state immunity came about there was no differentiation between a state representative's civil or commercial and criminal actions. In other words, all the official activities of the officials enjoyed immunity. This point can be deduced from the immunities enjoyed by diplomatic representatives or special missions.

As states involved themselves more and more in commercial activities and individual officials took advantage of their powers to do what they wished without restraint, the international community gradually began to differentiate between the different actions taken by the state and state officials. One way is to differentiate between two types of state behaviour, namely the behaviour of the rulers ('*act jure imperii*') and the behaviour of the management ('*act jure gestionis*'),[51] and another way is to differentiate between normal or legal activities of officials in fulfilling their jobs and activities that may constitute an international crime. The former differentiation served to advocate the restricted immunity theory of the 1960s and 1970s and encouraged it being put into practice, and the latter affirmed principles of irrelevance of official capacity that was established by the two international military tribunals with the end of World War II.

After World War II, in light of its cruelty and how massively destructive it was, the international community began to pursue the criminal responsibility of state leaders, government officials, and military and political leaders of the Axis Countries that were primarily responsible for starting the war, and committing acts of genocide and crimes against humanity. During the Nuremberg trials, the team of defence lawyers at the

---

[50] United Nations Convention on Jurisdictional Immunities of States and Their Property, 2004, Article 2(1)(b).

[51] Before the twentieth century, the Italian and Belgian courts had already developed a theoretical basis for immunity grounded on this differentiation. See Francesco Francioni, "International Law as a Common Language of National Courts", in *Texas International Law Journal*, 2001, vol. 36, issue 3, p. 595. For the Belgian case, see U. Verhoeven, "Immunity from Execution of Foreign States in Belgium Law", *Netherlands Year Book of International Law*, 1979, vol. 10, pp. 73, 76.

time argued that the activities of the accused were acts of state. This was rejected by the Tribunal in its judgment, stating:

> [...] crimes against international law are committed by men, not abstract entities, and only by punishing individuals who commit such crimes can the provisions of international law be enforced [...].[52]

According to the Tribunal, only by punishing the individual who had committed such crimes would the stipulations of international law be effectively carried out. Article 6 (responsibility of accused) of the International Military Tribunal for the Far East Charter states that,

> [...] neither the official position, at any time, of an accused, nor the fact that an accused acted pursuant to order of his government or of a superior shall, of itself, be sufficient to free such accused from responsibility for any crime with which he is charged, but such circumstances may be considered in mitigation of punishment if the Tribunal determines that justice so requires.

The above judgment and the regulations laid out in the Charter of the United Nations have not only clarified the legality of pursuing an official's individual responsibility in committing international crimes, it also marks the establishment of the principle of the irrelevance of official capacity. This principle was affirmed by the U.N., General Assembly in 1946 as one of the Nuremberg Principles.[53] The Rome Statute, which was adopted in 1998, has a similar provision stating that the rank or position of the actor will have no effect on the criminal responsibility thus pursued.[54] The above seems to make clear that, in the field of international criminal law, state officials cannot enjoy criminal immunity for international crimes, and are subject to jurisdiction of international tribunals. However, has international law completely denied the criminal immunity of state officials stationed abroad? The author believes that this conclusion cannot be reached so easily. Immunities from international tribunals'

---

[52] Antonio Cassese, "Affirmation of Principles of International Law Recognized by the Charter of the Nuremberg Tribunal, the General Assembly resolution 95(I)", available at http://untreaty.un.org/cod/avl/ha/ga_95-I/ga_95-I.html, last accessed on 13 October 2012.

[53] In 1946, the General Assembly adopted Resolution 95(1), "Affirmation of the Principles of International Law Recognized by the Charter of the Nuremberg Tribunal".

[54] Rome Statute, Article 27.

jurisdiction are not the same as immunities from foreign jurisdiction. Under some circumstances, the criminal immunity of state officials is still applicable.[55]

3.3.2. Analysis

In discussing the criminal immunity enjoyed by state officials abroad, two different situations need to be distinguished. One is the criminal immunity enjoyed by state officials when abroad, and the other is the criminal immunity enjoyed by state officials in international courts.

3.3.2.1. Regarding Criminal Immunity Enjoyed by State Officials in Other Countries

There is currently no treaty that clearly denies the principle of immunity before domestic courts handling international criminal cases, regardless of whether these are immunities enjoyed by states or state institutions.[56] Customary international law still acknowledges the immunity of a foreign state and its representatives, that is, state officials. This can be explained from a few different angles.

First of all, looking at the theoretical basis for the immunity enjoyed by state officials, we find that the goal and reason for granting state officials immunity is the same as for granting diplomats or consular officials immunity: The immunity is granted to the state which the official represents[57] with the intention that the official will be able to better carry out his function as a representative of his state, which promotes contact between states and the stability of international relations. Therefore, as long as there is no major change of the fundamental principle of equal sovereignty in the international legal system, the criminal immunity of officials should not be denied.

---

[55] This part does not discuss the topic of immunity enjoyed by state officials within their own country.

[56] J. Verhoeven, *United Nations Treaty Series*, vol. 1465, no. 24841, p. 125.

[57] There are primarily three kinds of theoretical basis for diplomatic privileges and immunities: (1) the theory of representation; (2) the theory of professional necessity; and (3) the theory of extraterritoriality. The former two are more widely accepted. Gong Renren, "Historical origins of the principle of jurisdictional immunities of States", in China Legal Science, 1991, vol. 5, p. 90.

Secondly, certain treaties that are aimed at combating criminal activity, such as the Convention on the Elimination of All Forms of Racial Discrimination, the Convention against Torture, and the Convention on the Prevention and Punishment of Crimes against Internationally Protected Persons, including Diplomatic Agents, require the punishment of individuals who commit related crimes, and have affirmed the principle of 'either extradite or prosecute' to that end. However, the 'right to prosecute' (or 'jurisdiction') which is included in this principle should be carried out only when the suspect is not extradited, with the precondition still being that jurisdiction of the state in which the official is a citizen or the state in which the crime was committed is respected. Moreover, under the principle of 'either extradite or prosecute', even if the forum state's jurisdiction is well-established, this does not deny the existence of immunity, and the lack of immunity does not imply that jurisdiction is admissible.[58]

Next, the immunity of state officials in foreign countries is only a procedural immunity, and does not entail the elimination of the responsibility or liability of those officials totally and thoroughly. This is to say that, the fact that officials enjoy criminal immunity in foreign state is only to spare them from the law enforcement procedures in that foreign state, and does not indicate that the behaviour of the officials conforms to national laws of the forum state. The objective of granting immunity is to maintain the stability of international relations, and is not to shield criminals. The state that assigns the officials may pursue their criminal responsibility according to its law, or choose to give up the immunity of its official so that the foreign state may exercise its jurisdiction. Therefore, even though many international treaties that are aimed at preventing and punishing certain serious crimes have provided the principle of 'either prosecute or extradite', by which a state may extend its jurisdiction over foreign officials, this should not influence the immunity provided by customary international law.

Fourth, international judicial practice has confirmed the criminal immunity enjoyed by officials in foreign state. The International Court of Justice affirmed that ministers of foreign affairs, heads of state and heads of government all enjoy immunity from the criminal jurisdiction of foreign nations in its judgment in the *Arrest Warrant* case. Besides these

---

[58] Preliminary Report on Immunity of State Officials from Foreign Criminal Jurisdiction, A/CN.4/601, para. 61.

three kinds of officials, the Court did not exclude criminal immunity for other officials in foreign states, and left room for interpretation by the international community in accordance with existing international law.[59] After the judgment in the *Arrest Warrant* case, some countries continued to confirm the principle of criminal immunity of officials in foreign states, for example, in the United Kingdom, expanding the kind of foreign officials who can enjoy criminal immunity to other high-ranking officials than heads of state, heads of the government, and foreign ministers, including defence and commerce ministers. Other than this, Belgium has also revised its national laws famous for universal jurisdiction, providing that jurisdiction can be exercised unless international law has not been violated.[60] In March 2012, the International Court of Justice in the case of *Germany v. Italy* confirmed that the activities of German Generals tried in an Italian domestic court were in fact international crimes, but even if one believes that the Italian court is trying cases involving violations of *jus cogens*, the immunity which is affirmed in customary international law is not affected. By denying the immunity enjoyed by Germany's armed forces under customary international law, the Italian court had in fact violated Italy's international obligation to Germany.[61]

3.3.2.2. The Criminal Immunity of State Officials before International Criminal Tribunals

In comparison with the criminal immunity before foreign states, it seems rather difficult for state officials to claim criminal immunity before international criminal tribunals, such as the two International Military Tribunals, the International Criminal Tribunal for the former Yugoslavia, and the International Criminal Court. It is particularly difficult when the state, as national state of the official or territorial state of the crime, is a party to the international criminal tribunal or has accepted its jurisdiction. This is because the jurisdiction of international criminal tribunals is granted by its State Parties, and is the result of a yielding of jurisdiction by the sovereign nation. Therefore, for the international criminal tribunals to exercise jurisdiction over a certain case, it can be understood that the State Party

---

[59] Judgment of 14 February 2002, *supra* note 40.

[60] A/CN.4/601, para. 39.

[61] Judgment of 3 February 2012 on Jurisdictional Immunities of the State (*Germany v. Italy: Greece intervening*), available at http://www.legal-tools.org/doc/674187/.

has already waived criminal immunity for its officials once and for all at the time of joining the treaty that establishes the tribunal.

The Rome Statute differentiates between criminal immunity enjoyed by officials before foreign states and before the Court itself. As stated in the Statute,

> [...] the Court may not proceed with a request for surrender or assistance which would require the requested State to act inconsistently with its obligations under international law with respect to the State or diplomatic immunity of a person or property of a third State, unless the Court can first obtain the cooperation of that third State for the waiver of the immunity.[62]

This, in reality, is the legal basis for States Parties of the Rome Statute to grant state officials of non-States Parties with immunity. For example, after the International Criminal Court issued an arrest warrant against Sudanese President Omar Al Bashir in 2009, he travelled to Chad and Kenya neither of which arrested him on the basis of Article 98 of the Rome Statute. In the Assembly of States Parties of the Rome Statute in 2009, African countries proposed to explore clarification of the relationship between Article 27 and Article 98 of the Rome Statute. The driving force behind this initiative was, on the one hand, to respond to the 'Article 98 agreements' concluded by the U.S. and other countries[63] and, on the other hand, to clarify the legal duties undertaken by the States Parties towards different subjects (that is, either the Court or third party) of the treaty concerning official immunity. Although the African proposal was not accepted at the meeting and had no opportunity to be discussed,[64] it

---

[62] Article 98(1) of the Rome Statute.

[63] This refers to the bilateral agreements between the U.S. and other nations which are aimed at avoiding the jurisdiction of the International Criminal Court over certain international crimes that the U.S. is involved in, on the basis of Article 98(2) of the Rome Statute. See ZHOU Zhenjie and QU Xuewu, "'Meiguo 98 tiao Xieding' Guojifa Xiaoli Pingxi" ("America's Article 98 Agreement" and an Analysis of the Effectiveness of International Law), available at http://www.iolaw.org.cn/2009/shownews.asp?id=3846, last accessed on 13 October 2012.

[64] There are two main reasons why most nations taking part in the meeting (primarily European countries) were unwilling to respond in a positive way: One was that they were not willing to depreciate the legal basis for the U.S.'s 'Article 98 agreements'; another was that they were not willing to reopen discussions and thus damage the balance achieved in the deliberations for the Rome Statute.

has clearly proved the existence of the two different kinds of criminal immunity of foreign officials. It also makes the point rather clear that, even for the ICC States Parties, granting criminal immunity to the officials of a third state in accordance with international legal norm other than the Statute is to a certain extent permitted under the Statute.

4

Has Non-Immunity for Heads of State Become a Rule of Customary International Law?

LIU Daqun[*]

I had the privilege and honour to work with late Judge LI Haopei when I joined the Treaty and Law Department of China's Ministry of Foreign Affairs more than 30 years ago. Later, I took over his position as a judge of the Appeals Chamber of the International Criminal Tribunals for the former Yugoslavia and for Rwanda. Judge LI Haopei's contribution to the development of international criminal law in China and to the work of the United Nations *ad hoc* Tribunals has been invaluable. Judge LI, who was an extremely wise and perceptive judge, as well as a scholar with an unparalleled understanding of international law, was a kind and gentle person, respected by his colleagues for his enlightening views and admired for his strong belief in the cause of justice. It is of particular significance to hold *FICHL LI Haopei Seminars* in China, where he spent most of his career, and in a time when international law is undergoing rapid development, especially in the area of immunity of heads of states.

Whether heads of states have immunity before criminal tribunals when facing prosecution of international crimes is currently a hotly debated topic in both academic and judicial circles. This subject is interesting as well as demanding – just as Cryer *et al.* aptly put it,

> [...] the interplay of international criminal law and immunities is complex, and the jurisprudence and authorities have been described as perplexing, contradictory, confused or incoherent.[1]

---

[*] **LIU Daqun** is Judge of the Appeals Chamber of the International Criminal Tribunals for the former Yugoslavia ('ICTY') and Rwanda ('ICTR'). The views expressed in this article do not reflect the views of any organisations or governments. The author would like to thank Mr. Chris Callan, an intern in ICTY, for his research and assistance. The author would also like to express his great pleasure in contributing to the *FICHL LI Haopei Lecture Series*.

[1] Robert Cryer, *et al.*, *An Introduction to International Criminal Law and Procedure*, second edition, 2010, p. 532, in turn citing Rosanne van Alebeek, "The Pinochet

This chapter will address the current legal status of heads of state immunity in relation to criminal prosecution for international crimes in both national and international courts, in order to explore whether the *non*-immunity of heads of state has become a rule of customary international law. Any discussion on immunities in civil proceedings and state immunity will be left aside since they are beyond the scope of this chapter.

4.1. Challenge to the Rule of Heads of State Immunity

Sovereign immunity is a well-established rule in international law. In 2002, the International Court of Justice ('ICJ') reaffirmed the importance of this principle in the *Arrest Warrant* case. Three judges in their joint separate opinion stress that "immunities are granted [...] to guarantee the proper functioning of the network of mutual inter-State relations, which is of paramount importance for a well-ordered and harmonious international system".[2] This reflects the principle of *par in parem imperium non habet*, the idea that an equal has no power over an equal, establishes that one state should not adjudicate on the conduct of another state. The principle is imperative in facilitating positive, workable international relations between states and maintaining global political stability and security.

Heads of states have historically been seen as the personification of the state and as a result were granted absolute immunity. This meant that a head of state could effectively act with impunity under international law, without fear of prosecution. The personal immunity (*ratione personae*), as compared to functional immunity (*ratione materiae*) attaches to limited and particular personals in a state, normally the heads of state or government as well as the Minister of Foreign Affairs in order to ensure the freedom to conduct the relations between States. The ICJ holds that this type of immunity applies not only in relation to official acts, but also in relation to private acts, stating that "throughout the duration of his or

Case: International Human Rights Law on Trial", in *British Yearbook of International Law*, 2001, vol. 71, no. 29, p. 47; J. Craig Barker, "The Future of Former Head of State Immunity After Ex Parte Pinochet", in *International and Comparative Law Quarterly*, 1999, vol. 48, p. 938.

[2] International Court of Justice, Arrest Warrant of 11 April 2000 (*Democratic Republic of the Congo v. Belgium*), Joint Separate Opinion of Judges Higgins, Kooijmans and Buergenthal, 14 February 2002, p. 86, para. 75, available at http://www.legal-tools.org/doc/23d1ec/.

her office, he or she when abroad enjoys full immunity from criminal jurisdiction and inviolability".[3] Over time, the inviolability of heads of state
as an individual has become divorced from the inviolability of the state
itself, and recently the impunity of heads of state has been challenged.

> In recent decades, with the advent of the human rights
> movement, States have taken stronger and stronger steps to
> prosecute international criminals. This emboldened State
> practice has brought to the fore many hidden or unresolved
> questions as to the boundaries between principles of ac-
> countability and immunity, and has engendered a reassess-
> ment and restriction of the scope of immunities.[4]

In fact, this trend started as early as 1919, following the end of
World War I, when the former German Kaiser William II was indicted by
the Allies for prosecution before a special tribunal under the terms of the
Treaty of Versailles.[5] Although he was never placed on trial, this appeared to herald a new approach to heads of state immunity, although it
should be noted that such trial could be only possible through the signing
of the Treaty and therefore through a waiver from Germany.

Later, after the Second World War, the International Military Tribunals ('IMT') sitting in Nuremberg and Tokyo were established. Article
7 of the Charter of the International Military Tribunal of Nuremberg states
that:

> The official position of defendants, whether as Heads of
> State or responsible officials in Government Departments,
> shall not be considered as freeing them from responsibility
> or mitigating punishment.[6]

The Nuremberg Tribunal reaffirmed this principle in its judgement
of 1 October 1946, stating that:

> The principle of International Law, which under certain cir-
> cumstances protects the representatives of a State, cannot be
> applied to acts which are condemned as criminal by Interna-

---

[3] International Court of Justice, Arrest Warrant of 11 April 2000 (*Democratic Republic
of the Congo v. Belgium*), Judgement of 14 February 2002, para. 54, available at
http://www.legal-tools.org/doc/c6bb20/.

[4] *Supra* note 1.

[5] Treaty of Versailles, Article 227, 28 June 1919.

[6] United Nations, Charter of the International Military Tribunal Article 7, 8 August
1945, in *UNTS*, vol. 82, p. 284.

tional Law. The authors of these acts cannot shelter themselves behind their official position in order to be freed from
punishment in appropriate proceedings.[7]

In 1950, the United Nations General Assembly adopted the "Principles of International Law Recognised in the Charter of the Nuremberg
Tribunal and in the Judgment of the Tribunal".[8] Of particular note, Principle III, which as Professor Cassese argues has come to acquire the status
of customary international law,[9] states:

The fact that a person who committed an act which constitutes a crime under international law acted as Head of State
or responsible Government official does not relieve him
from responsibility under international law.[10]

The *ad hoc* tribunals constituted by the United Nations Security
Council reapplied this principle, with the identical phrasing of both Article 7(2) of the International Criminal Tribunal for the former Yugoslavia
('ICTY') Statute and Article 6(2) of the International Criminal Tribunal
for Rwanda ('ICTR') Statute stating that the "official position of any accused person, whether as Head of State or Government or as a responsible
Government official, shall not relieve such person of criminal responsibility nor mitigate punishment".[11]

The ICTY held that these provisions were declaratory of customary
international law:

Individuals are personally responsible, whatever their official position, [...] even if they are heads of State or govern-

---

[7] The Trial of German Major War Criminals, Proceedings of the International Military
Tribunal sitting at Nuremberg, Part 22 (22 August 1946 – 1 October 1946), para. 447.

[8] General Assembly, Official Records, fifth session, Supp. No. 12, U.N. Doc. A/1316
(1950).

[9] Antonio Cassese, *International Criminal Law*, second edition, Oxford University
Press, 2008, p. 305.

[10] *Documents of the second session including the report of the Commission to the General Assembly*, Yearbook of International Law Commission, U.N. Doc.
A/CN.4/SER.A/1950/Add.1, 6 June 1957, vol. 2, no. 1, p. 375, available at
http://untreaty.un.org/ilc/publications/yearbooks/1950.htm, last accessed on 30 July
2012.

[11] Statute of the International Criminal Tribunal for the former Yugoslavia, Art. 7(2),
Security Council ('S.C.') Res. 827, U.N. Doc. S/Res/827, 25 May 1993; Statute of the
International Criminal Tribunal for Rwanda, Art. 6(2), S.C. Res. 955, U.N. Doc.
S/Res/955, 8 November 1994.

---

ment ministers: Article 7(2) of the Statute and article 6(2) of
the Statute of the International Criminal Tribunal for
Rwanda [...] are indisputably declaratory of customary international law.[12]

In its Draft Code of Crimes against the Peace and Security of Mankind,[13] the International Law Commission adopted the same principle.
Article 7 of the Draft Code, entitled "Official Position and Responsibility"
states that the "official position of an individual who commits a crime
against the peace and security of mankind, even if he acted as Head of
State or Government, does not relieve him of criminal responsibility or
mitigate punishment".

The Special Court for Sierra Leone ('SCSL') came to the conclusion that "the principle seems now established that the sovereign equality
of states does not prevent a Head of State from being prosecuted before an
international criminal tribunal or court".[14]

Similarly, the International Criminal Court ('ICC') itself concluded
that:

> The international community's commitment to rejecting im-
> munity in circumstances where international courts seek ar-
> rest for international crimes has reached a critical mass. If it
> ever was appropriate to say so, it is certainly no longer ap-
> propriate to say that customary international law immunity
> applies in the present context.[15]

---

[12] *Prosecutor v. Furundžija*, Case No. IT-95-17/1-T, Judgment, 10 December 1998,
para. 140, available at http://www.legal-tools.org/doc/e6081b/; *see also Prosecutor v.
Milošević*, Case No. IT-99-37-PT, Decision on Preliminary Motions, 8 November
2001, para. 28, available at http://www.legal-tools.org/doc/f15771/.

[13] *Report of the Commission to the General Assembly on the work of its forty-eighth
session*, 1996, 2(2), in *Yearbook of International Law Commission* vol. 1, no. 26,
U.N. Doc. A/CN.4/SER.A/1996/Add.1, Part 2, 1996, available at http://untreaty.un.
org/ilc/publications/yearbooks/1996.htm, last accessed on 30 July 2012.

[14] *Prosecutor v. Charles Ghankay Taylor*, Case No. SCSL-03-01-I-059, Decision on
Immunity from Jurisdiction, 31 May 2004, para. 52, available at http://www.legal-
tools.org/doc/3128b2/.

[15] *Prosecutor v. Omar Hassan Ahmad Al Bashir*, Case No. ICC-02/05-01/09, Decision
Pursuant to Article 87(7) of the Rome Statute on the Failure by the Republic of Malawi to Comply with the Cooperation Requests Issued by the Court with Respect to
the Arrest and Surrender of Omar Hassan Ahmad Al Bashir, 12 December 2011, para.
42, available at http://www.legal-tools.org/doc/476812/.

It would be tempting to use Professor Cassese's words to conclude that:

> In the present international community respect for human rights and the demand that justice be done wherever human rights have been seriously and massively put in jeopardy, override the principle of respect for state sovereignty. The new thrust towards protection of human dignity has shattered the shield that traditionally protected state agents.[16]

In international courts and tribunals, "practice has been consistent, in that no serving head of state has been recognised as being entitled to rely on jurisdictional immunities".[17] This is especially true for the contracting States Parties to the Rome Statute of the International Criminal Court ('Rome Statute' or 'ICC Statute'). With the ratification of the Rome Statute, they have accepted all the provisions in the Statute, including Article 27 on the irrelevance of official capacity.

4.2. Immunity before National Courts

Considering what has already been said about state sovereignty and the idea that one state should not adjudicate on the conduct of another state, the position on immunities taken by national courts, which exist on a horizontal level, is necessarily different from that of international courts or tribunals which operate on a vertical level. With respect to national criminal courts, "the operating principle in general international law is that a serving head of state is entitled to absolute immunity from the jurisdiction of such courts, unless it has been waived by the state concerned".[18] Sands, acting as *amicus curiae* before the Special Court for Sierra Leone ('SCSL'), argued that "before a national criminal court, a serving head of state is entitled to immunity under customary international law, even in respect of international crimes".[19]

---

[16] Antonio Cassese, 2008, *supra* note 9, p. 308.

[17] *The Prosecutor v. Charles Ghankay Taylor*, Case SCSL-2003-01-I, Submissions of the Amicus Curiae on Head of State Immunity, para. 2, available at http://www.legal-tools.org/doc/fdc405/.

[18] This question was at the heart of the decision by the SCSL in *Prosecutor v. Charles Ghankay Taylor*, Case No. SCSL-03-01-I-059, Decision on Immunity from Jurisdiction, 31 May 2004, para. 52, available at http://www.legal-tools.org/doc/3128b2/.

[19] *The Prosecutor v. Charles Ghankay Taylor*, Case SCSL-2003-01-I, Submissions of the Amicus Curiae on Head of State Immunity, para. 118(1), available at http://www.legal-tools.org/doc/fdc405/.

In the *Arrest Warrant* case, the ICJ made very plain that customary international law provided for absolute immunity for incumbent heads of state before foreign national courts, even where they were accused of international crimes. It said that:

> The Court has carefully examined State practice, including national legislation and those few decisions of national higher courts [...]. It has been unable to deduce from this practice that there exists under customary international law any form of exception to the rule according immunity from criminal jurisdiction and inviolability to incumbent Ministers for Foreign Affairs [or by analogy to heads of state], where they are suspected of having committed war crimes or crimes against humanity.[20]

It further said that:

> The Court has also examined the rules concerning the immunity or criminal responsibility of persons having an official capacity contained in the legal instruments creating international criminal tribunals [...]. It finds that these rules likewise do not enable it to conclude that any such an exception exists in customary international law in regard to national courts.[21]

This proposition found support from Lord Browne-Wilkinson in *Pinochet (No. 3)* who, on this point, explained that "[i]t is a basic principle of international law that one sovereign state does not adjudicate on the conduct of a foreign state".[22]

With respect to the proposition that incumbent heads of state have absolute personal immunity even if accused of committing an international crime,

> Judicial opinion and state practice on this point are unanimous, and no case can be found in which it was held that a state official possessing immunity *ratione personae* is subject to the criminal jurisdiction of a foreign state when it is

---

[20] *Supra* note 3, 2002, para. 58.

[21] *Ibid.*

[22] House of Lords, *Regina v. Bow Street Metropolitan Stipendiary Magistrate and Others, ex parte Pinochet Ugarte (No. 3)*, 2000, 1 AC 147, para. 201.

alleged that he or she has committed an international crime.[23]

It is a requirement of customary international law that a domestic court of one state must respect the immunity of the heads of another state, unless the second state waives this immunity. In Hissène Habré case before the domestic court of Senegal, Mr. Hissène Habré, the former head of state of Chad, did not benefit from any immunity. In an October 2002 letter to the Belgian judge investigating the charges against Habré, Chad's justice minister, Djimnain Koudj-Gaou, wrote, "Hissène Habré cannot claim to enjoy any form of immunity from the Chadian authorities". According to the ICJ, state representatives "cease to enjoy immunity from foreign jurisdiction if the State which they represent or have represented decides to waive that immunity".[24]

In the relationship between States Parties to the ICC Statute, one State Party may abrogate the head of state immunity of another State Party in order to fulfil its obligations under the Rome Statute. When a state ratifies the ICC Statute, it accepts all the obligations of the statute, including Article 27, which provides that heads of state of contracting parties are not immune from prosecution under the Rome Statute. Article 27(2) states that immunities, "whether under national or international law", shall not bar the Court from exercising its jurisdiction. This is particularly relevant to the process of arresting and surrendering indictees – if Article 27 applied only to trials before the ICC and not to the ability of national authorities from States Parties for the trial of the accused and for the implementation of arrest warrants, the whole structure of the ICC Statute would be meaningless.

As for the relationship between a contracting party and a non-contracting state, it is submitted that the immunity of officials from non-contracting states must still be respected under customary international law by domestic courts seeking to implement ICC arrest warrants, since the ICC Statute, as a treaty, cannot remove immunity of non-contracting states. According to Article 34 of the Vienna Convention on the Law of Treaties ('VCTL'), "a treaty does not create either obligations or rights

---

[23] Dapo Akande, "International Law Immunities and the International Criminal Court" (hereinafter 'Immunities and the ICC'), in *American Journal International Law*, 2004, vol. 98, p. 411.

[24] *Supra* note 3, 2002, para. 61.

for a third State without its consent". Although, Article 38 of the VCTL does not preclude "a rule set forth in a treaty from becoming binding upon a third State as a customary rule of international law, recognized as such",[25] non-immunity of the heads of state has not yet become a rule of customary international law.

4.3. Immunity of the Head of State before International Courts and Tribunals

The immunity of heads of states before international courts and tribunals is a very complicated issue. The recent case law in this area may be a good start for comments.

On 12 December 2011, the Pre-Trial Chamber ('PTC') of the ICC rendered the Decision Pursuant to Article 87(7) of the Rome Statute on the Failure by the Republic of Malawi to Comply with the Cooperation Requests Issued by the Court with Respect to the Arrest and Surrender of Omar Hassan Ahmad Al Bashir.[26] In the decision, having purportedly considered all the existing evidence, the Pre-Trial Chamber held "that customary international law creates an exception to Head of State immunity when international courts seek a Head of State's arrest for the commission of international crimes".[27] In support of this proposition, the PTC made a number of assertions. First it stated that "immunity for Heads of State before international courts has been rejected time and time again dating all the way back to World War I".[28] Second, it stated that "there has been an increase in Head of State prosecutions by international courts in the last decade [indicating that] initiating international prosecutions against Heads of State [has] gained widespread recognition as accepted practice".[29] Third, it stated that "the Statute now has reached 120 States Parties in its 9 plus years of existence, all of whom have accepted having

---

[25] See Articles 34 and 38 of the Vienna Convention of Law of Treaties.

[26] *Prosecutor v. Omar Hassan Ahmad Al Bashir*, Case No. ICC-02/05-01/09, Decision Pursuant to Article 87(7) of the Rome Statute on the Failure by the Republic of Malawi to Comply with the Cooperation Requests Issued by the Court with Respect to the Arrest and Surrender of Omar Hassan Ahmad Al Bashir, 12 December 2011, available at http://www.legal-tools.org/doc/476812/.

[27] *Ibid.* para. 43.

[28] *Ibid.* para. 38.

[29] *Ibid.* para. 39.

any immunity they had under international law stripped from their top officials".[30] Fourth, it said that since 120 states "have ratified this Statute and/or entrusted the Court with exercising 'its jurisdiction over persons for the most serious crimes of international concern'", it would be "facially inconsistent" for immunity to overrule this purpose.[31]

With due respect, I would like to make some comments on the findings of the PTC of the ICC. First, while it is reasonable to conclude that an individual head of state cannot escape criminal responsibility and that this can be considered a rule of customary international law, it does not mean that person no longer has immunity from the jurisdiction of the tribunal. As Akande writes, to "say that official capacity does not exclude criminal responsibility is not necessarily to say that the person may not be immune from the jurisdiction of particular tribunals".[32] After all, immunity acting as a procedural bar to prevent jurisdiction, does not pronounce on the legality or illegality of a particular act. It is submitted that the existence of a right does not necessarily mean that this right may be exercised. Although the subject matter jurisdiction of the ICC covers the international crimes listed in the Statute, the exercise of this jurisdiction might be barred by several factors, *inter alia*, head of state immunity.

The ICC's second argument is that:

> Subsequent to 14 February 2002, international prosecutions against Charles Taylor, Muammar Gaddafi, Laurent Gbagbo and the present case [Al Bashir] show that initiating international prosecutions against Heads of State have gained widespread recognition as accepted practice.[33]

With respect, the use of the term "widespread recognition" should be taken with a grain of salt. After all, this is something of a circular argument given that Muammar Gaddafi, Laurent Gbagbo and Al Bashir were

---

[30]   *Ibid.* para. 40.

[31]   *Ibid.* para. 41, citing Rome Statute of the International Criminal Court Art. 1, 17 July 1998, in *UNTS*, vol. 2187, p. 3 (hereinafter 'Rome Statute').

[32]   Dapo Akande, "ICC Issues Detailed Decision on Bashir's Immunity (…At long Last…) But Gets the Law Wrong", in *EJIL: Talk!*, 5 December 2011, available at http://www.ejiltalk.org/icc-issues-detailed-decision-on-bashir%e2%80%99s-immuni ty-at-long-last-but-gets-the-law-wrong/, last accessed on 13 October 2012 (hereinafter 'ICC Gets the Law Wrong').

[33]   *Prosecutor v. Omar Hassan Ahmad Al Bashir*, Case No. ICC-02/05-01/09, para. 39, *supra* note 26.

indicted by the ICC itself, albeit under a Security Council Referral. Further, at least in the case of Gaddafi and Gbagbo, it is arguable that they had lost their mandate for power by popular vote and would have had their immunity waived in any case. This leaves the case of Charles Taylor indicted as a serving head of state, which, by itself can hardly be used as widespread recognition of accepted practice. Moreover, the reasoning in the decision of the Special Court for Sierra Leone ('SCSL') has some fundamental flaws, since the SCSL only relies on its "truly international" nature and the immunity enjoyed by the sitting head of state according to international law does not apply before an international criminal court. As a matter of fact, the SCSL was not established by the Security Council pursuant to Chapter VII, as was the case with the ICTY and ICTR. Instead, the SCSL owes its existence to the treaty signed by the United Nations and the Government of Sierra Leone. Liberia was not a party to the treaty and did not waive the immunity of her head of state. The "truly international nature" of the Court can therefore hardly be a legitimate justification to abrogate the immunity of the heads of state of non-contracting states.

The ICC's conclusion that there is widespread recognition of the practice of initiating prosecutions against heads of state is all the more troubling considering that the PTC bases its third argument on the weight of state practice, pointing to the 120 States Parties to the Rome Statute, all of whom "have accepted having any immunity they had under international law stripped from their top officials".[34] It is true that those 120 States Parties have renounced the immunity of their own heads of state, but it would be a mistake to conclude that there is enough evidence of state practice to establish a new customary international law rule binding on all. As Schabas states, "the Court may have more than half the States in the world, but it does not represent half the population of the world".[35] Akande emphasises the importance of this point, stating:

> [...] that it is only parties to the ICC Statute that have waived the international law immunities [...] of their senior officials [...] nothing in the Statute can affect the immunities that the

---

[34] *Ibid.*, para. 40.

[35] William A. Schabas, *Obama, Medvedev and Hu Jintao may be Prosecuted by International Criminal Court, Pre-Trial Chamber* Concludes, PhD Studies in Human Rights, 15 December 2011, available at http://humanrightsdoctorate.blogspot.com/2011/12/obama-medvedev-and-hu-jintao-may-be.html, last accessed on 13 October 2012.

officials of nonparties would otherwise enjoy. Accordingly, Article 98 of the Statute represents an instruction to the Court and to ICC parties not to interfere with those officials of nonparties who ordinarily possess immunity in international law.[36]

Article 98(1) of the ICC Statute states:

> The Court may not proceed with a request for surrender or assistance which would require the requested State to act inconsistently with its obligations under international law with respect to the State or diplomatic immunity of a person or property of a third State, unless the Court can first obtain the cooperation of that third State for the waiver of the immunity.[37]

Indeed, the existence of both Article 27(2) and Article 98 of the Rome Statute may be a tacit acceptance by the drafters that the non-immunity of the head of state is not a rule of customary international law, as it gives deference to those non-States Parties.

Even among the States Parties to the Rome Statute, there are significant differences of opinion as to heads of state immunity, and therefore evidence of *opinio juris* negates the PTC's evidence of widespread state practice to a certain extent. For example, in the wake of the Pre-Trial Chamber's decision, the African Union Commission issued a press release[38] disagreeing with the decision. The African Union called on the Security Council to suspend the accusations, and that the Arab League also condemned the ICC's actions.[39] This is quite a significant show of

---

[36] *Immunities and the ICC*, 2004, *supra* note 23, p. 433.

[37] Rome Statute, *supra* note 31.

[38] Press Release, African Union Commission, On the decisions of Pre-Trial Chamber I of the International Criminal Court (ICC) pursuant to Article 87(7) of the Rome Statute on the alleged failure by the Republic of Chad and the Republic of Malawi to comply with the Cooperation Requests issued by the Court with respect to the Arrest and Surrender of President Omar Hassan Al Bashir or the Republic of The Sudan, African Union Press Release No. 002/2012, 9 January 2012, available at www.au.int/en/sites/default/files/PR-%20002-%20ICC%20English.pdf, last accessed on 13 October 2012.

[39] See http://news.bbc.co.uk/2/hi/7517393.stm, last accessed on 13 October 2012.

dissent toward the ICC's argument. According to Akande,[40] the PTC also fails to have regard to the national legislation of the States Parties, much of which draws a distinction between the immunity of the States Parties to the Statute and the immunities of the non-States Parties. This must further weaken the reasoning of the ICC.

While the ICJ in the *Arrest Warrant* case was seized of the question of the immunity of a Senior Official before a national court, it did make some comments, which suggested that immunity would not necessarily be a bar before international courts or tribunals. It stated that:

> The immunities enjoyed under international law by an incumbent or former Minister for Foreign Affairs do not represent a bar to criminal prosecution in certain circumstances [...] an incumbent or former Minister for Foreign Affairs may be subject to criminal proceedings before certain international criminal courts, where they have jurisdiction.[41]

It even went on to say that "Examples include the International Criminal Tribunal for the former Yugoslavia, and the International Criminal Tribunal for Rwanda [...] and the future International Criminal Court created by the 1998 Rome Convention".[42] On the surface, the ICJ appeared to draw a clear distinction between the level of immunity before a national court and the level of immunity before an international court. This has been read by some to mean that international tribunals must automatically overrule immunities. Such a reading would have been opposed by Judge Shahabuddeen, however, who stated in a case before the ICTY, "In my view, however, there is no substance in the suggested automaticity of disappearance of the immunity just because of the establishment of international criminal courts".[43]

On closer examination, the ICJ's statement appears to do nothing more than to confirm that specifically where an international court has jurisdiction, it is possible to remove immunities from a head of state, es-

---

[40] Dapo Akande and Sangeeta Shah, "Immunities of State Officials, International Crimes and Foreign Domestic Courts", in *European Journal of International*, 2010, vol. 21, Law 815.

[41] *Supra* note 3, 2002, para. 61.

[42] *Ibid.*

[43] *Prosecutor v. Krstić*, Case No. IT-98-33-A, Decision on Application for Subpoenas, Dissenting Opinion of Judge Shahabuddeen, 1 July 2003, para. 11, available at http://www.legal-tools.org/doc/7635c3/.

pecially in the case where the head of state of a State Party to the Rome Statute is indicted by the ICC. It does not explicitly say that immunities no longer exist before any international courts and tribunals, in particular with regard to non-contracting states.

Even if one were to assume that the ICJ meant to imply that there may be no head of state immunity before an international tribunal, its failure to fully define what constitutes an international court remains problematic. Indeed, taken to its full conclusion, no one could say that what Schabas hypothesises may not be true:

> [...] if there is no immunity before any international criminal court [...] would it be possible for Nauru, Monaco, Andorra, [...] and the Palestinian Authority to join together and create an international criminal tribunal where the President of the United States would be stripped of the immunity he would otherwise possess before the national courts of those countries?[44]

This might seem far-fetched, but undeniably there remain significant doubts over the status of head of state immunity in international law.

4.4. The Difference between the International *ad hoc* Tribunals and the ICC

When discussing the effectiveness of the international tribunals, as well as the issue of head of state immunity, it is normal to compare the situation of the ICTY and ICTR with that of the ICC. But in practice they are quite different. There are great differences in the creation of the ICTY, ICTR and ICC, which means that they cannot in general be considered like for like. The ICTY and ICTR were established by Security Council resolutions pursuant to Chapter VII of the U.N. Charter, and they are regarded as the subsidiary organs of the Security Council. Therefore, the ICTY and ICTR enjoy a legal basis that rests on Chapter VII of the U.N. Charter. Their judges can and have issued binding orders to states. When conducting statutory investigations on the territory of states, the prosecution services of these Tribunals have not sought permission as

---

[44] Schabas, 2011, *supra* note 35.

such from the states concerned. Under Article 25 of the U.N. Charter,[45] all U.N. member states are obliged to accept and implement the decisions of the Security Council adopted pursuant to Chapter VII, and this obligation prevails over other treaty obligations in accordance with Article 103 of the U.N. Charter.[46]

In contrast, the ICC cannot base its orders and decisions on Chapter VII of the U.N. Charter. The implementation of its work depends entirely on state co-operation, and three permanent members of the U.N. Security Council – China, Russia and the United States, among a number of powerful states, are not members of the ICC system. While the ICTY and ICTR established by the Security Council may execute its mandate under Chapter VII of the U.N. Charter, the ICC can only occasionally rely on the Council, and even not to the same extent.

Article 87(7) of the ICC Statute provides that:

> [w]here a State Party fails to comply with a request to coop-erate by the Court contrary to the provisions of this Statute [...] the Court may make a finding to that effect and refer the matter to the Assembly of States Parties or, where the Secu-rity Council referred the matter to the Court, to the Security Council.

In practice, however, the extent to which the Security Council will take action on these referrals remains to be seen. On 27 August 2010 and on 12 May 2011, Pre-Trial Chamber I of the ICC issued three decisions informing the Security Council and the Assembly of States Parties to the Rome Statute about Omar Al Bashir's visits to the Republic of Kenya, the Republic of Chad and Djibouti, "in order for them to take any measure they may deem appropriate".[47] On 25 October 2010 and on 1 December 2010, the Judges also issued two decisions requesting the Republic of Kenya and the Central African Republic to inform the Chamber about any

---

[45] Article 25 of the U.N. Charter reads: "The Members of the United Nations agree to accept and carry out the decisions of the Security Council in accordance with the present Charter".

[46] Article 103 of the U.N. Charter reads: "In the event of a conflict between the obligations of the Members of the United Nations under the present Charter and their obligations under any other international agreement, their obligations under the present Charter shall prevail".

[47] Report of the International Criminal Tribunal, United Nations General Assembly, sixty-sixth session, 19 August 2011, A/66/309, para. 25.

problem which would impede or prevent the arrest and surrender of Omar Al Bashir in the event that he visited these countries.[48] To date, the Security Council has taken no action at all in this matter. "In other words, the Security Council has not given the ICC a *carte blanche* in the matter of judicial cooperation".[49]

In contrast, the ICTY, the ICTY indicted 161 suspects and all of them have been arrested and surrendered to the seat of the Tribunal owning to the co-operation of all the states in the world. In the case of non co-operation, the Security Council did take action (although it is far from a firm precedent) to compel the former Yugoslavia to "cooperate fully"[50] with the ICTY, which leads to the arrest and transfer of the President of Serbia and Montenegro, Slobodan Milošević, to The Hague.

4.5. Security Council Referrals

The increasing prosecution of sitting heads of states before the ICC seemingly owes much to the process of Security Council referrals to the ICC in conjunction with Chapter VII of the U.N. Charter and Article 13(b) of the ICC Statute.

Referrals from the Security Council have been the most effective way for the ICC to have jurisdiction over the sitting head of state of a non-contracting state to the ICC. To date, the ICC has issued arrest warrants for two sitting heads of states, Sudanese President Al Bashir and Gaddafi of Libya, following UNSC resolutions referring the situations in Darfur and Libya to the Court. But neither was arrested and transferred to The Hague. One of the fugitives even travelled to several countries, some of which are States Parties to the ICC, and took part in many international conferences.[51] Under the Security Council referrals, there will be two scenarios, the prosecution and trial before the ICC and arrest and surrender of the fugitives to the seat of the Court, respectively involving two kinds of

---

[48]   ICC Press Release, 19 October 2011, ICC-CPI-20111019, PR 733.

[49]   Paola Gaeta, "Does President Al Bashir Enjoy Immunity From Arrest?", in *Journal of International Criminal Justice*, vol. 7, May 2009, pp. 315-332.

[50]   S.C. Res. 1199, on the situation in Kosovo (FRY), para. 13, U.N. Doc. S/RES/1199, 23 September 1998.

[51]   BBC News Africa, "Sudan's Bashir offers help to Libya during criticised visit", 7 January 2012, available at http://www.bbc.co.uk/news/world-africa-16454493, last accessed on 30 July 2012.

states, the States Parties to the ICC Statute and the non-contracting parties.

The ICC, in its decision to issue an arrest warrant for Al Bashir, stated that "the Security Council [...] has [...] accepted that the investigation into the said situation, as well as any prosecution arising therefrom, will take place in accordance with the statutory framework provided for in the Statute".[52] In other words, if a referral is made to the ICC, the Rome Statute provisions will become operative on the State concerned, regardless of whether it is a State Party to the Rome Statute. If the fugitive falls within the jurisdiction of the ICC, the ICC will apply Article 27 in every case referred. In effect those individuals indicted by the ICC after a situation has been referred would not be entitled to claim head of state immunity as a bar to jurisdiction before the ICC, even if they are not from States Parties.

Therefore, the point remains that the key state, that is, the state to which the head of state belongs, is bound to comply with the Court. If it is a State Party to the ICC, it is bound by its treaty obligations. If it is a non-contracting state, it is bound by the primacy of the U.N. Charter and by Articles 25 and 103 of the U.N. Charter to accept and carry out the decisions of the Security Council. Consequently the Rome Statute (including Article 27) will apply to that State, meaning that a sitting head of state can be legally indicted and subsequently will not be entitled to claim immunity as a bar to jurisdiction before the ICC.

Furthermore, it is generally understood that the Security Council may affect the rights of states when taking measures of which it deems to be necessary for the maintenance of international peace and security.[53] Consequently, the Security Council has the power to "decide explicitly or by implication that even immunities *ratione personae* do not constitute a bar to the cooperation of States in the execution of requests made by the

---

[52] *Prosecutor v. Omar Hassan Ahmad Al Bashir*, Case No. ICC-02/05-01/09-3, Decision on the Prosecution's Application for a Warrant of Arrest against Omar Hassan Ahmad Al Bashir (Public Redacted Version), 4 March 2009, available at http://www.legal-tools.org//e79f78/.

[53] Article 41 of the U.N. Charter reads: "The Security Council may decide what measures not involving the use of armed force are to be employed to give effect to its decisions, and it may call upon the Members of the United Nations to apply such measures".

Court for arrest and surrender".[54] "It is generally accepted that the Security Council in the exercise of its powers under Chapter VII of the U.N. Charter is competent to remove the immunity of serving heads of State".[55] This view is reinforced by the proposition that "[b]y referring a situation [...] the Security Council vests the ICC with the necessary authority to exercise its jurisdiction [...] and thereby makes article 27 applicable to office-holders of non-States parties".[56]

As for the arrest and surrender of the fugitives, the "statutory framework provided for in the Statute" also indicates the application of Article 98 for international co-operation, especially with the non-contracting state to the ICC Statute. In such case, the ICC should first obtain the co-operation of the state to which the indictee belongs for the waiver of the immunity.

As mentioned before, the ICC was set up by a treaty, which theoretically, only has the binding force over the States Parties, but not over the non-contracting states. As one scholar explains, a "referral by the Security Council is simply a mechanism envisaged in the Statute to trigger the jurisdiction of the ICC: it does not and cannot turn a state non-party to the Statute into a state party".[57] Nothing in the Statute supports the view that a referral by the Security Council turns the ICC into a subsidiary organ of the Security Council, as is the case with the ICTY and the ICTR. The obligations of States Parties to co-operate with the ICC remain 'only' treaty obligations, irrespective of how the jurisdiction of the Court has been triggered, including in the case of a Security Council referral.[58]

---

[54] Claus Kress and Kimberly Prost, "Article 98 (Cooperation with respect to waiver of immunity and consent to surrender)", in Otto Triffterer (ed.), *Commentary on the Rome Statute of the International Criminal Court: Observers' Notes, Article by Article*, second Edition, 2008, p. 1613.

[55] Dapo Akande, "The Bashir Indictment: Are Serving Heads of State Immune from ICC Prosecution?", in *Oxford Transitional Justice Research Working Paper Series*, 30 July 2008, p. 2, available at www.csls.ox.ac.uk/documents/Akande.pdf, last accessed on 13 October 2012.

[56] Tilman M. Dralle, "The Legal Nature of Security Council Referrals to the ICC and Muammar Gaddafi's Immunity from Arrest", June 2011, p. 3, available at http://www.tilman-dralle.de/pdf/Gaddafi_Immunity_International_Criminal_Court_Security_Council_Referral.pdf, last accessed on 13 October 2012.

[57] *Supra* note 46, p. 324

[58] *Supra* note 46.

It is submitted that the Statute will only be binding where the Security Council expressly requires all the member states of the United Nations to comply with ICC requests, in which case Article 103 of the U.N. Charter requires that member States give primacy to the obligations under the U.N. Charter. In every referral to date, the Security Council has expressly required the State of which the head of state is a national comply with the ICC requests,[59] without issuing the similar requests to the non-contracting states to the ICC Statute. According to paragraph 2 of Security Council Resolution 1593 (2005), only "Sudan and all the parties to the conflict" shall co-operate fully with the Court, while other states and regional and international organisations are just "urged" to co-operate with the ICC, which is not mandatory.

If the Security Council would like to make an arrest warrant effective, it may adopt a resolution requesting all states, including non-contracting states, to co-operate with the ICC and surrender the fugitives to the ICC. This might be the only effective way to compel a non-contracting state to carry out such an arrest warrant.

4.6. Conclusion

Sovereign immunity is a well-established rule of international law. Undoubtedly, there has been and continues to be a change in the balance between the law of immunities and international criminal law, in favour of the latter. The ICC was not wrong to point out that there are a greater number of prosecutions against heads of state. However, with significant doubts over the extent of state practice and *opinio juris* in this regard, it cannot yet be said that non-immunity for heads of state has become a rule under customary international law.

Taking into account customary international law and the latest developments in this area, if an indictee falls under the domestic jurisdiction of a state, and both that state and the state to which the indictee belongs are contracting parties to the ICC Statute, the host state may refuse the indictee's claim of immunity because of its treaty obligation under the Statute and the principle of complementarity. If the host state is a contracting party to the ICC Statute, while indictee is from a non-contracting

---

[59] *See, e.g.,* S.C. Res. 1593, para. 2, U.N. Doc. S/RES/1593, 31 March 2005 (stating that "the Government of Sudan [...] *shall cooperate fully* with and provide any necessary assistance to the Court and the Prosecutor pursuant" [emphasis added]).

state, it remains the case that head of state immunity under customary international law takes precedence over international criminal law unless the indictee's state waives her immunity, taking into consideration the findings of the ICJ in the *Arrest Warrant* case. If an indictee was brought before an international tribunal such as ICC, which has been given the mandate to disregard such immunity, the claim of immunity may probably be rejected, regardless of whether the indictee is from a contracting party to the ICC Statute. Finally, regarding the arrest and surrender of fugitives to the ICC, if both the requested state and the third state are contracting parties to the Statute, they should "co-operate fully with the Court in its investigation and prosecution of crimes within the jurisdiction of the Court". Especially, Article 86 and Article 27 of the Statute should be fully respected. In the case that the requested state is a contracting party to the Statute, while the third state is not, under Article 98(1) of the Rome Statute, the ICC cannot issue a request for surrender or assistance to a State Party "which would require the requested State to act inconsistently with its obligations under international law with respect to the State or diplomatic immunity of a person or property of a third State". The only way the Court can proceed with such a request is to get the third state to waive the immunity in question.[60]

A referral from the Security Council is the most effective way for the ICC to have jurisdiction over non-States Parties, since its Resolution adopted pursuant to Chapter VII could remove the immunity of the head of state of a non-contracting state to the Rome Statute. Whether the Security Council could or would like to adopt a resolution requesting all the states to co-operate with the ICC to arrest and transfer the fugitives or removing the immunity of the head of state depends on its political will. At the very least, the unanimous adoption of the Security Council Resolution referring the situation in Libya to the ICC provides some hope that this may be possible.[61]

---

[60] Rome Statute, Art. 98(1).
[61] S/Res/1970 (2011), 26 February 2011.

5

Immunity for State Officials from Foreign Jurisdiction for International Crimes

JIA Bingbing[*]

5.1. Introduction

Immunity for state officials is a part of state immunity and still generally obtains in criminal or civil proceedings instituted against them before national courts. The official capacity of the officials cannot be lightly assumed away in such proceedings, and the capacity attaches regardless of the perceived nature of the acts of such persons. A debate exists in practice and theory over the granting of state immunity in cases of international crimes. The current practice, however, still places state immunity on a higher level to other rules of international law that ground national jurisdiction, as opposed to international jurisdiction. This may be due to the unchanged foundation of the international order based in the U.N. Charter. Any denial of state immunity of foreign officials by a national court, without support of general state practice, will raise questions regarding the soundness of the fundamental principles of that order, and will not likely generate new rules of customary law in terms of state practice.

A word is first said of the usage to be employed in this context. Immunity for state officials, while slightly longish, is adequate for the present purposes, and it is also recognised that it is an aspect of state immunity.[1] Further, it is not considered to be equivalent to diplomatic im-

---

[*] **JIA Bingbing**, D.Phil. (Oxon.), is Professor of International Law at the Tsinghua University Law School since 2004. He was Legal Officer, the Appeals Chamber of the ICTY, 2002–2004; Legal Officer, Trial Chamber III of the ICTY, 2000–2002; Associate Legal Officer in the Appeals Chambers of the ICTY and of the ICTR, 1998–2000; and Law Clerk in the Appeals Chambers of the ICTY and ICTR, 1996–1998. He has published extensively in international law and serves as a member of several editorial boards.

[1] Arthur Watts, "The Legal Position in International Law of Heads of States, Heads of Governments and Foreign Ministers", in *Recueil des Cours*, 1994-III, vol. 247, p. 35.

munities. It arises where state officials, other than diplomats or head of state or government, are concerned in civil or criminal cases brought in foreign jurisdictions. Although the acts that give rise to the cases are those of individuals, these acts have been explicitly carried out in the official capacity so that they equally represent the acts of the state. In one authority's words, "[a] state can only act through servants and agents; their official acts are the acts of the state; and the state's immunity in respect of them is fundamental to the principle of state immunity".[2] Indeed, the Draft Articles of the ILC on Responsibility of States for International Wrongful Acts ('ILC Draft Articles') adopted by the International Law Commission ('ILC') in 2001, states in Article 4 that:

1. The conduct of any State organ shall be considered an act of that State under international law, whether the organ exercises legislative, executive, judicial or any other functions, whatever position it holds in the organization of the State, and whatever its character as an organ of the central government or of a territorial unit of the State.

2. An organ includes any person or entity which has that status in accordance with the internal law of the State.[3]

The fundamental principle of those draft articles is that "[e]very internationally wrongful act of a State entails the international responsibility of that State".[4] There is no question about the attributability of such responsibility to the State in question.

The 2004 U.N. Convention on Jurisdictional Immunities of States and Their Property (hereinafter 'the 2004 Convention') also provides, under Article 2(1)(b)(iv), that the term 'State' includes "representatives of the State acting in that capacity".[5] This convention chiefly provides for "the immunity of a State and its property from the jurisdiction of the courts of another State".[6] Again, the attributability of the responsibility for the official acts of individuals is beyond question, in that the immunity

---

[2] *Jones v. Ministry of the Interior of the Kingdom of Saudi Arabia and Another,* United Kingdom House of Lords, 2006, vol. 26, Opinions of 14 June 2006, para. 30 (*per* Lord Bingham of Cornhill).

[3] UNGA, A/RES/56/83, adopted 12 December 2001, with Annex.

[4] Article 1.

[5] UNGA, A/Res/59/38, adopted on 2 December 2004.

[6] Article 1.

of the officials derives from that of the State on whose behalf they act, to the extent as allowed by the 2004 Convention.

State immunity, in the light of the existing rules of attributability of state responsibility, can be either *ratione personae*, as in the case of, typically, heads of State,[7] or *ratione materiae*, or both, depending on the circumstances of each case in which immunity is pleaded. In practice, problems of immunities may arise in cases involving the class of officials other than heads of State or government or those covered by the law of diplomatic immunities and privileges, due to the apparent lack of specific rules to cover a wide range of positions, ranks, and titles held by such officials and known to governments of the world.

In principle, the personal scope of state immunity is to be determined by the rule of attribution of state responsibility in international law,[8] which point is confirmed by the ILC Draft Articles and the 2004 Convention. Where state immunity is assured, immunity for state officials is equally guaranteed as a corollary. The tension in this regard, however, lies with the cases in which immunity for state officials, though often to obtain, has been challenged, especially in national jurisprudence, on the ground of violations of peremptory rules of international law and of a distinction between the immunity of a state and that of its officials as persons. This state of tension has been the defining feature of the topic for the past twenty years.[9]

Before we proceed with the immunity theme, two jurisdictional issues faced by national courts are to be considered. After all, state immunity as a procedural bar is to be pleaded before national courts; whereas before international criminal tribunals or the International Criminal Court ('ICC'), it has had no standing due to a consistent pattern of practice that denies it in such *fora*. This practice of denial has a good claim to reflect

---

[7] *Cf.* Art. 3(2), the 2004 Convention. But practice may admit into this category other high-ranking officials: R. Kolodkin, "Second Report on Immunity of State Officials from Foreign Criminal Jurisdiction", U.N. Doc. A/CN.4/631, 10 June 2010, paras. 7 and 94(i).

[8] As, for instance, the ILC Special Rapporteur stated in his report on this matter, "an official performing an act of a commercial nature enjoys immunity from foreign criminal jurisdiction if this act is attributed to the State": R. Kolodkin, 2010, *supra* note 7, para. 94(e).

[9] A. Gattini, "War Crimes and State Immunity in the *Ferrini* Case", in *Journal of International Criminal Justice*, 2005, vol. 3, p. 233.

customary law. The two issues are the following: is the plea applicable to all plaints without any distinction between criminal and civil causes of action? This first issue closely links with the second, which entails an excursion into the contemporary controversy surrounding the application of the principle of universal jurisdiction ('U.J.').

5.2.   Criminal *versus* Civil Jurisdiction

Jurisdiction in international law is the authority or power of a state under the law to regulate conduct in matters not exclusively of domestic concern.[10] A discussion of issues of jurisdiction is essentially concerned with the limits of the legal competence of a State or other regulatory authorities to enact, apply, and enforce rules of conduct upon persons. In Mann's word,[11] it is referred to the function of law in regulating and delimiting the respective competences of States.[12] International law imposes limits on the exercise of state jurisdiction without differentiating whether it is concerned with criminal or civil matters.[13]

The fundamental question in this context is always whether there exists "a sufficiently close connection" between certain matters and a particular legal system seeking to govern them or a particular sovereign qualified to regulate them.[14] Similar rules that embody the connection exist in all fields of international law.[15] Conceptually, the matter seems to be

---

[10]   This is no different from the well-established meaning of the word in domestic law, such as the U.S. system: J. Beale, "The Jurisdiction of a Sovereign State", in *Harvard Law Review*, 1923, vol. 36, p. 241.

[11]   F.A. Mann, "The Doctrine of Jurisdiction in International Law", in *Recueil des Cours*, 1964-I, vol. 111, p. 15.

[12]   Quoting: C. Rousseau, "Principes de droit international public", in *Recueil des Cours*, 1958-I, vol. 93, p. 394.

[13]   *Cf.* Arrest Warrant of 11 April 2000, *Democratic Republic of the Congo v. Belgium*, Judgment of 14 February 2002 (hereinafter 'Arrest Warrant'), ICJ Reports, 2002, p. 3, para 51, available at http://www.legal-tools.org/doc/c6bb20/. The Institute of International Law also understood the term 'jurisdiction' as embracing "criminal, civil and administrative" matters: Third Commission, *Resolution on the Immunity fro Jurisdiction of the State and of Persons who Act on Behalf of the State in case of International Crimes*, IDI Napoli Session, 2009, Art. I(2), available at http://www.idi-iil.org/idiE/resolutionsE/2009_naples_01_en.pdf, last accessed on 13 October 2012.

[14]   F.A. Mann, "The Doctrine of International Jurisdiction Revisited after Twenty Years", in *Recueil des Cours*, 1984-I, vol. 186, p. 28.

[15]   *Ibid.*, p. 29.

---

quite straightforward. In his article, BIN Cheng draws a finer distinction between two elements of jurisdiction, namely, 'jurisfaction' and 'jurisaction'.[16] It is with the second element of jurisdiction that immunity is concerned, because it deals with the way in which state jurisdiction is exercised within and without a state's borders. In this general sense, there is no difference as far as is concerned the effect of immunity upon the exercise of any particular kind of state jurisdiction.[17] But for individuals in positions of government, it seems that the developments related to the criminal side of the competence are increasingly worrisome. This concern could be seen in the recent inclusion of the topic of U.J. in the agenda of the United Nations General Assembly ('UNGA'),[18] and in the Secretary-General's Report of 29 July 2010, with 44 governments' observations recorded.[19]

As recent practice that has involved the plea of state immunity occurs mostly in national jurisdiction, in which recourse to the principle of U.J. is often seen, a brief look at the practice is warranted.

5.3. Universal Jurisdiction

It is not intended to lay out the state of the current law of U.J.,[20] but to remark on two points that are necessary for further discussion. The first point has to do with the difficulty encountered by states seeking to develop rules for the exercise of U.J. in a domestic context. U.J. is to be exercised by the forum state where criminal or tort proceedings are initiated, and one question above all would require an immediate solution, namely, on what basis and against whom U.J. is exercised. Secondly, uncertainty

---

[16] B. Cheng, "The Extra-Territorial Application on International Law", in *Current Legal Problems*, 1965, vol. 18, p. 136.

[17] Arthur Watts, 1994-III, *supra* note 1, p. 106: immunity from suit applies to officials in respect of matters arising on their official visits and for matters arising prior to the visits.

[18] The UNGA adopted Resolution 64/117 on 16 December 2009, requesting the Secretary-General to invite member States to submit observations on a series of issues falling under the agenda item of the scope and application of the principle of universal jurisdiction for the sixty-fifth session of the UNGA.

[19] Those observations can be found at http://www.un.org/en/ga/sixth/65/ScopeAppUni Juri.shtml, last accessed on 13 October 2012.

[20] S.H. Yee, "Universal Jurisdiction: Concept, Logic and Reality", in *Chinese Journal of International Law*, 2011, vol. 10, pp. 503–530.

clearly surrounds any claim in practice for a larger scope for U.J. than that of and through treaty-based mechanisms. If that claim is made, immunity will become its first hurdle.

The first point concerns an ongoing dispute between those states exercising U.J. and those whose nationals are at the receiving end of the exercise. While jurisdiction, and especially its implementation in respect of criminal matters, have never been short of controversy, the active resort to U.J. – as distinct from other heads of jurisdiction that have already enjoyed wide acceptance among states as a matter of customary law – by a few countries in recent years over alleged international crimes has touched a raw nerve of the states whose nationals have been affected. This development has highlighted one aspect of the debate at the international level: namely, where treaties are non-applicable, is there a customary law basis for the exercise of U.J.?[21] If the customary basis is not recognised, U.J. cannot be exercised in that situation. Otherwise, immunity comes into play on an equal footing to the alleged customary law basis of U.J.

The preceding discussion gives rises to the second point. It appears that the law of U.J. as a whole is uncertain at its present stage of development, as testified to by the decision in the *Arrest Warrant* case.[22] In the *Arrest Warrant* case, the International Court of Justice, or ICJ, could not find any customary rule that denied immunity to a serving foreign minister while he was suspected of having committed war crimes or crimes against humanity.[23] The Court stated that:

> [...] although various international conventions or the prevention and punishment of certain serious crimes impose on States obligations of prosecution or extradition, thereby requiring them to extend their criminal jurisdiction, such extension of jurisdiction in no way affects immunities under customary international law, including those of Ministers for Foreign Affairs. These remain opposable before the courts of

---

[21] *Cf.* Institute of International Law, *Resolution on Universal Criminal Jurisdiction with Respect to the Crime of Genocide, Crimes against Humanity and War Crimes*, adopted 26 August 2005 during the Krakow session, *Annuaire* (Tome II), vol. 71, p. 297.

[22] Arrest Warrant, *supra* note 13, para. 15 (which shows that there was no link between Belgium and the crimes alleged of the Congolese Foreign Minister).

[23] *Ibid.*, para. 58.

> a foreign State, even where those courts exercise such a ju-
> risdiction under these conventions.[24]

The judgment, by a vote of 13 to 3, found that:

> [...] the issue against Mr. Abdulaye Yerodia Ndombasi of
> the arrest warrant of 11 April 2000, and its international cir-
> culation, constituted violations of a legal obligation of the
> Kingdom of Belgium towards the Democratic Republic of
> the Congo, in that they failed to respect the immunity from
> criminal jurisdiction and the inviolability which the incum-
> bent Minister for Foreign Affairs of the Democratic Republic
> of the Congo enjoyed under international law.[25]

It then required Belgium to cancel the warrant and to so inform the parties to which it had been circulated. What has transpired from the case is that the claim by some countries to exercise U.J. in spite of that uncertainty in state practice lies at the root of the recent cases in which the plea of state immunity has been invoked.

The implications of the findings of the Court are thought-provoking.[26] For, U.J. based in treaty in general and on the conventional obligation of *aut dedere aut judicare* in particular has to give way to the customary rules of immunity. Is customary law superior to treaties? If so, what is the reason? Furthermore, the first point raised above seems to add another twist to this question. Supposing the law of immunities and that of U.J. are both customary in nature, can they cancel each other out, thus implying an equality in terms of validity? Or the customary law of immunity prevails over that of U.J., thus implying a hierarchy within customary law, leaving aside the issue of *jus cogens*? Those questions could only be answered after we consider, in the next section, the nature of the state immunity law.

In brief, the current practice in respect of U.J. is as inconsistent as it is still developing.[27] Apart from a list of well-known treaties,[28] the evolv-

---

[24] *Ibid.*, para. 59.

[25] *Ibid.*, para. 78.

[26] For instance, Antonio Cassese, "When may Senior State Officials Be Tried for International Crimes? Some Comments on the Congo v. Belgium Case", in *European Journal of International Law*, 2002, vol. 13, pp. 853–875.

[27] *The AU-EU Expert Report on the Principle of Universal Jurisdiction*, Council of the European Union Secretariat, Brussels, 16 April 2009, 8672/1/09 Rev.1, para. 24, pp. 24–25.

ing nature of that practice can also be seen through the litigations in the U.S. brought on the basis of the *Alien Tort Statute* and claims for civil damages elsewhere in the world for international crimes.[29] Universal civil or tort jurisdiction, as an alternative to criminal jurisdiction, may likewise trigger the plea of state immunity by the respondent. To illustrate, in a case involving a claim for civil liability for torture by state officials, *Jones v. Saudi Arabia*, the House of Lords of the U.K. upheld state immunity,[30] but it also intended to deny it in criminal proceedings where the Convention against Torture (or 'CAT'),[31] in its view, created an exception to the general rules of immunity.[32] The British court would only recognise an exception to state immunity by virtue of a specific multilateral treaty to which the U.K. is a party.[33] What is the rationale of the immunity for state-officials that makes it so powerful a plea in national courts?

5.4. Immunity for State Officials

The rationale of state immunity as a whole has been well explained by Marshall CJ in *The Schooner Exchange v. McFadddon*:

> This perfect equality and absolute independence of sovereigns, and this common interest compelling them to mutual intercourse, and an interchange of good offices with each other, have given rise to a class of cases in which every sovereign is understood to waive the exercise of a part of that complete exclusive territorial jurisdiction, which has been stated to be the attribute of every nation.[34]

---

[28] S.H. Yee, 2011, *supra* note 20, pp. 512–519.

[29] *Cf.* H. Fox, *The Law of State Immunity*, second edition, Oxford University Press, 2008, pp. 356–362, 583–590.

[30] *Supra* note 2, para. 33 (*per* Lord Bingham of Cornhill): "Where applicable, state immunity is an absolute preliminary bar, precluding any examination of the merits. A state is either immune from the jurisdiction of a foreign court or it is not".

[31] "Convention against Torture and other Cruel, Inhuman or Degrading Treatment or Punishment", in *United Nations Treaty Series*, 1984, vol. 1465, p. 85 (entry into force 26 June 1987).

[32] *Supra* note 2, para. 33 (*per* Lord Bingham of Cornhill).

[33] Whereas the ICJ did not consider that such treaties as the ICC Statute would be sufficient, in terms of customary law, to displace immunity: Arrest Warrant, para. 58 ("It finds that these rules likewise do not enable it to conclude that any such an exception exists in customary international law in regard to national courts.").

[34] *The Schooner Exchange v. McFaddon*, 1812, 7 *Cranch* 116.

The European Court of Human Rights has reached a similar conclusion, that:

> [...] sovereign immunity is a concept of international law, developed out of the principle par in parem non habet imperium, by virtue of which one State shall not be subject to the jurisdiction of another State. The Court considers that the grant of immunity to a State in civil proceedings pursues the legitimate aim of complying with international law to promote comity and good relations between States through the respect of another State's sovereignty.[35]

Immunity for the officials other than heads of state or government is mainly functional in nature,[36] especially when that immunity is relevant to matters arising during official visits or missions.[37] The ICJ noted in 2008 that international law did not recognise personal immunities of the officials as concerned in *Djibouti v. France* case, namely, the *procureur général* and the Head of National Security of the Republic of Djibouti.[38] There is also the scholarly view that the 2004 Convention endorses the functional immunity for acts performed in an official capacity.[39]

But the scope of this functionality is in fact larger, as the ICJ stated in 2002, in respect of a matter that did not arise during any official visits, that:

> The Court accordingly concludes that the functions of a Minister for Foreign Affairs are such that, throughout the duration of his or her office, he or she when abroad enjoys full immunity from criminal jurisdiction and inviolability. That immunity and that inviolability protect the individual concerned against any act of authority of another State which

---

[35] *Al-Adsani v. U.K.*, Application No 35763/97, Judgment of 21 November 2001, *International Law Reports* vol. 123, p. 24, para. 54.

[36] *Cf.* Art. 3(1), the 2004 Convention. Also see, Djibouti and France's submissions in: Certain Questions of Mutual Assistance in Criminal Matters, *Djibouti v. France*, ICJ Reports 2008, p. 177, paras. 187 and 189.

[37] Arthur Watts, 1994-III, *supra* note 1, pp. 103, 107. Also see, R. Kolodkin, 2010, *supra* note 7, para. 94(h).

[38] ICJ Reports, 2008, p.177, para. 194.

[39] D. Stewart, "The Immunity of State Officials under the UN Convention on Jurisdictional Immunities of States and Their Property", in *Vanderbilt Journal of Transnational Law*, 2011, vol. 44, p. 1056.

---

would hinder him or her in the performance of his or her duties.[40]

This confirms the view that incumbent foreign ministers, as heads of state and government and diplomatic agents, enjoy personal immunity under both treaties and customary law.[41] The Court did not define, and there has been no certainty with regard to, the class of officials that may come under this type of immunity.

The functional character aside, the absoluteness of immunity from criminal jurisdiction accruing to State officials is unmistakable.[42] It is not possible that, if immunity of a foreign government from criminal jurisdiction before a court of the forum state is assured, international law withholds that immunity from those officials who have carried out the instructions of that government that give rise to the exercise of that jurisdiction. Even their acts beyond governmental instructions are recognised by the law to be covered by immunity, due to the official capacity in which the acts were carried out.[43] Officials are servants, agents or organs of a government; and in view of the recent cases from the ICJ, high-ranking officials may just be able to presume that they are clothed with immunity due to official capacity.[44] This could be another guise of personal immunity, in that the official capacity is determined by the rank of the official concerned in this regard. To recognise his or her immunity, the court relies on the official capacity as provided by the rank. The rank naturally attaches to the person in question, and the two cannot be separated without a proper process of demotion by the government which appoints the person to the office. A foreign court cannot presume lightly that the person is not protected by immunity. The preceding view also applies to the situation in which the person acts in a presumably private capacity. The official cap

---

[40] Arrest Warrant, *supra* note 13, para. 54; see also, *ibid.*, Joint Separate Opinion of Higgins, Kooijmans, and Buergenthal, para. 75.

[41] *Cf.* C. Keitner, "Foreign immunity after *Samantar*", in *Vanderbilt Journal of Transnational Law*, 2011, vol. 44, pp. 841–842.

[42] R. Kolodkin, 2010, *supra* note 7, p. 54.

[43] Art. 7, ILC Draft Articles: "The conduct of an organ of a State or of a person or entity empowered to exercise elements of the governmental authority shall be considered an act of the State under international law if the organ, person or entity acts in that capacity, even if it exceeds its authority or contravenes instructions".

[44] Arrest Warrant, *supra* note 13, para. 59. The statement of the Court in the paragraph did not distinguish between acts in official and in private capacity.

stays on the person's head until it is legally removed. It is, however, recognised that there is a debate over the personal immunity of officials below the rank of foreign minister.[45] As things stand,[46] immunity of this type has been upheld in favour of the officials implicated in criminal or civil damage cases initiated in several countries.[47] In parallel to this fact, it may be noted that state immunity is increasingly relied on by officials or agents or their governments in cases in which the accused are not present in the forum state, and their deeds have been committed outside that country.[48] This increase in the use of the plea of state immunity results from the widening use of national jurisdiction over foreign state officials.

As for the concerns with impunity that may ensue, international law does not leave the matter undecided to the detriment of the victims, reflecting the maxim that *ubi jus ibi remedium*. The ICJ explicitly stated in the *Arrest Warrant* case that:

> [...] while jurisdictional immunity is procedural in nature, criminal responsibility is a question of substantive law. Jurisdictional immunity may well bar prosecution for a certain period or for certain offences; it cannot exonerate the person to whom it applies from all criminal responsibility.[49]

---

[45] R. Kolodkin, 2010, *supra* notes 7, paras. 35 and 94; R. van Alebeek, *The Immunity of States and Their Officials in International Criminal Law and International Human Rights Law*, Oxford University Press, 2008, pp. 192–195.

[46] Art. 31(1), *Convention on Special Missions*, adopted 8 December 1969 by the UNGA, entry into force 21 June 1985, in *UNTS*, vol. 1400, p. 231. As of writing, it had 38 States Parties: see further http://treaties.un.org/pages/ViewDetails.aspx?src=TREATY &mtdsg_ no= III-9&chapter=3&lang=en, last accessed on 29 March 2012.

[47] C. Tomuschat, "The International Law of State Immunity and its Development by National Institutions", *Vanderbilt Journal of Transnational Law*, 2011, vol. 44, pp. 1133–1139 (the Italian Corte di Cassazione's jurisprudence is noted as one of a kind in this field, failing to garner support in other legal systems).

[48] The *Lozano* case (or the *Calipari* case), Corte di Cassazione (Sez I penale), 24 July 2008, No. 31171, reported by G. Serra in *Italian Yearbook of International Law*, 2008, vol. 18, pp. 346–351. The Corte stated to the effect that, as a matter of universally accepted custom, acts by states organs in the discharge of their functions are immune from civil or criminal jurisdiction of a foreign State: quote by P. Palchetti, "Some Remarks on the Scope of Immunity of Foreign State Officials in the Light of Recent Judgments of Italian Courts", in *Italian Yearbook of International Law*, 2009, vol. 19, p. 87.

[49] Arrest Warrant, *supra* note 13, para. 60.

Indeed, the Court had the firm view that state immunity does not serve as an exonerating factor in terms of the individual responsibility – if proved beyond reasonable doubt – of the person enjoying the immunity. In the instant case, the ICJ recognised that prosecution may still be mounted if the person in question ever found himself in four specific situations.[50] Logically, there is no problem with this approach, for immunity and responsibility are two separate categories, unconnected with each other.[51]

More importantly, as will be mentioned in next section, state immunity may be subject to exceptions contained in treaties to which the forum state and the state whose officials are subject to complaints before the former's courts are both parties.[52]

The ultimate effect of the plea of State immunity is therefore explained as such that "[w]here state immunity is applicable, the national court has no jurisdiction to exercise"[53], and that "[w]here applicable, state immunity is an absolute preliminary bar, precluding any examination of the merits. A state is either immune from the jurisdiction of a foreign court or it is not".[54]

5.5. Immunity *versus* Treaty Crimes

It is a fact that treaties on criminal matters do not often provide for the level of immunity to be enjoyed by a person who may fall under the purview of the treaties. This is for good reason, as has been shown in the quotes in the preceding section from the English case. But there are treaties that do refer to rules of the international law of immunity. Article 98(1) of the Rome Statute of the International Criminal Court (hereinafter 'Rome Statute') provides:

> The Court may not proceed with a request for surrender or assistance which would require the requested State to act inconsistently with its obligations under international law with respect to the State or diplomatic immunity of a person or property of a third State, unless the Court can first obtain the

---

[50] *Ibid.*, para. 61.

[51] *Ibid.*, para. 59.

[52] As for the view that immunity is exception to state jurisdiction, see Section 5.8. below.

[53] *Jones v. Saudi Arabia*, 2006, *supra* note 2, para. 24 (*per* Lord Bingham of Cornhill).

[54] *Ibid.*, para. 33.

cooperation of that third State for the waiver of the immunity.

The clause probably covers both customary rules of state or diplomatic immunity and treaties. The rule of the law of treaties that deals with
the status of third states is responsible for the provision of Article 98(1),[55]
even though Article 27 of the Rome Statute declares that the Statute applies to "all persons without any distinction based on official capacity",
and that immunities under national or international law "shall not bar the
Court from exercising its jurisdiction over such a person". While the
crimes proscribed under the Statute may have parallel existences in the
Statute and customary law, the Statute does not see its jurisdiction going
beyond itself, and in light of Article 98(1), it actually treats the crimes as
treaty-based. However, as the Statute concedes by virtue of Article 98(1),
neither the substantive crimes under the Statute nor the statutory jurisdiction over them can give the ICC the extra authority to proceed with a case
involving a third State in spite of the law of immunity.

This digression to the Rome Statute raises yet another question.
Many of the crimes of the Statute partake of a *jus cogens* character independently of the Statute.[56] Could that undermine state immunity? It goes
without saying that the Rome Statute itself and the ICC cannot do so due
to the terms of Article 98(1). Do national courts dealing with allegations
of such crimes find themselves in any different situation?

Before we take on the question just raised, there is another point
about the relations between immunity and treaty-based jurisdiction. As
Lord Bingham observed in *Jones v. Saudi Arabia*, with regard to the
famed *Pinochet* case (No. 3),

> [...] the essential ratio of the decision, as I understand it, was
> that international law could not without absurdity require
> criminal jurisdiction to be assumed and exercised where the
> Torture Convention conditions were satisfied and, at the
> same time, require immunity to be granted to those properly
> charged.[57]

---

[55] Art. 34, Vienna Convention on the Law of Treaties, 1969.

[56] F.i.D. Shelton, "International Law and 'Relative Normativity'", in M. Evans (ed.),
International Law, second edition, Oxford University Press, 2008, p. 165.

[57] *Supra* note 2, 2006, para. 19 (*per* Lord Bingham of Cornhill).

The convention in question took away immunity as far as contracting parties to the convention are concerned, and the courts of those countries cannot consequently recognise immunity in the circumstances. Thus, immunity may be subject to the exception of a multilateral treaty to which both the forum state and the state that claims immunity before the former's court are parties. The reason is likely to be that a treaty as *lex specialis* can circumvent the customary law rules of immunity between the forum state and the state that claims immunity on behalf of its representatives or agents. This line of reasoning seems to be irreproachable, but its applicability is likely to depend on the actual terms of relevant treaties. Some treaties, for instance, are understood to require a contracting party to enforce its terms on the premise that the deeds that require the party to implement the terms are committed on its soil or within the scope of its jurisdiction.[58] The 2004 Convention has also affirmed this venue of court proceedings in relation to the plea of state immunity. Article 12 provides:

> Unless otherwise agreed between the States concerned, a State cannot invoke immunity from jurisdiction before a court of another State which is otherwise competent in a proceeding which relates to pecuniary compensation for death or injury to the person, or damage to or loss of tangible property, caused by an act or omission which is alleged to be attributable to the State, if the act or omission occurred in whole or in part in the territory of that other State and if the author of the act or omission was present in that territory at the time of the act or omission.

Further, were it applied to a case like the *Arrest Warrant* case, the existence of a treaty-based crime may not persuade the Court in accepting the reasoning to the detriment of the customary rule of state immunity.

5.6. Immunity *versus* Violations of *Jus Cogens*

The conclusion of the recent case law, national or international, which involves the law of state immunity, is that immunity still shrouds state officials from even cases involving alleged breaches of *jus cogens*, and the cases may be criminal or civil. Further, immunity as a procedural bar

---

[58] *Ibid.*, para. 20 (referring to the U.S.' understanding II(3) regarding Art. 14(1) of the Convention against Torture 1984, available at http://treaties.un.org/pages/ViewDetails.aspx?src=TREATY&mtdsg_no=III-9&chapter=3&lang=en, last accessed on 13 October 2012.

does not allow a forum state's courts to deal with a substantive law issue, such as the existence *vel non* of an international crime.[59] But differing views are not unknown.[60] In *Al-Adsani v. U.K.*, the European Court of Human Rights (Grand Chamber) held that:

> The Court, while noting the growing recognition of the over-riding importance of the prohibition of torture, does not accordingly find it established that there is yet acceptance in international law of the proposition that States are not entitled to immunity in respect of civil claims for damages for alleged torture committed outside the forum State.[61]

The seven dissenting judges, however, did not subscribe to this "understatement"; rather, they dissented on this very point, by holding that a *jus cogens* rule, such as the prohibition against torture, lifted the jurisdictional bar of state immunity, by reason of the former's character as a *jus cogens* rule, which is placed higher in the hierarchy of rules of international law.[62] If, on the strength of state practice, such a hierarchy exists between the rule against torture and the rule of state immunity, this statement holds true. The majority obviously did not think so.

It is clear that, at their current stage of development, rules of *jus cogens* are to be found in the substantive part of international law, but that rules of U.J. and state immunity partake more of a procedural character. State practice has yet to recognise any obligation *erga omnes* to exercise U.J. over claims arising from alleged breaches of peremptory norms of international law. The gap between the latter norms and their enforcement by states individually is plain to see. This is the case even though there is in reality an obvious link between the doctrine of U.J. and *jus cogens*, in that the exercise of U.J. is currently deemed as mainly concerned with violations of international law which affect "the interests of the interna-

---

[59] The European Court of Human Rights took a slightly different view of this: *Al-Adsani v. U.K.*, 2001, *supra* note 35, para. 58.

[60] It is arguable that *jus cogens* may remove immunity: Antonio Cassese, *International Law*, second edition, 2005, p. 208.

[61] *Al-Adsani v. U.K.*, 2001, *supra* note 35, para. 66. The Court accepted that torture was prohibited by *jus cogens*: *ibid.*, para. 61.

[62] *Ibid.*, pp. 49–50, paras. 1–3.

tional community as a whole", which characteristic is essential for the identification of a *jus cogens* rule.[63]

The question relevant to this section, then, is whether an alleged violation of *jus cogens* can found the personal and subject-matter jurisdiction of a court, national or international, over it. That question has been considered by the ICJ in the case between the Democratic Republic of the Congo and Rwanda.[64] Regarding the argument made by the Congo to found the Court's jurisdiction on the basis of the *jus cogens* against genocide, the ICJ held that:

> [...] the fact that a dispute relates to compliance with a norm having such a character [--jus cogens], which is assuredly the case with regard to the prohibition of genocide, cannot of itself provide a basis for the jurisdiction of the Court to entertain that dispute. Under the Court's Statute that jurisdiction is always based on the consent of the parties.[65]

A similar conclusion was reached by the Court in respect of the same argument made in relation to Rwanda's reservation to the Convention on Racial Discrimination.[66]

What is interesting is the view of the Court that jurisdiction is not affected by the nature of a dispute that pertains to a norm of the *jus cogens* type. Given the difference between substantive and procedural law, where the ICJ could not found its jurisdiction procedurally, it cannot consider the merits of the dispute. A violation of *jus cogens* rules is not *sub judice* until the ICJ passes the stage of jurisdiction and admissibility. Indeed, it would seem to follow from the finding of the Court that the jurisdiction over *jus cogens* violations would not exist even *without* the plea of state immunity, because of the lack of the consensual basis between the parties for the Court to claim jurisdiction.

This state of the law of state immunity has been reaffirmed during the proceedings of the *Case concerning Jurisdictional Immunities of the*

---

[63] Art. 53, Vienna Convention on the Law of Treaties of 1969. Also see, *Barcelona Traction* (second phase) (*Belgium v. Spain*), ICJ Reports 1970, pp. 3, 32.

[64] *Armed Activities on the Territory of the Congo* (New Application: 2002) (*Democratic Republic of the Congo v. Rwanda*), Jurisdiction and Admissibility, Judgment, ICJ Reports, 2006, p. 6.

[65] *Ibid.*, para. 64.

[66] *Ibid.*, para. 78.

State (Germany v. Italy: Greece Intervening) , just decided by the ICJ.[67]
The case deals with, among others, the conflict between state immunity
and certain *jus cogens* rules. In the Application of 22 December 2008,
Germany stated that:

> In the instant case, the dispute concerns in particular the ex-
> istence, under customary international law, of the rule that
> protects sovereign States from being sued before the civil
> courts of another State.[68]

And that:

> Germany's only objective is to obtain a finding from the
> Court that to declare claims based on those occurrences as
> falling within the domestic jurisdiction of Italian courts, con-
> stitutes a breach of international law.[69]

The conflict with the rules of immunity has been summed up in the Italian
statement in its Counter-Memorial of 22 December 2009:

> Italy subscribes to the idea that immunity and jus cogens
> rules on human rights and humanitarian law can generally
> coexist in the international legal system. However, there is a
> substantive inconsistency in the legal system if immunity is
> used by a State responsible for grave breaches of interna-
> tional law in order to avoid its responsibility.[70]

The argument was reasonable enough, but there is one problem.
Supposing the plea of state immunity is a procedural bar to jurisdiction,
no court can proceed to the merits stage of a claim without facing the plea
first. To argue about a substantive inconsistency would be equivalent of
saying that *jus cogens* prevail over the plea, and can found jurisdiction
regardless. Then, the first phase before the Court regarding jurisdiction
and admissibility is superfluous. That would be unlikely to be accepted by
states or international judicial bodies whose jurisdiction is, as a matter of
principle, consensual, in view of the current structure of the international

---

[67] *Jurisdictional Immunities of the State* (*Germany v. Italy: Greece Intervening*), General List No. 143, Judgment of 3 February 2012, available at http://www.legal-
tools.org/doc/674187/. The written and oral pleadings in this case are available at
http://www.icj-cij.org/docket/index.php?p1=3&p2=3&code=ai&case=143&k=60, last
accessed on 13 October 2012.

[68] Germany's Application, para. 2.

[69] *Ibid.*, para. 3.

[70] Para. 4.67.

judicial order. The revision of the consensual nature of such order is by no means impossible,[71] but its complete removal cannot be attained without changing, above all, the Statute of the ICJ. The removal itself would surely be a change of the foundation of the U.N. Charter.

Applying its reasoning in the *Arrest Warrant* and *Armed Activities* cases, the ICJ stated in its judgment of 3 February 2012, with regard to the relations between the law of state immunity and the *jus cogens* of international crimes that:

> The two sets of rules address different matters. The rules of State immunity are procedural in character and are confined to determining whether or not the courts of one State may exercise jurisdiction in respect of another State. They do not bear upon the question whether or not the conduct in respect of which the proceedings are brought was lawful or unlawful.[72]

The distinction between procedural and substantive law was unmistakably dominant in the reasoning. The Court then stated:

> A jus cogens rule is one from which no derogation is permitted but the rules which determine the scope and extent of jurisdiction and when that jurisdiction may be exercised do not derogate from those substantive rules which possess jus cogens status, nor is there anything inherent in the concept of jus cogens which would require their modification or would displace their application.[73]

To resolve this issue by reliance on the distinction referred to above may require further study to justify its singular role in stopping a case of this type from moving beyond the jurisdiction phase.

5.7. International Jurisdiction

What has been said above in respect of the relations between state immunity and national jurisdiction is not necessarily applicable in the context of international criminal jurisdiction, as the matter has been treated differently in inter-state relations and the bodies of international criminal jus-

---

[71] The *United Nations Convention on the Law of the Sea*, Section 2, Part XV.

[72] *Supra* note 39, para. 93.

[73] *Ibid.*, para. 95.

tice.[74] The difference lies, above all, with the issue of attributability of a wrongful deed committed by a state official. However, in the international context, individual responsibility as a matter of substantive law is not affected by the availability of immunity to the individual official in question. There, the situation has long become clear, in that immunity, personal or functional, has been denied since the Nuremberg Charter.[75]

A related question is with the referral power of the U.N. Security Council as envisaged by the Rome Statute. Such a resolution of referral can divest an official of even a non-State Party to the Statute of the plea of immunities in his defence,[76] but may also reiterate the immunities enjoyed by a non-State Party's officials in spite of the referral.[77] The customary law of state immunity will, in short, be qualified by the resolution.

5.8. Conclusions: A Hierarchy of Rules?

From the proceeding survey of the current judicial practice, it seems that a more fundamental question has been latent therein. There is the presumption that in the international legal order, there is a hierarchy of rules. Rules are therefore categorised according to certain biding principles of the system, and some rules are superior to all the rest. The question, as shown above in the vibrant mixture of cases for and against state immunity, is more with which are the rules of *jus cogens* than whether *jus cogens* trump ordinary rules of customary law and treaties. If the position against state immunity is being advocated by a single jurisdiction, it is not to be taken as authoritative in the determination of the state of the law in this regard, even less so where the contrary practice in recognising that immunity remains, as it is, overwhelming.

It is suggested that, while the scope of *jus cogens* is generally vague, some rules of this category have withstood the test of time to remain as part of the foundation of the contemporary international order. It

---

[74] G. Schwarzenberger, *International Law as Applied by International Courts and Tribunals*, vol. II, The Law of Armed Conflict, Stevens and Sons, 1968, p. 518.

[75] Art. 7, the Nuremberg Charter; Art. 6, the Tokyo Charter. Also see, Antonio Cassese, *International Criminal Law*, Oxford University Press, 2003, pp. 267–271.

[76] *Cf.* Dapo Akande, "The Legal Nature of Security Council Referrals to the ICC and its Impact on Al Bashir's Immunities", in *Journal of International Criminal Justice*, 2009, vol. 7, pp. 340–342.

[77] UNSC, S/RES/1593 (2005) (re Darfur situation), operative paragraphs 2 and 6.

is also suggested that the rules would contain such as the one of sovereignty equality. That may indeed be an explanation for the curious reality that immunity can become a formidable wall to resist the surging waves of personal complaints and foreign prosecutions, both of which can be and have been clearly grounded in international law.[78] Not so long ago, a powerful explanation for this reality has been given by an authority in the following terms:[79]

> State immunity is a procedural rule going to the jurisdiction of a national court. It does not go to substantive law; it does not contradict a prohibition contained in a jus cogens norm but merely diverts any breach of it to a different method of settlement. Arguably, then, there is no substantive content in the procedural plea of State immunity upon which a jus cogens mandate can bite.

However, the authority has left many questions unanswered. It may therefore be inquired, besides those questions raised by her,[80] as to whether inter-state relations are in possession of a degree of superiority over the needs to punish serious international crimes. The answer is probably in the affirmative for the moment, as evidenced by the recent cases of U.J., and by the terms of Article 98(1) of the Rome Statute.[81] What is the possible reason?

The system of nation-states has been and remains a basic structure underlying the international legal order; no alternative building blocks have been found to be capable of replacing it. The system of international law, being the language that are spoken in communication with nations, peoples, entities, organisations, and individuals, is premised on the primacy of national sovereignty and of course, the equality of sovereign

---

[78] Claus Kreß and Kimberly Prost, "Article 98", in Otto Triffterer (ed.), *Commentary on the Rome Statute of the International Criminal Court: Observers' Notes, Article by Article*, second edition, C.H. Beck, 2008, p. 1609.

[79] H. Fox, *The Law of State Immunity*, Oxford University Press, 2002, p. 525. This view has not been revised in the second edition of her treatise: second edition, 2008, pp. 151–152.

[80] Some have been addressed by subsequent practice: H. Fox, 2008, *supra* note 29, pp. 152–156.

[81] J. Kleffner, "The Impact of Complementarity on National Implementation of Substantive International Criminal Law", in *Journal of International Criminal Justice*, 2003, vol. 1, pp. 105–106.

states.[82] Immunity derived from such fundamentals could not possibly be abandoned without shaking the very foundation of the current international order as moulded by the U.N. Charter. *Jus cogens*, it may be remembered, emanates from that order, and norms of this category would have to be created, applied and revised on that and only that basis. Otherwise, there will be no *jus cogens* norms that can have a meaningful and effective existence, if they are wrought by others than states. Further to this premise, it may also be added that for states at different stages of development following their vow to abide by the obligations of the U.N. Charter upon entry into that legal order, it is not through the variation of the basic principles of the current Charter by unilateral action independent of the Charter, but rather, the amendment procedures entrenched in the Charter, that the basic principles of the Charter may be revised to reflect the changing times, or *jus cogens* may be established with universal recognition.

To achieve the above goal, it is helpful to consider state immunity as an exception to the even more fundamental feature of sovereignty – jurisdiction.[83] However, the practice, for one reason or another, has hardened the granting of various degrees of state immunity into a rule of customary law,[84] changeable through customary law, no less. It takes concrete form, for instance, not only in the 2004 Convention,[85] but in numerous national legislations, let alone international and national case-law.[86] Further, if state immunity as such is conceived for the collective benefits of inter-state relations, which are typically bilateral, there may just be another question arising as to whether the collective benefits of often two countries enjoy a higher status in relation to other rules of international law. In other words, there would still be a hierarchy involved in this consideration. In addition, how to assess the benefits or their reverse, the harms, arising in such inter-state relations could give rise to more ques-

---

82 Art. 2(1), the U.N. Charter.

83 L. Caplan, "State Immunity, Human Rights, and Jus Cogens: A Critique of the Normative Hierarchy Theory", in *American Journal of International Law*, 2003, vol. 97, pp. 751–757.

84 *Ibid.*, 776.

85 *Cf.* Art. 5 of the convention, as a general principle, that "[a] State enjoys immunity, in respect of itself and its property, from the jurisdiction of the courts of another State subject to the provisions of the present Convention".

86 L. Caplan, 2003, *supra* note 83, pp. 765–770.

tions in practice, as subjectivity will inevitably creep in when the assessment is made before a court.

The reality of the current state of the law of state immunity, including immunity of state officials, is not that different from what obtained when modern international law reached its early stage of maturity before 1945. While the world community has come a long way since the 1960s, states, due to different stages of development, still look up to the U.N. Charter as the basic instrument that regulates inter-state relations. The speed with which the world has advanced may not be that fast. At that moment, the very authority on the law of state immunity uttered the following inimitable words:

> One sovereign being in no respect amenable to another, and being bound by obligations of the highest character not to degrade the dignity of his nation, by placing himself or its sovereign rights within the jurisdiction of another, can be supposed to enter a foreign territory only under an express license, or in the confidence that the immunities belonging to his independent sovereign station, though not expressly stipulated, are reserved by implication, and will be extended to him.[87]

---

[87] *Supra* note 34.

6

International Criminal Court: A Judicial Guarantee for International Peace and Security?

GUO Yang[*]

6.1. Introduction

On 11 June 2010, after two-week heated negotiations, around 4,600 delegates from States, intergovernmental and non-governmental organisations concluded the First Review Conference of the Rome Statute of International Criminal Court[1] (hereinafter referred to as the 'Statute' or 'Rome Statute') in Kampala, Uganda. The Conference adopted by consensus the Amendments to the Statute so as to integrate into the Statute the definition of the 'crime of aggression' and the conditions under which the International Criminal Court (hereinafter referred to as 'ICC' or the 'Court') could exercise its jurisdiction over the crime.[2]

Based on Article 6 of the Charter of the International Military Tribunal (London, 8 August 1945)[3] and the jurisprudence of the Nuremberg

---

[*]   **GUO Yang**, Ph.D. candidate, China University of Political Science and Law; Legal Officer, Regional Delegation for East Asia of the International Committee of the Red Cross ('ICRC'). The opinions expressed in this chapter are those of the author and not necessarily the institution he works for.

[1]   On 17 July 1998, the international community adopted the Rome Statute, the legal basis for establishing the first permanent International Criminal Court. The Statute entered into force on 1 July 2002 and the ICC was established accordingly. The Court has jurisdiction over the crime of aggression, the crime of genocide, crimes against humanity and war crimes. Available at http://www.icc-cpi.int/Menus/ICC/about+the+Court/, last accessed on 13 October 2012; see also the Rome Statute, Article 5, fn. 1.

[2]   ICC Press Release, ICC-ASP-20100612-PR546; for a detailed description of the negotiation, see Claus Kreß and Leonie von Holtzendoff, "The Kampala Compromise on the Crime of Aggression", in *Journal of International Criminal Justice*, 2010, vol. 8.

[3]   Agreement for the Prosecution and Punishment of the Major War Criminals of the European Axis, and Charter of the International Military Tribunal, London, 8 August 1945, available at http://www.icrc.org/ihl.nsf/FULL/350?OpenDocument, last accessed on 13 October 2012.

Trial, the Amendments define the 'crime of aggression' as an act of aggression in a manifest violation of the U.N. Charter committed by political or military leader. As for the conditions under which the Court may exercise its jurisdiction with respect to the crime, the Amendments provide that the Security Council of the U.N. may, acting under Chapter VII of the U.N. Charter, refer a situation of aggression to the Court; and the latter can therefore entertain its jurisdiction with respect to the States in question. The Amendments further authorise the Prosecutor to, subject to the approval of the Pre-Trial Division, proceed with an investigation on the crime of aggression upon State referral or *proprio motu* even if the Security Council, after being informed of the situation, does not make determination of aggression within six months. However, under the aforementioned circumstances, the Court has no jurisdiction over the crime of aggression committed by nationals of non-States Parties or within the territory of non-States Parties and it also has no jurisdiction over the crime with respect to States Parties that have made a declaration of non-acceptance of the Court's jurisdiction over the crime.[4]

The adoption of the Amendments was acclaimed by some States and scholars as a breakthrough for the development of international criminal law, but received criticism and doubts from other States and scholars as well. Its significance as a milestone for international criminal law lies in that it will serve as a warning to aggressive States and their leaders. It is an achievement of more than sixty years of efforts by the international community in the maintenance of international peace and security through justice following the trials at Nuremberg and Tokyo. Criticisms went firstly to the content of the definition, which is considered ambiguous and not in line with the essential criminal law principles of legality and specialty. It was also argued that the definition will make more difficult the use of force to end the very crimes the Court is charged with prosecuting, namely war crimes, crimes against humanity and crimes of genocide. It would thus divert the Court from its core mission of protection of human rights. In particular, the provisions which authorise the Prosecutor to proceed with an investigation of the crime without a deci-

---

[4] Review Conference, RC/Res.6 Annex I, available at http://www.icc-cpi.int/iccdocs/asp_docs/Resolutions/RC-Res.6-ENG.pdf, last accessed on 17 October 2012.

sion from the Security Council are considered as a serious challenge to the current regime of international peace and security.[5]

Through an analysis of different opinions on the definition of the crime and the conditions for the Court's jurisdiction in the Amendments, the author of this chapter modestly presents his thoughts on these issues.

6.2. Definition of the Crime of Aggression

Negotiations on the crime of aggression were among the most difficult parts of the making of the ICC. Being concerned that the legal constraints imposed by this crime would hamper their freedom of military humanitarian interventions, some States argued that aggression should not be included in the Court's jurisdiction. Arab States seemed eager to define the crime on the basis of UNGA Resolution 3314 (XXIX) so as to ensure that the right of self-determination was recognised as an exculpatory defence against the crime. States from the European Union and the Non-Aligned Movement made it clear that the Statute was unacceptable without jurisdiction over the crime of aggression.[6] By the end of the United Nations Diplomatic Conference of Plenipotentiaries on the

---

[5] Kreß and von Holtzendoff, 2010, *supra* note 2; David Scheffer, "State Parties Approve New Crimes for International Criminal Court", in *ASIL Insight*, 22 June 2010, vol. 14, issue 16; Benjamin B. Ferencz, "Ending Impunity for the Crime of Aggression", in *Case Western Reserve Journal of International Law*, 2009, vol. 41, p. 281; "Statement by Chinese Delegation after the Adoption of the Crime of Aggression at the Review Conference", in *Chinese Journal of International Law*, 2010, p. 475 (the speaker of this Statement is not identified in the Journal). 杨力军: "论《国际刑事法院罗马规约》中的侵略罪", 载于《中国国际法年刊（2010）》, 世界知识出版社 2011 年版, 第 25–46 页(YANG Lijun, "On the Crime of Aggression under the Rome Statute", in *Chinese Yearbook of International Law*, World Affairs Press, 2010, p. 25–46); 周露露: "试析侵略罪条款的法律影响——以国际刑事法院管辖侵略罪的条件为视角", 载于《中国国际法年刊（2010）》, 世界知识出版社 2011 年版, 第 47–54 页 (ZHOU Lulu, "An Analysis on the Impacts of the Provisions on Crime of Aggression—in the Perspective of the Conditions for the Court's Jurisdiction", in *Chinese Yearbook of International Law*, World Affairs Press, 2010, pp. 47–54); 王秀梅: "侵略罪定义及侵略罪管辖的先决条件问题", 载于《西安政治学院学报》2012 年 3 月版, 第 102–106 页 (WANG Xiumei, "Definition of Crime of Aggression and the Conditions for the Court's Jurisdiction", in *Journal of Xi'an Politics Institute*, March 2012, pp. 102–106.

[6] Benjamin B. Ferencz, "Enabling the International Criminal Court to Punish Aggression", in *Washington University Global Studies Law Review*, 2007, vol. 6, p. 558.

Establishment of an International Criminal Court in Rome in 1998, there were still many irreconcilable points of view over the crime of aggression, in particular in regard of the proper role of the Security Council in determining an act of aggression and how to define the crime so as to satisfy the principle of legality.[7] In order to break the stalemate and adopt the Statute, States finally came up with a compromise by listing the crime of aggression, along with genocide, crimes against humanity and war crimes, as the crimes within the Court's jurisdiction, but at the same time stipulating that the Court could not exercise its jurisdiction over the crime of aggression until a provision defining the crime and setting up the conditions for jurisdiction was adopted in accordance with the Statute.[8] Following this compromise, the Preparatory Commission for the ICC[9] and the Special Working Group on the Crime of Aggression ('SWGCA')[10] were established by the Diplomatic Conference and the Assembly of State Parties to the Statute in 1998 and 2002 respectively to seek a reconciliation of the conflicting views over the crime. States Parties as well as non-States Parties were invited to take part in all the sessions of these two institutions. After ten years of hectic efforts at the Preparatory Commission and the SWGCA, proposals on the provisions on aggression were finally drafted at the SWGCA in 2009[11], submitted to the Statute's First Review Conference for discussion in 2010, and were adopted by the State Parties by consensus at the last moment of the Conference.

---

[7] Michael O'Donovan, "Criminalizing War: Toward a Justifiable Crime of Aggression", in *British Columbia International and Comparative Law Review*, 2007, vol. 30, pp. 515–517.

[8] Paragraph 2 of Article 5 of the Statute (before modification). It reads: "The Court shall exercise jurisdiction over the crime of aggression once a provision is adopted in accordance with articles 121 and 123 defining the crime and setting out the conditions under which the Court shall exercise jurisdiction with respect to this Crime. Such a provision shall be consistent with the relevant provisions of the Charter of the United Nations". Now this clause was deleted in accordance with RC/Res.6, Annex I of 11 June 2010. See, footnote I of Article 5 of the Statute.

[9] Final Act of the United Nations Diplomatic Conference of Plenipotentiaries on the Establishment of an International Criminal Court, Annex I, Resolution F, para. 7, U.N. Doc. A/CONF.183/10, 17 July 1998.

[10] Continuity of work in respect of the crime of aggression, ICC-ASP/1/Res.1, adopted at the third plenary meeting on 9 September 2002.

[11] Report of the Special Working Group on the Crime of Aggression, Doc. ICC-APS/7/SWGA/2 (2009).

As for the definition of the crime of aggression, the key issue that needs to be determined is the link between 'acts of aggression' of a State and individual criminal responsibility. The strengthening of accountability for acts of aggression with an enforcement measure based on individual criminal responsibility is considered as a major contribution of the Nuremberg and Tokyo Trials to international criminal law.[12] Acts of aggression are breaches of international peace and security that can only be committed by a State. On the other hand, the perpetrator of the crime of aggression can only be an individual. These are the customary rules established by the military trials following World War II.[13] Therefore, acts of aggression are the precedent for the crime of aggression and the latter is a corollary of the former.[14] The crime of aggression introduced by the Amendments confirms these principles established by the World War II trials.

6.2.1. Act of Aggression

Paragraph 2 of Article 8 *bis* introduced by the Amendments provides that:

> For the purpose of this Statute, 'act of aggression' means the use of armed force by a State against the sovereignty, territorial integrity or political independence of another State, or in any other manner inconsistent with the Charter of the United Nations. Any of the following acts, regardless of a declaration of war, shall, in accordance with United Nations General Assembly Resolution 3314 (XXIX) of 14 December 1974, qualify as an act of aggression:
>
> 1. The invasion or attack by the armed forces of a State of the territory of another State, or any military occupation, however temporary, resulting from such invasion

---

[12] Roger S. Clark, "Amendments to the Rome Statute of the International Criminal Court Considered at the first Review Conference on the Court, Kampala, 31 May – 11 June 2010", in *Goettingen Journal of International Law*, 2010, vol. 2, p. 695.

[13] G.A. Resolution 95(1): Affirmation of the Principles of International Law Recognized by the Charter of the Nuremberg Tribunal; see also, Antonio Cassese, "Affirming of the Principles of International Law Recognized by the Charter of the Nuremberg Tribunal", in *United Nations Audiovisual Library of International Law*, 2009, available at http://untreaty.un.org/cod/avl/pdf/ha/ga_95-I/ga_95-I_e.pdf, last accessed on 17 October 2012.

[14] Ferencz, 2007, *supra* note 6, pp. 561–562.

or attack, or any annexation by the use of force of the territory of another State or part of thereof;

2. Bombardment by the armed forces of a State against the territory of another State or the use of any weapons by a State against the territory of another State;

3. The blockade of the ports or coasts of a State by the armed forces of another State;

4. An attack by the armed forces of a State on the land, sea or air forces, or marine and air fleet of another State;

5. The use of armed forces of one State which are within the territory of another State with the agreement of the receiving State, in contravention of the conditions provided for in the agreement or any extension of their presence in such territory beyond the termination of the agreement;

6. The action of a State in allowing its territory, which it has placed at the disposal of another State, to be used by the other State for perpetrating an act of aggression against a third State;

7. The sending by or on behalf of a State of armed bands, groups, irregulars or mercenaries, which carry out acts of armed force against another State of such gravity as to amount to the acts listed above, or its substantial involvement therein.[15]

---

[15] *Supra* note 5. The English version of the Statute has been modified according to the Resolution. However, the Chinese translation of the Resolution concerning the act of aggression ("侵略行为"是指一国使用武力或以违反《联合国宪章》的任何其他方式侵犯另一国的主权、领土完整或政治独立的行为") is inconsistent with the English version (the official Chinese version available at http://www.icc-cpi.int/iccdocs/asp_docs/Resolutions/RC-Res.6-CHN.pdf, last accessed on 13 October 2012). From the Chinese translation we may conclude that violations against the sovereignty, territory integrity or political independence in a manner other than the use of armed forces (*i.e.*, the so-called economic aggression) could also qualify as act of aggression. However, from the acts of aggression listed afterwards, the elements of crime of aggression annexed to the Resolution and opinions expressed during the process of negotiation, the reasonable conclusion should be that the act of aggression, as a precondition for the crime of aggression, is targeting at the use of armed forces by State. Therefore, the appropriate Chinese version of the act of aggression should be: 侵略行为是指一国使用武力侵犯另一国的主权、领土完整或政治独立或以违反《联合国宪章》的其他方式使用武力的行为。

This clause is actually a combination of Articles 1 and 3 of UNGA Resolution 3314 (XXIX), which was considered as the best compromise the SWGCA could reach since they reflected current customary international law.[16] In terms of structure, the definition is a combination of a generic description and a list of specific acts. The proponents of this methodology argued that the generic description would allow the Court to fit unforeseen situations of aggression into the definition, while the list is specific enough to provide practical guidance. Thus, it could not only satisfy the principle of legality but also encompass unforeseen scenarios at the time of negotiation, which is important to the Court's proper function of retribution and deterrence.[17] In particular, the reference to Resolution 3314 in the sentence, namely 'in accordance with the United Nations General Assembly Resolution 3314 (XXIX) of 14 December 1974', is of creative ambiguity in that it allows the Court, subject to the relevant provisions of the Statute, to rely on articles other than those of 1 and 3 in the Annex of the Resolution for the purpose of determining an act of aggression.[18]

However, the integration of the Articles and the reference to the UNGA Resolution of 3314 (XXIX) was criticised as well.[19] First, Resolution 3314 was adopted to provide guidance for the Security Council – an international executive organ – in its determination of the existence of an act of aggression and thus, was clearly political not legal in nature. It was not aimed at establishing individual criminal responsibility and there-

---

[16] Roger S. Clark, "Negotiating Provisions Defining the Crime of Aggression, its Elements and the Conditions for ICC Exercise of Jurisdiction over It", in *European Journal of International Law*, 2009, vol. 20, p. 1103; Major Kari M. Fletcher, "Defining the Crime of Aggression: Is There an Answer to the International Criminal Court's Dilemma?", in *Air Force Law Review*, 2010, vol. 65, p. 259.

[17] Devyani Kacker, "Coming Full Circle: The Rome Statute and the Crime of Aggression", in *Suffolk Transnational Law Review*, 2010, vol. 33, p. 264; O'Donovan, 2007, *supra* note 7, pp. 524–529.

[18] Claus Kreβ and Leonie von Holtzendorff, "The Kampala Compromise on the Crime of Aggression", in *Journal of International Criminal Justice*, 2010, vol. 8, p. 1191; however, it is asserted the Article 2, which accords *prime facie* effect to any first use of armed force, shall not guide the judicial work of the Court.

[19] Oscar Solera, "The Definition of the Crime of Aggression: Lessons Not-Learned", in *Case Western Reserve Journal of International Law*, 2010, vol. 42, pp. 804–810; Major Kari M. Fletcher, 2010, *supra* note 16, p. 260; Michael J. Glennon, "The Blank-Prose Crime of Aggression", in *Yale Journal of International Law*, 2010, vol. 35, p. 97.

fore, does not satisfy the principle of legality. Because of its ambiguity, the International Law Commission refused to integrate this definition into its Draft Code of Crimes against the Peace and Security of Mankind. Even the Security Council has never made any reference to the definition in its resolutions on situations when it has made a determination of aggression. Secondly, the reference made to the Resolution also creates confusion as to the real role of the Resolution. If the reference is interpreted as the integration of the Annex of the Resolution as whole, then the list of acts of aggression should be open and non-exhaustive because the Security Council, based on Article 4 of the Annex, may determine that acts other than those listed in Article 3 constitute aggression. Therefore, what would happen if the Security Council decides to add a new act of aggression to the list? If the Court follows the Council's new decision, its independence will be put at risk, the ambiguity of the definition will be further enhanced and the principle of legality will suffer further damage, which is clearly in violation of Article 22 of the Statute.[20] But if the Court refuses to take into consideration of the new acts of aggression defined by the Security Council, the reference will then loose its value. Last but not least, the combination of the generic description and the list could also lead to confusion in term of application. If the list is considered as exhaustive and the only crimes to be addressed by the Court, the generic description will be made redundant; however, if the generic description is considered to be clear enough to satisfy the principle of legality, the list will then be redundant. In this regard, it is suggested the list, according to the spirit of the Resolution, shall be open and illustrative but should be subject to the limitation set up by the generic description.[21]

Clearly, the purpose of defining 'act of aggression' is to assess the legality of the use of forces by States, based on Article 2(4) of the U.N. Charter. Article 2(4) explicitly prohibits the threat or use of force against

---

[20] Article 22 of the Statute; it concerns the principle of *nullum crimen sine lege*. Paragraph 1 of the Article provides that "a person shall not be criminally responsible [...] unless the conduct in questions constitutes, at the time it takes place, a crime within the jurisdiction of the Court". Paragraph 2 of the Article requires that "in case of ambiguity, the definition shall be interpreted in favour of the person being investigated, prosecuted or convicted". Therefore, if the act of aggression determined by the Security Council is not within the list, it could be argued that it is also not a crime listed within the Statute and thus, not within the jurisdiction of the Court either; see Fletcher, 2010, *supra* note 16, p. 260.

[21] Kacker, 2010, *supra* note 17, pp. 264–265.

---

the territorial integrity, or political independence of any State, or in any other manner inconsistent with the Purpose of the United Nations. However, the generic definition of 'act of aggression' in the Amendments contains some departure from Article 2(4), due to its importation of Resolution 3314. Firstly, it qualifies 'force' with 'armed' and thus, was considered by some scholars to have limited its scope of application, that is, acts of force other than armed force, such as economic force or computer attacks would not come within the scope of the definition. Secondly, beside the protection of political independence and territorial integrity, the definition in the Amendment also protects 'sovereignty', which is far from being specific and would expand the scope of the prohibition in Article 2(4). Thirdly, the meaning of the phrase 'in other manner inconsistent with the U.N. Charter' needs to be clarified. Last but not least, by choosing 'act of aggression' rather than 'war of aggression' as used by the Nuremberg Charter, this relatively low-threshold of acts of aggression in the Amendments could provide opportunity for abuse of procedure before the Court through referring any dispute involving use of armed force to the Court. All these ambiguities impose doubts on the judicial applicability of the definition. This might then make the list of acts of aggression a valuable supplement. However, even though the list is specific, it only addresses traditional armed conflicts among States and cannot accommodate emerging forms of use of forces, such as terrorist attack or aiding armed insurgents.[22] It was even argued that "sovereignty, territorial integrity and political independence" are not the only assets the crime of aggression should protect. All cases of use of forces in international relations are against the purpose or spirit of Article 2(4). Therefore, the definition of aggression should be "the use of force against another State".[23]

As far as the structure of the definition is concerned, the combination of a generic description and a specific list, as argued by some scholars, could incorporate the strengths of both approaches.[24] However, this methodology is a Sword of Damocles for it can still be argued that it takes

---

[22] *Ibid.*, p. 269; Glennon, 2010, *supra* note 20, pp. 96–99. Some scholars are of the opinion that the term of 'force' in Article 2(4) does not cover any possible kind of force, but is, according to the correct and prevailing view, limited to armed force. See Bruno Simma, *The Charter of the United Nations: A Commentary*, second Edition, Oxford University Press, 2002, p. 117.

[23] Solera, 2010, *supra* note 19, pp. 813–815.

[24] Kacker, 2010, *supra* note 17, p. 264.

the weaknesses of both as well. Putting two definitions with built-in ambiguities and limits side by side can still double ambiguities or limits. Taking into consideration that ambiguity created by compromise is the nature of the international law-making process and is faced by all the international institutions, technical ambiguities could be clarified through the Court's cautious jurisprudence in the future.

The content of the definition of 'act of aggression' actually indicates the extent to which the States are willing to subject the use of force to the legal review by the Court. It is clear from the Amendments that States intend only to address the issue of use of force among themselves, namely inter-state armed conflicts, under the umbrella of 'act of aggression'. This then requires a State act as a peculiar element on the crime of aggression compared to other crimes under the Statute.[25] In the context of the current international security context, this definition fulfils the purpose of Article 2(4) and the U.N., that is, "to save succeeding generations from the scourge of war, which twice in our lifetime has brought untold sorrow to mankind".[26]

However, it has been argued that the situation of international security has changed compared to the time when the U.N was founded. As stated in the report entitled *A more secure world: Our shared responsibility* by the Secretary-General's High-level Panel on Threats, Challenges and Change, there were fewer inter-state wars in the past 60 years and the war between great powers was avoided. Internal armed conflicts, terrorism and trans-national organised crime are now the threats to security faced by the international community. These non-traditional security threats are mainly or substantially generated by non-State actors. The rules regulating use of force by non-State actors have not been developed to the same level as those for States. Therefore, it is recommended that legal reform be adopted to tackle such non-traditional threats.[27] According to a survey done by the International Institute of Strategic Studies, there are currently eighty-four different non-State actor groups in the Middle East and North Africa alone.[28] Some of these groups, such as Al-Qaida,

---

[25] Kreß and von Holtzendorff, 2010, *supra* note 18, p. 1190.

[26] Preamble and Article 1 of the U.N. Charter.

[27] *A more secure world: Our shared responsibility*, A/59/565, 13 December 2004.

[28] Steve Beytenbrod, "Defining Aggression: An Opportunity to Curtail the Criminal Activities of Non-State Actors", in *Brook Journal of International Law*, 2011, vol. 36, no. 2, p. 648.

have the capacity to launch an attack against States on their own. It has also been argued that international practice shows that non-State actors could launch an armed attacked in the sense of Article 51 of the U.N. Charter and thus, States could invoke a right of self-defence against those non-State armed attacks.[29] Therefore, to adopt a definition still limiting an 'act of aggression' as an illegal use of force among States equals turning a blind eye to the already changed international security situation. The opportunity to progressively develop international criminal law was missed. On the other hand, a definition of 'act of aggression' highlighting a State's act is also at variance with the principles of international criminal law established since the Nuremberg Trial. These principles include that non-State actors can incur criminal responsibility, both independently and through a joint crime with a State. International criminal law focuses on the individual, irrelevant of his or her affiliation.[30]

As far as acts of aggression are concerned, the scenario that a State commits aggression through non-State actors could be classified within the situation defined by sub-paragraph (g) of the list. An independent 'aggression' committed by non-State actors seemingly falls out of both the list and the definition. In this regard, it should be born in mind that as a secondary rule, the criminalisation of acts of aggression is subject to the limitation set up by the primary rule regulating the use of force, namely Article 2(4) of the Charter, which was considered the starting point to reach consensus. Before the primary rules have developed to reflect contemporary developments, it is unrealistic to cure imperfection through the backdoor of the secondary rule, namely international criminal law.[31]

6.2.2. Crime of Aggression

The 'crime of aggression' is defined by paragraph 1 of Article 8 *bis* as:

> [...] planning, preparation, initiation or execution, by a person in a position effectively to exercise control over or to direct the political or military action of a State, of an act of ag-

---

[29] Claus Kreβ, "Some Reflection on the International Legal Framework Governing Transnational Armed Conflicts", in *Journal of Conflict and Security Law*, 2010, vol. 15, pp. 247–248.

[30] Beytenbrod, 2011, *supra* note 28, pp. 674–675.

[31] Kreβ and von Holtzendorff, 2010, *supra* note 18, pp. 1190, 1193.

> gression which, by its character, gravity and scale, consti-
> tutes a manifest violation of Charter of the United Nations.

This definition is based on Article 6 of the 1946 London Charter of the International Military Tribunal ('IMT'). The Charter defined 'crime against peace' as "planning, preparation, initiation or waging of a war of aggression, or a war in violation of international treaties, agreements or assurances [...]".[32]

The definition of the crime of aggression presents the following characteristics.

6.2.2.1. A Leadership Crime

According to the definition, a crime of aggression can only be committed by those persons who hold a position allowing them to effectively exercise control or direct the political or military action of a State. It can be concluded that only those persons in a *de jure* or *de facto* leadership position have the chance to fulfil the 'effective control or direct' criteria. This leadership element is in accordance with the nature and purpose of the crime. Acts of aggression as acts of a State are of a collective nature and the purpose of the criminalisation of aggression is to prevent and punish the use of armed force as a tool of State foreign policy. Therefore, the perpetrators of the crime can only be those persons who have the capacity to influence, shape or control the military or political policy of States and the leadership element then becomes the connecting point between the individual criminal liability and the act of aggression. The requirement of the leadership element for the crime of aggression was affirmed by the jurisprudence of the Nuremberg Trial and General Assembly 95(1), as well as recognised by scholars.[33] The leadership element of the crime is further strengthened and clarified by inclusion of Article 25, paragraph 3 *bis*, according to which, in respect of the crime of aggression, persons charged with any form of responsibility, namely committing, ordering, soliciting, inducing, aiding, *et cetera*, shall be those who can also effectively exercise control over or direct the political or military action of a

---

[32] *Supra* note 2; Article 6, Charter of the International Military Tribunal. London, 8 August 1945.

[33] Larry May, *Aggression and Crimes Against Peace*, Cambridge University Press, 2008, pp. 232–233; Claus Kress, "The Crime of Aggression before the First Review of the ICC Statute", in *Leiden Journal of International Law*, 2007, vol. 20, p. 855.

State.[34] Accordingly, secondary perpetrators do not fall within the jurisdiction of the Court, that is, an ordinary soldier of the aggressor state cannot be criminalised as an aider under Article 25.[35] Taking into consideration the reality that broad categories of persons are nowadays more or less involved in the State's efforts put into the war (that is, the farmer cultivates food for the army, and citizens work in the ammunition factory, *et cetera*), the limits put on by the leadership element seem fitting and proper. The collective nature of aggression should not impose a collective penalty to all of those involved, especially those only involved remotely.

Even though there is no disagreement on the leadership element as a requirement for the crime, there are controversies over the scope of this element. The opponents of the terms of 'control' or 'direct' are of the opinion that these terms are a misinterpretation of the jurisprudence of the Nuremberg Trial.[36]

Firstly, the Nuremberg Tribunal applied a 'shape' or 'influence' standard rather than that of 'effective control or direct' to define the responsible persons for the crime. The application of such standard for the crime could be summarised as: (1) the person had the knowledge that an aggressive war was intended; (2) the person who possess such a knowledge must be in a position to shape or influence the aggressive policy, namely have the ability to further, hinder or prevent the policy; (3) the person defined by (1) and (2) took action to further the aggressive policy. Therefore, a person without the ability to shape or influence an aggressive policy, who just takes part in the furtherance of the policy, cannot be charged with crime of aggression because his act shows that there is a lack of criminal intent for the aggression.[37] The standard of 'shape or influence' is seemingly less strict than that of 'effective control or direct'. By applying the former, the persons who are not part of State apparatus, such as influential economic actors, could be charged with the crime. By applying the latter, only those forming the leadership circles of a State could be charged because the term 'control' refers to power over the

---

[34] *Supra* note 4; R.C. Res. 6 and Article 25(3) *bis*.

[35] Kreβ and von Holtzendorff, 2010, *supra* note 18, p. 1189.

[36] Kevin Jon Heller, "Retreat From Nuremberg: The Leadership Requirement in the Crime of Aggression", in *European Journal of International Law*, 2007, vol. 18, p. 479.

[37] *Ibid.*, p. 487.

commission of the acts and the term 'direct' connotes actual direction at an operative level.[38] On the other hand, the case law of the International Military Tribunals clearly established that not only the leaders of the aggressor State but also persons in the private economic sector as well as citizens of a third State can be charged with the crime of aggression, and, as stated above, no requirement of 'effective control or direct' was imposed on those persons. Therefore, the standard of 'effective control or direct' is not a proper reflection of the precedents established by the IMT.[39] In order to address this discrepancy, it was suggested to clearly state in the *travaux préparatoires* that the intent of the drafters behind the 'effective control or direct' standard is to adopt comprehensively the Nuremberg positions.[40]

It was also argued that the 'effective control or direct' standard is anything but clear. In a democratic society, "it is almost impossible to pinpoint responsibility for a certain action to just a few individuals since large numbers of bureaucrats are usually involved in preparing and shaping decisions".[41] However, it was stressed by some scholars that the leadership element is Article 8*bis* should focus on *de facto* control or direction, not on formal status. Therefore, it could extend to business or even religious leaders. It is a stricter but proper standard compared to that of the Nuremberg Trial because the latter is too broad in that it could cover too large a group of persons in democratic societies. But the extension of this requirement to all forms of participation under Article 25 is considered by the same scholars as an improper reduction of the effects of this clause.[42]

6.2.2.2. *Actus Reus* and *Mens Rea* of the Crime

The term '*actus reus*' refers to the wrongful deed that comprises the physical components of a crime. It was argued that an 'act of aggression' requires co-ordination and co-operation among varied parties and some of these activities are not obviously illegal, such as financial preparation,

---

[38] *Ibid.*, p. 491.

[39] Heller, 2007, *supra* note 36, pp. 480–486.

[40] Kress, 2007, *supra* note 33, p. 855.

[41] Glennon, 2010, *supra* note 19, p. 100.

[42] Kai Ambos, "The Crime of Aggression after Kampala", in *German Yearbook of International Law*, 2010, vol. 53, pp. 463–509.

production of ammunitions and even move or mobilisation of the armed forces. Only being put into the overall context of the aggression can their illegal nature be ascertained? Therefore, only participation in planning the aggression can qualify as *actus reus* with respect to the crime of aggression.[43] The Amendment follows this logic but, based on Article 6 of the Nuremberg Charter, expands the scope of participation to cover planning, preparation, initiation and execution.

It was suggested during the negotiation to delete the terms 'plan, prepare, initiate or execute' because Article 25 addresses all kinds of participation in the crime and the use of these terms could blur the difference between the primary and secondary perpetrators. Those insisting on the use of these terms argued that they reflected the typical form of the crime, highlighted the action to be criminalised and thus, could play an effective deterrence role. It was also stressed by the negotiators that the mere planning without actual execution of the aggression planned should not be charged since mere planning cannot be considered as a use of armed force inconsistent with the U.N. Charter and cannot satisfy the requirement that the Court shall only prosecute the gravest breaches of international law.[44] On the other hand, it could be concluded from the list of acts of aggression and the discussions during the negotiations that an attempted aggression is not intended for prosecution nor an inchoate conspiracy to commit aggression without a following, actual act of aggression.[45] The Elements of crime adopted at the Review Conference affirm that the crime of aggression is based on act of aggression that has been committed.[46]

The term '*mens rea*' refers to the wrongful state of mind that comprises the mental component of a crime. According to the jurisprudence of the Nuremberg Trial, the mere knowledge of the aggressive policy was not enough to impose criminal responsibility on a person. The perpetrator must aim at advancing the policy by what he or she chose to do. Without this intent, there will be no sufficient link between the perpetrator's action and the perpetration of the war and thus, it would be unfair to convict

---

[43] May, 2008, *supra* note 33, pp. 230, 232–233.

[44] Kacker, 2010, *supra* note 17, pp. 266–267.

[45] Clark, 2009, *supra* note 16, pp. 1108–1109.

[46] *Supra* note 4, paragraph 3 of the Elements in Annex II requires that "The act of aggression [...] was committed".

such a person.[47] In this regard, the negotiators agreed that Article 30 of the Statute should be applied to the crime of aggression. This Article requires that a person shall be criminally responsible only if the crime is committed with intent and knowledge. Knowledge means awareness that a circumstance exists or a consequence will occur in the ordinary course of events. The term 'intent' connotes that a person means to engage in the conduct or cause the consequence or is aware that the consequence will occur in the ordinary course of events.[48] The requisite criminal intent is essential to the crime of aggression because all nations are preparing for war in one or another way, but not all of them are doing the preparation with the intention for an aggressive war.[49] Also as stated earlier, an act of war involves varied parties, but not all of them are participating with the intent to further the aggressive policy. Only those who, not only possessing the awareness of the aggressive plan, but also meaning to further the plan through what they choose to do or not to do, can be charged with the crime of aggression. It shall also be noted that the knowledge of the aggressive context refers to the awareness of the factual circumstances establishing the illegality of the use of force and not a legal evaluation of those factual circumstances.[50]

It was suggested that the crime of aggression contains a specific intent for the perpetrators of the crime who would always aim at obtaining a strategic advantage over opponents or changing the *status quo*.[51] This proposal, which would greatly narrow down the scope of the crime, was not accepted by the negotiating States.

6.2.2.3. The Threshold Clause

Paragraph 1 of Article 8*bis* contains what is known as a 'threshold clause', which is meant to grant jurisdiction to the Court only in the cases where the act of aggression "by its character, gravity and scale, constitutes a manifest violation of the Charter of the United Nations". Therefore, some acts may constitute 'act of aggression' according to paragraph 2, but

---

[47] May, 2008, *supra* note 33, pp. 251, 254.

[48] Paragraph 2 of Article 30 of the Statute.

[49] Fletcher, 2010, *supra* note 16, p. 259.

[50] Ambos, 2010, *supra* note 42; *supra* note 5, paragraphs 5 and 6 of the Elements in Annex II of the RC/Res. 6.

[51] Solera, 2010, *supra* note 19, pp. 815–819.

not 'crime of aggression' in paragraph 1 of the same article if they do not violate the Charter manifestly.

In the process of negotiations, this threshold clause was considered valuable in that it limits the Court's jurisdiction to the most serious acts of aggression and it is also a compromise of years of heated negotiations allowing for widest possible support. In order to address this issue of gravity, it was further recommended to clarify the test for the crime as follows:

1. The commission of aggression must be widespread or systematic;

2. It involves a relatively large number of victims or imposes severe injury upon civilian populations or combatants in violation of the laws and customs of armed conflicts.

Therefore, a so-called minor use of forces such as border skirmishes or cross border artillery attack and other similar situations could be excluded from the definition of the crime.[52]

However, the opponents of the insertion of such a threshold clause argued that the Preamble, Articles 1, 5 and 17 of the Statute have already required that only the most serious crimes be included in the Court's jurisdiction; it is unreasonable and illogical to further classify the acts of aggression into manifest or non-manifest violations of the Charter since they are all violations of the Charter and thus, merit the same treatment.[53] On the other hand, the qualifiers provided by the threshold clause do not provide the requisite specificity or precision. Applying it to the same case by different persons could lead to different conclusions. They are of a subjective nature, fail to provide 'ascertainable standards of guilt' and therefore do not satisfy the criminal law principles of legality or specialty.[54]

As for the question whether the same standard shall be applied to act of aggression and the crime of aggression, it is worth noting that act of aggression aims at establishing State responsibility for the illegal use of force, while the crime of aggression is meant to impose criminal respon-

---

[52] Keith A. Petty, "Criminalizing Force: Resolving the Threshold Question for the Crime of Aggression in the Context of Modern Conflict", in *Seattle University Law Review*, 2009, vol. 33, p. 118.

[53] Fletcher, 2010, *supra* note 17, pp. 257–258; Kacker, 2010, *supra* note 18, pp. 267–268.

[54] Glennon, 2010, *supra* note 20, pp. 101–102.

sibility on individual persons. The former presents a nature of civil law while the latter is criminal law in nature. It is worthwhile to apply a less strict standard for act of aggression as that would make it difficult for States to justify illegal use of force, while a restrictive definition of crime of aggression will be more in line with the requirement of criminal justice, in particular the protection of human rights.[55]

6.2.3. Understandings Regarding the Crime of Aggression: Is Humanitarian Intervention Excluded?

During the process of negotiations, it was asserted that the crime of aggression should only cover manifest and undisputed violations of the Charter and exclude the borderline or grey area cases, such as humanitarian intervention, anticipatory self-defence and mere border incursion for anti-terror warfare.[56] It was even argued that an exception of humanitarian necessity should be established for the crime of aggression under the Statute.[57]

Out of concerns for unilateral humanitarian intervention, the U.S. Delegation insisted at the Conference that the crime of aggression under Article 8*bis* should not cover military action aiming to prevent war crimes, crimes against humanity or genocide because they are not manifest violations of the U.N. Charter and seek to prevent the very crimes the Statute is designed to deter.[58] Upon U.S. insistence, understandings regarding the crime of aggression were adopted, the following points of which are particularly noteworthy:[59]

> 6. [...] aggression is the most serious and dangerous
> form of illegal use of force; and that a determination
> whether an act of aggression has been committed re-

---

[55] May, 2008, *supra* note 34, Chapter 5 and pp. 213–214.

[56] Andreas Paulus, "Second Thoughts on the Crime of Aggression", in *European Journal of International Law*, 2010, vol. 20, no. 4, p. 1121; Elizabeth Wilmshurst, "Aggression", in R Cryer, *et al.* (eds.), *An Introduction to International Criminal Law and Procedural*, 2007, p. 268.

[57] Christopher P. Denicola, "A Shield for the Knight of Humanity: the ICC should Adopt a Humanitarian Necessity Defense to the Crime of Aggression", in *University of Pennsylvania Journal of International Law*, 2008, vol. 30, p. 641.

[58] Statement by the U.S. Delegation, available at http://www.state.gov/s/l/releases/remarks/142665.htm, last accessed on 17 October 2012.

[59] *Supra* note 4, RC/Res.6, Annex III.

---

quires consideration of all the circumstances of each particular case, including the gravity of the acts concerned and their consequences, in accordance with the Charter of the United Nations.

7. [...] in establishing whether an act of aggression constitutes a manifest violation of the Charter of the United Nations, the three components of character, gravity and scale must be sufficient to justify a manifest determination. No one component can be significant enough to satisfy the manifest standard by itself.

Can unilateral humanitarian intervention be excluded from the scope of the crime of aggression based on these understandings? Firstly, unilateral humanitarian intervention involves use of armed force against sovereignty and territorial integrity without U.N. authorisation. It could be reasonably described as a violation of the U.N. Charter. It is also difficult to differentiate, in terms of gravity, character or scale, acts of humanitarian intervention from acts of aggression listed in paragraph 2 of Article 8*bis*. Therefore, acts of humanitarian intervention could constitute acts of aggression, which seems to make paragraph 7 of the Understandings a useless justification for humanitarian intervention.[60] The proponent for the 'humanitarian intervention exception' may still argue that the intervention is to prevent international crimes, that it aims to produce positive consequences for the international community and for the population of the State in questions as well and, thus, should be excluded from the scope of the crime based on paragraph 6 of the Understandings. However, paragraph 6 requires that the determination of the gravity and consequences be made in accordance with the U.N. Charter. The unilateral humanitarian intervention, as stated before, clearly does not accord with the rules regulating use of force provided by the U.N.[61]

---

[60] Larry May, "The International Criminal Court and the Crime of Aggression: Aggression, Humanitarian Intervention and Terrorism", *Case Western Reserve Journal of International Law*, 2009, vol. 41, p. 334. Prof. Glennon is of the opinion that no legal consideration may serve as a justification for aggression under Article 8*bis*; Glennon, 2010, *supra* note 19, pp. 88–90.

[61] The insertion of "in accordance with the Charter of the United Nations" was done upon the insistence of the Iranian Delegation to limit its scope to what is permitted under the Charter; see, William A. Schabas, "Kampala Diary 10/6/10 The ICC Review Conference: Kampala 2010", available at http://iccreviewconference.blogspot.com/, last accessed on 31 July 2012.

In addition, the legal status and effects of the Understandings for the Court are unclear. Firstly, the Understandings are not part of the Statute and cannot be considered as a treaty. Therefore, they do not belong to the applicable law of the Court as provided by Article 21 of the Statute and are not binding on the Court.[62] It should also be noted that the Understandings are not necessarily a reflection of the attitudes and understandings of the States Parties to the Statute since it was adopted under the insistence of a non-State Party. Under these circumstances, there exist reasonable doubts as to whether the Understandings could be relied upon as reference for the interpretation of the Article 8*bis*.

6.3. Conditions for the Court's Jurisdiction over the Crime of Aggression

6.3.1. Introduction

The conditions for the Court to exercise its jurisdiction over the crime of aggression are provided as follows in Article 15*bis* and *ter*:[63]

> Article 15 *bis* Exercise of jurisdiction over the crime of aggression (State referral, *proprio motu*)
>
> 1. The Court may exercise jurisdiction over the crime of aggression in accordance with article 13, paragraphs (a) and (c), subject to the provisions of this article.
>
> 2. The Court may exercise jurisdiction only with respect to crimes of aggression committed one year after the ratification or acceptance of the amendments by thirty States Parties.
>
> 3. The Court shall exercise jurisdiction over the crime of aggression in accordance with this article, subject to a decision to be taken after 1 January 2017 by the same majority of States Parties as is required for the adoption of an amendment to the Statute.
>
> 4. The Court may, in accordance with article 12, exercise jurisdiction over a crime of aggression, arising from an act of aggression committed by a State Party,

---

[62] According to Article 21 of the Statute, the applicable law for the Court includes in the first place, the Statute, Elements of Crimes, its rules of Procedure and Evidence and in the second place, applicable treaties and principles and rules of international law.

[63] *Supra* note 4, Annex I, RC/Res.6.

unless that State Party has previously declared that it does not accept such jurisdiction by lodging a declaration with the Registrar. The withdrawal of such a declaration may be effected at any time and shall be considered by the State Party within three years.

5. In respect of a State that is not a party to this Statute, the Court shall not exercise its jurisdiction over the crime of aggression when committed by that State's nationals or on its territory.

6. Where the Prosecutor concludes that there is a reasonable basis to proceed with an investigation in respect of a crime of aggression, he or she shall first ascertain whether the Security Council has made a determination of an act of aggression committed by the State concerned. The Prosecutor shall notify the Secretary-General of the United Nations of the situation before the Court, including any relevant information and documents.

7. Where the Security Council has made such a determination, the Prosecutor may proceed with the investigation in respect of a crime of aggression.

8. Where no such determination is made within six months after the date of notification, the Prosecutor may proceed with the investigation in respect of a crime of aggression, provided that the Pre-Trial Division has authorized the commencement of the investigation in respect of a crime of aggression in accordance with the procedure contained in article 15, and the Security Council has not decided otherwise in accordance with article 16.

9. A determination of an act of aggression by an organ outside the Court shall be without prejudice to the Court's own findings under this Statute.

10. This article is without prejudice to the provisions relating to the exercise of jurisdiction with respect to other crimes referred to in Article 5.

Article 15 *ter* Exercise of jurisdiction over the crime of aggression (Security Council referral)

1. The Court may exercise jurisdiction over the crime of aggression in accordance with article 13, paragraph (b), subject to the provisions of this article.

2. The Court may exercise jurisdiction only with respect to crimes of aggression committed one year after the ratification or acceptance of the amendments by thirty States Parties.

3. The Court shall exercise jurisdiction over the crime of aggression in accordance with this article, subject to a decision to be taken after 1 January 2017 by the same majority of States Parties as is required for the adoption of an amendment to the Statute.

4. A determination of an act of aggression by an organ outside the Court shall be without prejudice to the Court's own findings under this Statute.

5. This article is without prejudice to the provisions relating to the exercise of jurisdiction with respect to other crimes referred to in Article 5.

Under Article 15*bis* and *ter* the Court may exercise its jurisdiction over the crime of aggression under the following circumstances: acting under Chapter VII, the Security Council of the U.N. may refer a situation concerning aggression to the Court; a State Party may refer a situation concerning aggression to the Court or the Prosecutor of the Court may initiate an investigation *proprio motu*. These clauses are actually affirmations of Article 13 of the Statute and received general consensus during the negotiations.[64]

However, as for the scope of the jurisdiction, an important distinction was made between, on one hand, State referral or the Prosecutor's initiation of an investigation and, on the other hand, the Security Council's referral. Under the former scenario, in order to protect the non-States Parties' nationals from the jurisdiction of the Court with respect to the crime of aggression, paragraph 2 of Article 15*bis* provides that the Court cannot exercise its jurisdiction when the crime is committed by a non-State Party's national or on a non-State Party's territory. This amendment was considered to have provided the protection long sought by non-State Parties. At the same time, paragraph 4 of Article 15*bis* expunges those States Parties having declared their non-acceptance of the new crime of

---

[64] Fletcher, 2010, *supra* note 16, p. 247; Kacker, 2010, *supra* note 17, p. 272.

aggression from the Court's jurisdiction. These concessions are expected to be able to facilitate the acceptance of the amendment. Under the latter scenario, that is referral from the Security Council acting under Chapter VII of the Charter, the Court may exercise its jurisdiction over the crime of aggression with respect to any State, whether it has accepted the Court's jurisdiction or not.[65]

As for the State referral or investigations initiated by the Prosecutor, if the latter believes that there is a reasonable basis to proceed with the investigation, he or she shall first ascertain whether the Security Council has made a determination of an act of aggression with respect to the State concerned. The Prosecutor shall also notify the Security Council of the situation. When the Security Council has made a determination of an act of aggression with respect to the State, the Prosecutor may proceed with the investigation but the determination is not binding for the State. If the Security Council does not make such a determination within six months after the receipt of the Prosecutor's notification, the Prosecutor may proceed with the investigation provided that he or she gets the authorisation from the Pre-Trial Division, but the Security Council could defer the investigation under Article 16 of the Statute. Consensus was also reached during the Review Conference that the authorisation from the Pre-Trial Division shall be a majority agreement of all the judges constituting the Division.[66]

6.3.2. Analysis

During the process of negotiations on the crime of aggression, the conditions for the Court's jurisdiction on the crime, in particular whether the Court should proceed with the investigation in the absence of a determination of aggression by the Security Council, was considered as the 'question of questions'.[67] This question is actually tackling the issues of what role the Security Council should play in the case of a State referral or a Prosecutor's *proprio motu* investigation. The core issue is whether the Court should independently proceed with an investigation in the absence of a determination of aggression by the Security Council. The essence of the issue is how to keep the balance between the independence of the

---

[65] Scheffer, 2010, *supra* note 5.

[66] *Ibid.*

[67] Kreβ and von Holtzendorff, 2010, *supra* note 18, pp. 1208.

Court and the authority of the Security Council with respect to the determination of aggression. States – in particular the permanent members of the Security Council – were deeply divided on this issue during the negotiations.

It is understandable that there will be no conflict between the Security Council and the Court when the former refers a situation to the latter. In these circumstances, the States concerned are also under obligation to co-operate with the Court since the referral is made by the Security Council acting under Chapter VII of the Charter.[68]

Therefore, the real question is what kind of role the Security Council should play in the case of a State referral or an investigation initiated by the Prosecutor. In order to address this issue, the Amendment firstly requires that the Prosecutor should ascertain whether the Security Council has made a determination of aggression with respect to the State in question or not. If the Security Council had made such a determination, the Prosecutor can then proceed with the investigation but the determination of the Council is not binding on the Court.

The above-mentioned seemingly reasonable solution still creates problems in practice. Firstly, since its inception, the Security Council has only issued determinations of acts of aggression with respect to situations concerning South Africa and Angola (1967), Israeli bombing of the headquarters of the Palestine Liberation Organization ('PLO') in Tunisia (1985), and an armed aggression by mercenaries against Benin (1977). 'Threat to international peace or security' is the term more frequently used by the Council for situations of conflicts.[69] Therefore, due to the scarce practice of the Council with respect to such determinations, we could reasonably foresee that the chances for the Prosecutor to proceed on the basis of the Council's determination are rather slim. As for the Council's determinations of 'threat to international peace and security' or 'breach of peace', they cannot serve as a basis for the Prosecutor to proceed with an investigation since there is no such authorisation in the Stat-

---

[68] Ferencz, 2009, *supra* note 5, p. 286; Kacker, 2010, *supra* note 17, p. 277.

[69] Troy Lavers, "Determining the Crime of Aggression: Has the Time Come to Allow the International Criminal Court its Freedom?", in *Albany Law Review*, 2008, vol. 71, pp. 304–305; *supra* note 17: according to Devyani Kacker, there are only 31 resolutions of the Council condemning acts of aggression, most of which concern South Africa and Rhodesia (pp. 275–276).

ute.[70] It shall be further noted that the determination of the Council is only a matter of procedure and not binding on the Court. Thus, if the determination of the Council and the Court are in conflict, the reputation and credibility of both institutions will be at risk. What should the Court do if the Council decides that no aggression has taken place in a given situation? Can such a determination serve as a justified defence for the State or defendant before the Court? The logical answer to these questions should be that the determination of the non-existence of aggression is also not binding for the Court, just as that of the existence of aggression. Then, faced with the embarrassing situation that the Prosecutor proceeds with the investigation despite its determination of the non-existence of aggression, the Security Council could possibly rely on Article 16 of the Statute to defer the proceedings before the Court.

However, it is in fact equally difficult for the Council to make a determination of non-existence of aggression as is aggression. The more frequent scenario we could foresee is that the Council could not make any decision due to the internal political dynamics within the Council. It is exactly out of this concern that the Amendments further authorise the Prosecutor to proceed with the investigation if the Council has not made a determination of aggression within six months after being notified of the situation. This clause is the one that aroused the most heated debate over the authority of the Council and the independence of the Court during the negotiations.

Those who support an exclusive authority of the Council with respect to the determination of aggression argued that Articles of 20 and 39 of the Charter grant exclusive authority to the Council in terms of determination and enforcement with respect to maintenance of international peace and security. Article 5 of the Statute provides that the crime of aggression under the Statute shall be in line with the Charter. Therefore, a determination of aggression by the Council shall be the precondition for

---

[70] It was suggested that when the Security Council makes a determination of threat to international peace and security or breach of peace, the procedural shall be launched to determine whether aggression has been committed or not for the sake of prosecution of the crime under the ICC. And the determination of aggression could be done by the International Court of Justice or the ICC; see David Scheffer, "A Pragmatic Approach to Jurisdictional and Definitional Requirements for the Crime of Aggression in the Rome Statute", in *Case Western Reserve Journal of International Law*, 2009, vol. 41, pp. 404–408.

the Court to exercise its jurisdiction over the crime of aggression. On the other hand, aggression is normally a highly controversial political issue and the Court, a judicial organ, is not a suitable institute to deal with this political problem. The Council is the right political institution to address the issue of aggression, and its determination can facilitate the maintenance of international peace and security and the co-operation of the States needed by the Court with respect to prosecution of the crime of aggression.[71]

Those who oppose the 'dictatorship' of the Council with respect to the crime of aggression and insist on the independence of the Court argued that the Council's authority to determine acts of aggression is established under the Charter for international peace and security purposes, and not for the purpose of individual criminal responsibility. The former is a political issue and the latter is a legal one. The Council, as a political organ, is not suitable for the legal assessment of the crime of aggression. What is more, the Charter only grants 'primary' but not 'exclusive' authority to the Council with respect to the maintenance of international peace and security. To make the Council's determination of an act of aggression a precondition for the Court's jurisdiction actually violates the principle of equal sovereignty of the Charter for it puts the permanent members of the Council in an advantageous position over other members of the U.N. In practice, the institutions of the U.N. other than the Council, such as the ICJ and the General Assembly, have made declarations of aggression in situations concerning Korea, Namibia and in the cases of *Nicaragua v. U.S.* (1986), '*oil platform* case' (*Iran v. U.S.*, 2003), and *Congo v. Uganda* (2005). To require the Court to abide by a decision of a political organ will reduce the accused's chance of defence before the Court and thus, harm the principle of justice as well as the independence and credibility of the Court. The discussions during the negotiations indicated that insistence of the exclusive authority of the Council with respect to act of aggression would break the consensus and also could not get the support of the majority. It was also agreed during the negotiations that the Court would not be bound by decisions of an organ outside of the Court and the Council is also not bound by the Articles on the crime of aggression in the Statute. The relationship between the Court and the Council shall be firstly independent from each other in terms of their respective

---

[71]   Fletcher, 2010, *supra* note 16, p. 250; Kacker, 2010, *supra* note 17, pp. 277–278.

functions, but also complementary to each other in that one is to make peace through justice and the other does the same through international politics.[72]

Some scholars are of the opinion that there always exists a dilemma for the relations between the Court and the Council: to integrate the Council into the Court procedure may violate the principle of criminal justice, while to exclude it from the procedure might create even more problems. As a political organ, the Security Council has a lot of discretion for its decisions and function and does not show a coherent practice, which makes the Council's decision very unpredictable and hard for States to rely on as guidance for their action. Therefore, to integrate the Council's decision as part of the decision of the Court would violate the principle of specialty of criminal justice. But as stated before, to authorise the Prosecutor to proceed with the case in disregard of the decisions of the Council will put the reputation and credibility of both institutions at risk if their decisions conflict each other. It will also put the States into a dilemma when faced with conflicting decisions because they are required to give priority to the obligations from the Council under Article 103 of the Charter, which could hinder their co-operation with the Court. On the other hand, inactions by the Council does not necessarily mean that it has no opinion on the issue, but could imply that an aggression has taken place, that it has doubts on the matter, or that it has other concerns over its action for the sake of international peace and security. The intervention of the Court under these circumstances might not be a contribution to peace and security. Last but the least, it is inappropriate for the Statute to impose a time limit for the Council's action, as such a limitation could only be established by modification of the Charter.[73]

---

[72] Mark S. Stein, "The Security Council, the International Criminal Court, and the Crime of Aggression: How Exclusive is the Security Council's Power to Determine Aggression?" in *Indiana International and Comparative Law Review*, 2005–2006, vol. 16, no. 1; Niels Blokker, "The Crime of Aggression and the United Nations Security Council", in *Leiden Journal of International Law*, 2007, vol. 20, pp. 867–894; Fletcher, 2010, *supra* note 16, p. 250; Kacker, 2010, *supra* note 17, p. 27 Kreβ and von Holtzendorff, 2010, *supra* note 18, p. 1208; Lavers, 2008, *supra* note 69.

[73] Glennon, 2010, *supra* note 19, pp. 102–109; Kacker, 2010, *supra* note 17, p. 277; the cases of Sudan and Congo were cited to show that for the sake of international peace and security, the Security Council does not take action.

The Amendments adopted at the Conference show that those supporting the independence of the Court have prevailed and the Court will become an institution additional to the Council assessing the legality of States' use of force.

Last but not least, the limits imposed on the Court's jurisdiction over the crime of aggression are worth noting. Firstly, the number of States concerned could be limited. As stated before, not only non-State Parties are excluded from the Court's jurisdiction, but also not all States Parties are covered by the jurisdiction of the Court over the crime of aggression. According to the Resolution adopting the Amendments, the latter are subject to ratification or acceptance and will enter into force in accordance with Article 121, paragraph 5.[74] Therefore, the Amendments were considered by the drafters as amendments to the crimes under the Statute and only accepting States Parties are bound. In this regard, it was suggested that the Amendments should enter into force for all States Parties either under paragraph 3 of Article 121, which requires adoption of the amendment by consensus or a two-thirds majority, or under paragraph 4 of the same Article, which requires acceptance by a seven-eighth majority. The reason for using the procedure under Article 121(3) is that Article 5(2) of the Statute simply requires adoption of the crime of aggression, which is exactly addressed by Article 121(3). State Parties have accepted the Court's jurisdiction under Article 5 – including the crime of aggression – when they became parties to the Statute. Therefore the Amendments are not really an amendment to Article 5 as defined by Article 121(5), and thus should not be subject to further acceptance by States Parties. The reason for using the procedure under Article 121(4) is that due to domestic requirements the Amendments could be subject to ratification or acceptance by the States Parties. Only a procedure for entry into force for all the States Parties can satisfy equality among them, which is also the intention of the Statute drafters.[75] Due to policy considerations, these suggestions were not adopted by the negotiators.[76]

---

[74] *Supra* note 4, OP1.

[75] Astrid Reisinger Coracini, "The International Criminal Court's Exercise of Jurisdiction Over the Crime of Aggression – at Last…in Reach…Over Some", in *Goettingen Journal of International Law*, 2010, vol. 2, no. 2, pp. 763–766.

[76] *Ibid.*

Secondly, a temporal limitation is also imposed on the Court's jurisdiction. The Court may exercise its jurisdiction only with respect to a crime of aggression committed one year after the acceptance of the Amendments by thirty States Parties, which is further subject to a decision to be taken after 1 January 2017 by the same majority of States Parties required for the adoption of an amendment to the Statute.[77] Accordingly, even if thirty States Parties have accepted the Amendments before 31 December 2016, the Court cannot exercise its jurisdiction over crime of aggression if the States Parties cannot reach a decision after 1 January 2017. And *vice versa,* even if the States Parties can reach such a decision after 1 January 2017, the Court can still be prevented from entertaining its jurisdiction over the crime if less than thirty States Parties have accepted the Amendments. Taking into consideration the fact that, at the time of writing, only one State Party has accepted the Amendments[78] two years after their adoption, and the divide among States during the negotiations, it is hard to foresee when the Court can exercise its jurisdiction over the crime of aggression.

6.4. Conclusion

The States' views on the crime of aggression are a reflection of their policy of war or use of armed force, which is further dependent on their global perspective on inter-state relations. If States hold the perception that their relations are competitive in nature and a zero-sum game, conflicts between the States shall, then, be a normal feature of international relations and war can be used as tool of foreign policy. As a result, aggression is considered as neutral in legal terms and a reality for inter-state relations. This is the situation of the nineteenth century during which war was firmly ensconced as a routine feature of international life and was considered an institution of international law. If States view their relations as basically of peaceful co-existence, then to breach such a peaceful situation requires some justification. A breach of peace without justification will be condemned, even punished, by the international community of States. Born in ancient times, and waning during the eighteenth and nineteenth centuries, the just-war ideology has had its revival under the U.N.

---

[77] Paragraphs 2 and 3 of Article 15*bis* and *ter.*

[78] Liechtenstein is the first State that has ratified the Amendment and deposited its instruments of ratification to the U.N. on 8 May 2012, ICC-ASP-20120509-PR793.

Charter, namely armed force can only be used for the sake of peace and security, in case of self-defence, or collective security.[79] Accordingly, the criminalisation of aggression and the ensuing individual responsibility have also been established as a basic institution of modern international law.[80]

However, as an enforcement mechanism of the international security regime, the criminalisation of aggression could not be isolated from the reality of the international politics. When the victorious States were reconstructing the international security regime, they were not willing to rely totally on an international organisation for their security and were keen to reserve their prerogative of use of force because it concerns their safety and survival. Therefore, whether to use force or not is more a policy consideration and it is much better or easier to address this issue through political channels.[81] At the same time, the privileges enjoyed by the great powers within the collective security regime – the Security Council – are primary considerations for these powers' undertakings in the name of international peace and security because those privileges shelter them for their military actions. Therefore, the idea that another institution, in addition to the Security Council, is to be established to evaluate the use of force by the State will definitely be opposed by those powers.[82] Lastly, to put issues of both *jus ad bellum* and *jus in bello* [83] into the jurisdiction of the same Court could arouse dilemmas for their application: when a State involved in an armed conflict faces a potential charge

---

[79] Stephen C. Neff, *War and Law of Nations*, Oxford University Press, 2005. The author gives a detailed description of historical development of the nature of war: war as instrument of justice (just war), war as an institution of international law and neo just war under the U.N. Charter.

[80] Henry L. Stimson, *The Nuremberg Trial: Landmark in Law*, Foreign Affairs, 1947.

[81] Ferencz, 2009, *supra* note 5, p. 286; Noah Weisbord, "Conceptualizing Aggression", in *Duke Journal of Comparative and International Law*, vol. 20, pp. 1–3.

[82] Ferencz, 2009, *supra* note 5, p. 286.

[83] *Jus ad bellum* and *jus in bello* are considered to be two separate branches of rules regulating armed conflicts. The former addresses situations under which the resort to armed forces is allowed while the latter deals with the behaviour of the parties to the conflicts, such as prohibition of attacking civilians and protection of prisons of war, *etc*. Violation of the former could constitute crime of aggression and violation of the latter could constitute war crimes. See, Robert Kolb and Richard Hyde, *An Introduction to the International Law of Armed Conflicts*, Hart Publishing, 2008, Chapter 2 and 3.

---

of aggression, can we still expect that State to abide by the rules of armed conflicts during a war where it is deemed to be the aggressor?[84] Therefore, taking into consideration the reality of international politics and the concerns and divides among States over the regulation of the use of force, the difficulties of the negotiations do not come as a surprise.[85]

The military trials after the WWII and the foundation of the U.N. have established a common maxim for international law and politics, that is, war as an instrument of State foreign policy is abolished and declared illegal and the core interest of the international community is to save the generations to come from the scourge of war. Thus, the U.N. endeavours to prevent war through political channels while the international criminal justice aims at punishing those who have seriously violated the rules regulating the use of force. They are complementary to each other in protecting the core interest of the international community.[86]

Last, but not least, it is not only the responsibility of the Great Powers to maintain international peace and security, but the desire and responsibility of all States. The establishment of the International Criminal Court marked a breakthrough for the development of international criminal law since WWII. Since its inception, the Court has become an indispensable player in international relations through its judicial activities.[87] In spite of all the difficulties, the Amendments were adopted. It will not only enhance the Court's capacity with regard to international peace and security, but also complete the regime of collective security with a judicial tool. Therefore, the adoption of the Amendments may be deemed not only as a warning to 'aggressive policy makers', but also as a response to the inefficiency of the Security Council, which is controlled by the Great Powers and refuses to be reformed to address the changing security situation. Even though we still need to wait and see whether the Court will live up to the expectations of the supporters of the Amendments after 1 January 2017, we are at least assured that the State leaders will now think twice

---

[84] Andres Paulus, "Second Thoughts on the Crime of Aggression", in *European Journal of International Law*, 2009, vol. 20, p.1127.

[85] Glennon, 2010, *supra* note 19.

[86] William Eldred Jackson, "Putting the Nurnberg Law to Work", in *Foreign Affairs*, 1947.

[87] David Kaye, "Who's Afraid of the International Criminal Court?", in *Foreign Affairs*, May/June 2011.

before they resort to force in dealing with international disputes, which will definitely not make the world less safe than it is today.

7

Universal Jurisdiction
for Core International Crimes

Erkki Kourula[*]

7.1. Introduction

Universal jurisdiction is a valuable tool in the fight against impunity. Although it is not a new concept under international law, there still exists a divergence of views on its purpose, definition, usefulness and indeed its exercise in practice. This chapter does not aim to exhaustively discuss all issues pertaining to universal jurisdiction. Having first addressed the issue from a more general perspective, it primarily discusses some of the challenges that have emerged in recent years as far as the application of universal jurisdiction is concerned in the prosecution of core international crimes, from the perspective of the differing approaches taken in national jurisdictions (and, for example, by the E.U. and A.U. in general), and the differing political perspectives, to the role of international courts and tribunals in the overall fight against impunity for such crimes. Issues addressed include the lack of a uniform position on universal jurisdiction as between States in general, the question of 'overlapping' jurisdictions and subsidiarity, immunities of State officials, and the overall feasibility of prosecutions based on universal jurisdiction.

---

[*] **Erkki Kourula** serves as Judge of the Appeals Chamber of the ICC. He holds a Ph.D. in international law from the University of Oxford. He has held various research positions in international law, including international humanitarian law and human rights, and has acted as a professor of international law. He has been Director General for Legal Affairs of the Ministry of Foreign Affairs of Finland, as well as a judge in Finland dealing with criminal cases. Judge Kourula followed closely the developments leading to the establishment of the ICTY and ICTR and was actively involved in the negotiations of the Rome Statute (1995–1998) as head of the Finnish Delegation to the Preparatory Committee and the Rome Conference on the Establishment of the ICC.

7.2. The Idea of Universal Jurisdiction

Under international law, the concept of universal jurisdiction enables domestic courts to punish perpetrators of those crimes which are so heinous that they are considered to amount to crimes against the international community as a whole, irrespective of where they occurred or the nationality of the perpetrator or victims.[1] In other words, universal jurisdiction provides a basis for ensuring responsibility regardless of the place where the crime was committed and irrespective of any link of active or passive nationality, or other grounds of jurisdiction recognised by international law. As such, universal jurisdiction is an important tool for ending the impunity of perpetrators of the most serious crimes of international concern. The term 'universal jurisdiction' has been defined as follows:

> [...] universal criminal jurisdiction is the assertion by one state of its jurisdiction over crimes allegedly committed in the territory of another state by nationals of another state against nationals of another state where the crime alleged poses no direct threat to the vital interests of the state asserting jurisdiction. In other words, universal jurisdiction amounts to the claim by a state to prosecute crimes in circumstances where none of the traditional links of territoriality, nationality, passive personality or the protective principle exists at the time of the commission of the alleged offence.[2]

---

[1]   Malcolm N. Shaw, *International Law*, sixth edition, Cambridge University Press, 2008, p. 668.

[2]   A.U.-E.U. Expert Report on the Principle of Universal Jurisdiction, issued 16 April 2009, 8672/1/09, REV 1, available at http://ec.europa.eu/development/icenter/reposi tory/troika_ua_ue_rapport_competence_ universelle_EN.pdf, last accessed on 30 July 2012 (hereinafter 'A.U.-E.U. Expert Report'), Annex, para. 8. For other definitions of universal jurisdiction see *e.g.*: Principle 1.1 of The Princeton Principles on Universal Jurisdiction, 2001, available at http://lapa.princeton.edu/hosteddocs/unive_jur.pdf, last accessed on 27 August 2012; *Resolution on 'Universal Jurisdiction with regard to the crime of genocide, crimes against humanity and war crimes'*, Institute of International Law, 2005, para. 1; F. Jessberger, "Universal Jurisdiction", in Antonio Cassese *et al.* (eds.), *The Oxford Companion to International Criminal Justice*, Oxford University Press, 2009, p. 555; Cedric Ryngaert, *Jurisdiction in International Law*, Oxford University Press, 2008, p. 101; Gerhard Werle, *Principles of International Criminal Law*, TMC Asser Press, The Hague, 2005, p. 59; Christopher C. Joyner, "Arresting Impunity: The Case for Universal Jurisdiction in Bringing War Criminals To Accountability", in *Law and Contemporary Problems*, vol. 59, no. 4, pp. 164 *et seq.*; Antonio

---

The concept of universal jurisdiction is said to be based on customary[3], as well as conventional[4], international law. Conventional sources, referring to universal jurisdiction when a suspect is present on the territory of a State, include the Convention against Torture of 1984, the Convention against Enforced Disappearance of 2006 and the grave breaches provisions of the 1949 Geneva Conventions.[5] A related concept, often also contained in such conventions, is that of *aut dedere aut judicare*, that is, the obligation for States to either prosecute the case in question or extradite the person to a State that will prosecute.[6] As has been stated, "a state party to one of the treaties in question is not only bound to empower its criminal justice system to exercise universal jurisdiction but is further bound actually to exercise that jurisdiction by means of either considering prosecuting or extraditing". [7]

7.3. Challenges in the Exercise of Universal Jurisdiction in Relation to Core International Crimes

Achieving the goal of putting an end to core international crimes and prosecuting those responsible for them is now aimed at on both the international and national levels.[8]

Internationally, the advent of international criminal institutions such as the International Criminal Tribunals for the former Yugoslavia and Rwanda ('ICTY' and 'ICTR', respectively) and, importantly, the perma-

Cassese, "Is the Bell Tolling for Universality? A Plea for a Sensible Notion of Universal Jurisdiction", in *Journal of International Criminal Justice,* 2003, vol. 1, p. 589; Christopher K. Hall, "The Role of Universal Jurisdiction in the International Criminal Court Complementarity System", in Morten Bergsmo (ed.), *Complementarity and the Exercise of Universal Jurisdiction for Core International Crimes*, Torkel Opsahl Academic EPublisher, Oslo, 2010, pp. 202 *et seq.*

3   See R. Cryer, H. Friman, D. Robinson and E. Wilmshurst, *International Criminal Law and Procedure*, Cambridge University Press, 2007, p. 44; Werle, 2005, *supra* note 2, p. 59. A.U.-E.U. Expert Report, Annex, para. 9, see *supra* note 2.

4   See A.U.-E.U. Expert Report, Annex, para. 9, see *supra* note 2; see also Philippe Sands, "International Law Transformed? From Pinochet to Congo...?", in *Leiden Journal of International Law*, 2003, vol. 16, pp. 42 *et seq.*

5   A.U.-E.U. Expert Report, Annex, para. 9, see *supra* note 2.

6   *Ibid.*, para. 11; Hall, 2010, pp. 204–205, see *supra* note 2.

7   A.U.-E.U. Expert Report, Annex, para. 11, see *supra* note 2.

8   *Ibid.*, para. 28.

nent International Criminal Court ('ICC'), has signalled a clear commitment by the international community to end impunity for such crimes. The Preamble to the Rome Statute states, *inter alia,*

> **Determined** to put an end to impunity for the perpetrators of these crimes and thus to contribute to the prevention of such crimes.

The ICC's role is intended to form part of the overall goal to end impunity. Part, in the sense that it was not intended that it should act alone. The Preamble also states:

> **Affirming** that the most serious crimes of concern to the international community as a whole must not go unpunished and that their effective prosecution must be ensured by taking measures at the national level and by enhancing international cooperation,
>
> [...]
>
> **Recalling** that it is the duty of every State to exercise its criminal jurisdiction over those responsible for international crimes,
>
> [...]
>
> **Emphasizing** that the International Criminal Court established under this Statute shall be complementary to national criminal jurisdictions.

In this sense, the ICC is intended to act alongside States who are primarily entrusted with the task of prosecuting the crimes falling within the jurisdiction of the Court; at this time, genocide, crimes against humanity and war crimes.[9] The question arises as to the extent to which those States have to date achieved this goal and how their role interplays with that of the ICC. In addition, one may question whether the ICC's jurisdiction and the application of the principle of universal jurisdiction overlap. Are these two systems compatible? Is international justice best served by having both systems function simultaneously?

There are arguments both in favour of the exercise of universal jurisdiction and arguments against. Included in the former, are the fact that often the crimes in question are committed in places "where they cannot be prevented or punished easily", or are "committed within the territory of

---

[9]   Article 5 of the Rome Statute.

a particular state caught up in internal conflict".[10] States where crimes are committed may also lack the resources to investigate and prosecute the crimes or be unwilling or unable to do so.[11] The exercise of universal jurisdiction may also act as a catalyst for investigations or prosecutions internationally or nationally,[12] it can "help to fill a small part of the global impunity gap"[13], and it can create a change in how these crimes are seen both by the public and governments.[14] Arguments against the exercise of universal jurisdiction include the fear that prosecutions based on universal jurisdiction would be politically motivated or infringe on State sovereignty, that the principle of double jeopardy may be jeopardised (and that "[u]niversal jurisdiction favours the rights of the victim over the rights of the accused")[15], and that the place of local concern should have primacy. ("The very idea that a totally disconnected country would bring the case is an offence to the jurisdictions that have the primary responsibility to resolve the conflicts inherent in the trial."[16])

In 2008, ministers of the A.U. and E.U. met to discuss "universal jurisdiction in the context of the relationship between the A.U. and E.U.", agreeing "to set up a technical ad hoc expert group to clarify the respective understanding on the African and EU side on the principle of universal jurisdiction".[17] The resulting report aimed at describing the exercise of universal jurisdiction, outlining the understandings of the African and European States[18] and making recommendations.[19]

---

[10] Joyner, pp. 166–167, see *supra* note 2.

[11] AMICC, Questions & Answers on the ICC and Universal Jurisdiction.

[12] Hall, 2010, pp. 212 *et seq.*, see *supra* note 2.

[13] Hall, 2010, pp. 214 *et seq.*, see *supra* note 2.

[14] Hall, 2010, p. 202, see *supra* note 2.

[15] George P. Fletcher, "Against Universal Jurisdiction", in *Journal of International Criminal Justice*, 2003, vol. 1, p. 580.

[16] Fletcher, 2003, p. 583, see *supra* note 15.

[17] A.U.-E.U. Expert Report, paras. 1 and 2, see *supra* note 2. Six independent experts were appointed: Professor Antonio Cassese (Italy), Professor Pierre Klein (Belgium), Dr. Roger O'Keefe (Australia), Dr. Mohammed Bedjaoui (Algeria), Dr. Chaloka Beyani (Zambia) and Professor Chris Maina Peter (Tanzania); all experts served in their personal capacities. See A.U.-E.U. Expert Report, paras. 5–7.

[18] A.U.-E.U. Expert Report, Annex, paras. 33–38 in respect of African concerns and paras. 39–45 in respect of European concerns, see *supra* note 2.

[19] *Ibid.*, para. 4.

In relation to African concerns, it was reported that, although they welcomed the principle in and of itself, there were constraints and concerns as to its application: "national legal and international constraints on the capacity of many African States"[20] to prosecute the crimes were said to exist while in addition it was reported that, as observed by some members of the International Law Commission, the "assertion by national courts of the principle of universal jurisdiction has led to misunderstandings and to aggravation of inter-state tensions, and has given rise to perceptions of abuse on political or other grounds".[21] African States considered that "they [had] been singularly targeted in the indictments and arrests of their officials and that the exercise of universal jurisdiction by European states [was] politically selective against them".[22] They also had concerns about the manner of issuance of indictments (frequently by "low-level judges, often sitting alone"), the public issuance of indictments and disregard for immunities of sitting state officials.[23]

As far as European States were concerned, the report found that they "view the exercise of universal jurisdiction as an essential weapon in the fight against impunity for serious crimes of international concern"[24] and "an important measure of last resort" in situations where "the state where the crime has allegedly been committed and the state(s) of nationality of the suspect and victims are manifestly unwilling or unable to prosecute".[25] The E.U. experts, in response to some of the African concerns, noted that "criminal proceedings initiated against African State officials on the basis of universal jurisdiction represent[ed] only a part of the total number of times when universal jurisdiction [was] invoked as a basis for jurisdiction by EU Member States" and that proceedings had been instituted or sought against nationals from other regions of the world, although "[i]n many cases, proceedings [had] been discontinued out of respect for the immunities accorded state officials by international law".[26] The report found that E.U. Member States:

---

20 *Ibid.*, para. 33.
21 *Ibid.*, para. 34.
22 *Ibid.*, para. 34.
23 *Ibid.*, paras. 35–38.
24 *Ibid.*, para. 39.
25 *Ibid.*, para. 39.
26 *Ibid.*, para. 40.

> [...] emphasize the need for African states to institute pro-
> ceedings against suspected perpetrators of serious crimes of
> international concern, whether on the basis of universal ju-
> risdiction or of other, more traditional bases of jurisdiction,
> *e.g.* territoriality, nationality, passive personality, *etc.*[27]

Although the report noted extradition requests made by some African States expressing their intent to prosecute such crimes, generally
based on territoriality or nationality, the inability of the requested state to
comply was noted, because they could not "satisfy themselves that certain
fundamental human rights guarantees would be respected on the surrender" of those persons.[28]

Out of this report came a number of recommendations (17 in all)
which the experts were required to make "with a view to fostering better
mutual understanding between the AU and EU regarding universal jurisdiction".[29] Generally, it was recommended that States should strive to put
an end to core international crimes and prosecute those responsible, to
prosecute treaty crimes when party to such treaties and to ensure that they
have implementing legislation in place.[30]

The scope and application of the principle of universal jurisdiction
is also under discussion within the Sixth Committee of the General Assembly. The issue was included on the agenda of the sixty-fourth session
in 2009[31] and since then has been discussed at the sixty-fifth and sixty-
sixth sessions in 2010 and 2011, respectively.[32] In the latter session, it
was noted that "there was controversy surrounding the principle":

> Some delegations noted that universal jurisdiction involved
> complex issues of a legal, political and diplomatic nature.
> Indeed, delegations expressed different views on the scope
> of universal jurisdiction and its application, highlighting that
> it was in these aspects that most concerns existed. It was also

---

[27] *Ibid.*, para. 44.

[28] *Ibid.*, para. 45.

[29] *Ibid.*, para. 46.

[30] *Ibid.*, paras. 46 *et seq.*

[31] See http://www.un.org/en/ga/sixth/64/UnivJur.shtml#, last accessed on 29 August
2012.

[32] See http://www.un.org/en/ga/sixth/65/ScopeAppUniJuri/shtml and http://www.un.org/
en/ga/sixth/66/ScopeAppUniJuri/shtml, last accessed on 27 August 2012.

noted that the principle was viewed as some as incipient, lacking clarity in its scope and how it was applied.[33]

Issues discussed ranged from "the importance of agreeing on a definition of universal jurisdiction and the need to distinguish it from other related concepts, such as international criminal jurisdiction, the obligation to extradite or prosecute, as well as other related principles and rules of international law", the crimes covered by the principle, the application of universal jurisdiction (including the emphasis on "the need for the judicious and responsible application of the principle"), immunities and the conditions for the application of universal jurisdiction.[34] A working group would be established at the sixty-seventh session, in 2012, "to continue to undertake a thorough discussion of the scope and application of universal jurisdiction".[35]

Some of the above concerns are discussed below. One may see that although moves have been taken at the national level to prosecute those responsible for core international crimes on the basis of universal jurisdiction, differing approaches of States create challenges.

Although many States have now enabled domestic courts to expand their jurisdiction and prosecute international crimes under the universality principle,[36] the manner in which this has been approached has differed.[37] Some examples of cases brought or sought under universal jurisdiction are[38] the cases of: President Augusto Pinochet in London and Spain;[39] Sister Maria Kisito and Sister Gertrude, in Belgium; Nikola Jorgić and Novislav Djajić in Germany; in Chad Hissène Habré in Belgium; Donald

---

[33] See http://www.un.org/en/ga/sixth/66/ScopeAppUniJuri/shtml, last accessed on 27 August 2012.

[34] *Ibid.*

[35] *Ibid.*

[36] See Hall, 2010, pp. 217–223, see *supra* note 2.

[37] For an overview of the approaches taken in African and E.U. States, see A.U.-E.U. Report, Annex, paras. 15– 27, see *supra* note 2. See also Naomi Roht-Arriaza, "Universal Jurisdiction: Steps Forward, Steps Back", *Leiden Journal of International Law*, 2004, vol. 17, p. 375; Hall, 2010, pp. 217 *et seq.* and pp. 226 *et seq.*, see *supra* note 2.

[38] AMICC, "Questions & Answers on the ICC and Universal Jurisdiction". See also Katherine Gallagher, "Universal Jurisdiction in Practice: Efforts to Hold Donald Rumsfeld and Other High-level United States Officials Accountable for Torture", in *Journal of International Criminal Justice*, 2009, vol. 7, no. 5, p. 1087.

[39] Sands, 2003, p. 37, see *supra* note 5.

Rumsfeld in Belgium. In terms of legislative moves, those taken by, for example, Belgium and Spain have been well-documented, and more expansive legislation in those jurisdictions has since been amended and reduced in scope.[40] In general, legal limitations to the exercise of universal jurisdiction that may be found in national legislation may include: that the person is present on the territory of the prosecuting State; that prosecution be initiated by the Attorney General; that there is respect for immunities; that universal jurisdiction only applies to crimes committed in a specific conflict; that the crimes may only be prosecuted in the higher courts.[41]

Looking more closely at one of these limitations, in terms of the requirement of presence, under the broad notion (or what has been named 'absolute universal jurisdiction'), the State may prosecute the person irrespective of where the crime occurred or the nationality of the perpetrator or victim, as well as regardless of the presence of the accused on the territory of that State.[42] Under the narrow notion ('conditional universal jurisdiction'),[43] the State may prosecute the person only if he or she is present on the territory of that State.[44] The issue essentially is whether, for the exercise of universal jurisdiction, the presence of the accused on the territory (so-called *'forum deprehensionis'*) is required as a condition.[45] Different degrees of 'presence' are also argued for, for example, simple capture or residence, with one writer stating that "[i]t would be self-defeating to add conditions which would render universal jurisdiction akin to a tra-

---

[40] See e.g. Cassese, 2003, p. 589, see *supra* note 2; Roht-Arriaza, 2004, p. 375, see *supra* note 37; Gallagher, 2009, pp. 1087, see *supra* note 38; Roozbeh (Rudy) B. Baker, "Universal Jurisdiction and the Case of Belgium: A Critical Assessment", in *ILSA Journal of International and Comparative Law*, 2009–2010, vol. 16, no. 1, p. 141.

[41] A.U.-E.U. Expert Report, Annex, paras. 18 and 24, see *supra* note 2; see also Hall, 2010, pp. 223 *et seq.*, see *supra* note 2.

[42] Antonio Cassese, *International Criminal Law*, first edition, Oxford University Press, 2003, pp. 286–287.

[43] See Cassese, 2003, pp. 284–292, see *supra* note 42; see also Cassese, 2003, pp. 589–595, see *supra* note 2.

[44] Cassese, 2003, pp. 285–286, see *supra* note 43; Cassese, 2003, pp. 592–593, see *supra* note 2. Antonio Cassese, "When may senior state officials be tried for international crimes? Some comments on the Congo v. Belgium Case", in *European Journal of International Law*, 2002, vol. 13, no. 4, pp. 855 *et seq.*

[45] A.U.-E.U. Expert Report, Annex, para. 10, see *supra* note 2.

ditional connecting factor, and thus lose its specificity and raison d'être".[46]

Another problem arises in the face of overlapping claims to jurisdiction over a suspected person. In this sense, the question arises as to whether it can be determined that a particular State has a principal interest in exercising its jurisdiction if the State where the crime was committed or the State of nationality of the suspect or victim(s) is willing and able to exercise jurisdiction, in addition to a State claiming the right under universal jurisdiction over the crime in question. Does a State claiming the right to exercise universal jurisdiction have any obligation to defer to a State with a "closer" connection to the crime? The A.U.-E.U. Expert Report states:

> Positive international law recognises no hierarchy among the various bases of jurisdiction that it permits. In other words, a state which enjoys universal jurisdiction over, for example, crimes against humanity is under no positive legal obligation to accord priority in respect of prosecution to the state within the territory of which the criminal acts occurred or to the state of nationality of the offender or victims.[47]

Principal 8 of the Princeton Principles on Universal Jurisdiction allows the custodial state to make a decision on whether to prosecute or extradite based on a list of criteria, including the place of commission of the crime and nationality of the suspect and victims, though there is no obligation to extradite.[48] It has been argued that if more than one State wishes to prosecute,

> [...] the state with custody seeking to exercise universal jurisdiction would normally have a better claim than the territorial state to act on behalf of the international community, since the presence of the suspect outside the territorial state

---

[46] Georges Abi-Saab, "The Proper Role of Universal Jurisdiction", in *Journal of International Criminal Justice*, 2003, vol. 1, p. 596.

[47] A.U.-E.U. Expert Report, Annex, para. 14, see *supra* note 2; see also Cedric Ryngaert, "Applying the Rome Statute's Complementarity Principle: Drawing Lessons from the Prosecution of Core Crimes by States Acting under the Universality Principle", in *Criminal Law Forum*, 2008, vol. 19, no. 1, p. 153, which concludes that, although desirable, the application of the subsidiarity principle is not required by international law.

[48] Available at http://lapa.princeton.edu/hosteddocs/unive_jur.pdf, last accessed on 27 August 2012.

creates a presumption that the authorities of the territorial state are not acting with due diligence to investigate and prosecute. Failure to transmit an extradition request would be compelling evidence that the territorial state was not serious.[49]

Such a view is, however, not uncontested, arguments being made for example that the principle of subsidiarity has already developed as a legal concept.[50] In terms of the merits of such a concept, it can be argued that, in practice, in prosecuting serious crimes of international concern, States should accord priority to territoriality as a basis of jurisdiction "as a matter of policy", in view of the fact that the object of such crimes principally is the State where the crimes have been committed and that therefore that State has to be considered as the one most directly affected by the crime. The ninth recommendation of the A.U.-E.U. Report finds as follows:

> In prosecuting serious crimes of international concern, states should, as a matter of policy, accord priority to territoriality as a basis of jurisdiction, since such crimes, while offending against the international community as a whole by infringing universal values, primarily injure the community where they have been perpetrated and violate not only the rights of the victims but also the general demand for order and security in that community. In addition, it is within the territory of the state of alleged commission that the bulk of the evidence will usually be found.[51]

Under this concept, the exercise of universal jurisdiction is, therefore, premised on the failure of the territorial or national State (the State having a primary interest) to start proceedings, and should, therefore, not be activated if one of those States initiates proceedings. This idea comes across in paragraphs 3(c) and (d) of the Resolution on "Universal criminal jurisdiction with regard to the crime of genocide, crimes against humanity and war crimes" of 2005, issued by the Institute of International Law:

---

[49] Hall, 2010, p. 230, see *supra* note 2.

[50] Claus Kreβ, "Universal Jurisdiction over International Crimes and the Institut de Droit international", in *Journal of International Criminal Justice*, 2006, vol. 4, no. 3, pp. 589–595. See also Cassese, 2003, pp. 593–594, see *supra* note 2. See also Abi-Saab, 2003, p. 596, see supra note 46.

[51] A.U.-E.U. Expert Report, Annex, R9, see *supra* note 2.

    c)   Any State having custody over an alleged offender should, before commencing a trial on the basis of universal jurisdiction, ask the State where the crime was committed or the State of nationality of the person concerned whether it is prepared to prosecute that person, unless these States are manifestly unwilling or unable to do so. It shall also take into account the jurisdiction of international criminal courts.[52]

    d)   Any State having custody over an alleged offender, to the extent that it relies solely on universal jurisdiction, should carefully consider and, as appropriate, grant any extradition request addressed to it by a State having a significant link, such as primarily territoriality or nationality, with the crime, the offender, or the victim, provided such State is clearly able and willing to prosecute the alleged offender.[53]

It is argued, in favour of subsidiarity, that:

> The territorial or national State may indeed be a better forum in light of the proximity of the evidence, the knowledge of the accused and the victims, and the better perspective which it has on all circumstances surrounding the crime. [...] Moreover, the entrenchment of the rule of law in States with historically weak judicial systems, typically developing countries, requires that bystander States with stronger judicial systems, typically industrialized countries, enable the former States to assume their responsibility in putting an end to a culture of impunity [ ] Although prosecutions on the basis of the universality principle may have a catalytic effect on home State prosecutions, bystander States should exercise appropriate restraint in case the home State is able and willing to investigate and prosecute a situation in which a core crime has been committed.[54]

It has also been argued by the same author that:

> [...] subsidiarity should not be resorted to by national prosecutors and courts as a welcome tool to get rid of diplomati-

---

[52]   Available at http://www.idi-iil.org/idiE/resolutionsE/2005_kra_03_en.pdf, last accessed on 13 October 2012.

[53]   *Ibid.*; see also A.U.-E.U. Expert Report, Annex, para. 46, R12, see *supra* note 2.

[54]   Ryngaert, 2008, pp. 157–158, see *supra* note 47.

cally awkward cases. Subsidiarity should instead be understood as a *responsibility* or even *duty*, of bystander States to mete out justice, in the interests of the victims and the international community, where the territorial or national State has failed or refused to do so.[55]

It is noteworthy that the subsidiarity principle has been implicitly referred to by three judges in the *Arrest Warrant* case. In their separate opinion they noted that a "State contemplating bringing criminal charges based on universal jurisdiction must first offer to the national State of the prospective accused person the opportunity itself to act upon the charges concerned".[56] Another example of the subsidiarity principle in practice was the decision of the *Audencia Nacional* in the case of the *Decision of the Spanish Supreme Court concerning the Guatemala Genocide Case*, where the Spanish Supreme Court concluded that the Spanish Courts could apply universal jurisdiction only if neither the territorial State nor the perpetrator's home State genuinely exercised jurisdiction.[57]

The idea is not wholly different to that enshrined in the Rome Statute.[58] In terms of subsidiarity as between States and complementarity as between the ICC and national jurisdictions, both are intended to provide a legal basis for the investigation and prosecution of international crimes of the most serious concern when this is not taking place elsewhere. As seen above, the ICC "shall be complementary to national criminal jurisdictions".[59] Under this principle, national courts in principle have priority over the jurisdiction of the ICC, and the Court is intended to act as a last resort when national legal systems of States are, *inter alia*, unable or un-

---

[55] *Ibid.*, pp. 156–157.

[56] International Court of Justice, *Case Concerning the Arrest Warrant of 11 April 2000 (Democratic Republic of the Congo v. Belgium)*, Judgment, 14 February 2002, ICJ Reports 2002, Joint separate opinion of Judges Higgins, Kooijmans and Buergenthal, p. 80, para. 59, available at http://www.legal-tools.org/doc/23d1ec/.

[57] Spanish Supreme Court, *Decision of the* Spanish Supreme Court *concerning the Guatemala Genocide Case*, 25 February 2003, Decision No. 327/2003, available at http://www.derechos.org/nizkor/guatemala/ doc/stsgtm.html, last accessed on 30 July 2012.

[58] See also Ryngaert, 2008, p. 153, see *supra* note 47.

[59] Preamble and Article 1 of the Rome Statute; see also Sands, 2003, pp. 40 *et seq.*, see *supra* note 4.

---

willing to exercise jurisdiction.[60] The idea is, therefore, that in principle national jurisdictions will step up and that only in the event that they do not, will the ICC. For example, Article 17(1)(a) of the Rome Statute provides that, a case shall be determined inadmissible where "[t]he case is being investigated or prosecuted by a State which has jurisdiction over it, unless the State is unwilling or unable genuinely to carry out the investigation or prosecution".

In terms of which States could challenge the admissibility of a case before the ICC, Article 17 of the Rome Statute clearly refers to "a State which has jurisdiction over" the case. It remains to be seen how the ICC will interpret this should a challenge come from a State based on a claim of universal jurisdiction, something which to date has not happened; it could be argued that if a State claims to have universal jurisdiction over a case which also falls within the jurisdiction of the ICC, and if the situation satisfies the requirements of Article 17 of the Rome Statute, the ICC could declare a case to be inadmissible before it. Indeed it has been argued, "when the term 'jurisdiction' of states is used in the Rome Statute, it means jurisdiction permitted or required under international law, including universal jurisdiction [save in certain cases in articles 18 and 19]".[61] In this case, the scope for national prosecutions of the crimes falling within the jurisdiction of the ICC would be great and, together with the words of the Rome Statute preamble (see above), could indeed encourage States to exercise their (universal) jurisdiction over these serious international crimes. It is argued that "an interpretation providing the broadest possible protection of victims of crimes under international law over alternative interpretations which would restrict the scope of the obligations recognised by states" is favoured.[62] On the other hand, it has also been argued in terms of complementarity, that although there is priority of jurisdiction of national courts where they "have a traditional connecting fac-

---

[60] Article 17 of the Rome Statute; see also International Criminal Court, *The Prosecutor v. Germain Katanga et al.,* Judgment on the Appeal of Mr. Germain Katanga against the Oral Decision of Trial Chamber II of 12 June 2009 on the Admissibility of the Case, ICC-01/04-01/07-1497, 25 September 2009, available at http://www.legal-tools.org/doc/ba82b5/.

[61] Hall, 2010, pp. 207 and 209 *et seq.*, see *supra* note 2.

[62] Hall, 2010, p. 212, see *supra* note 2; see also Louise Arbour, "Will the ICC have an Impact on Universal Jurisdiction", in *Journal of International Criminal Justice*, 2003, vol. 1, p. 585.

tor with the crime", there would be no priority of jurisdiction of a national court when based on universal jurisdiction:

> [...] in exercising universal jurisdiction the state does not act in its own name *uti singulus,* but in the name of the international community (as with the institution of *action popularis*). However, once this community develops its own specialized organs to fulfil precisely these same tasks, they take precedence over states acting as their surrogates.[63]

As far as immunities of State officials are concerned, as seen in the A.U.-E.U. Expert Report, African concerns were that:

> [...] in so far as the indictment of sitting state officials is concerned, there is disregard for immunities enjoyed by state officials under international law. Consequently, any such indictment severely constrains the capacity of African states to discharge the functions of statehood on the international plane.[64]

The A.U.-E.U. Expert Report ultimately recommends as follows:

> [...] those national criminal justice authorities considering exercising universal jurisdiction over persons suspected of serious crimes of international concern are legally bound to take into account all the immunities to which foreign state officials may be entitled under international law and are consequently obliged to refrain from prosecuting those officials entitled to such immunities.[65]

Concerns in this regard have also been expressed during the discussions of the Sixth Committee. It was stated that,

> [...] there was a delicate balance to be struck between the prevention of impunity and the free exercise of sovereignty by agents of the State, whereby immunity of State officials would be the exception to the applicability of jurisdiction.[66]

As far as immunities are concerned, the Case Concerning the Arrest Warrant of 11 April 2000 (*Democratic Republic of the Congo v. Belgium*)

---

[63] Abi-Saab, 2003, p. 601, see *supra* note 46.

[64] A.U.-E.U. Expert Report, Annex, para. 38, see *supra* note 2.

[65] A.U.-E.U. Expert Report, Annex, R8, see *supra* note 2.

[66] Available at http://www.un.org/en/ga/sixth/66/ScopeAppUniJuri/shtml, last accessed on 27 August 2012.

of 14 February 2002 of the International Court of Justice is relevant wherein it was found, *inter alia*, that:

> [...] the functions of a Minister for Foreign Affairs are such that, throughout the duration of his or her office, he or she when abroad enjoys full immunity from criminal jurisdiction and inviolability. That immunity and that inviolability protect the individual concerned against any act of authority of another State which would hinder him or her in the performance of his or her duties. [67]

As far as the Rome Statute is concerned, Article 27 is entitled "[i]rrelevance of official capacity" (see also Article 98) and provides:

1. [The Rome] Statute shall apply equally to all persons without any distinction based on official capacity. In particular, official capacity as a Head of State or Government, a member of a Government or parliament, an elected representative or a government official shall in no case exempt a person from criminal responsibility under this Statute, nor shall it, in and of itself, constitute a ground for reduction of sentence.

2. Immunities or special procedural rules which may attach to the official capacity of a person, whether under national or international law, shall not bar the Court from exercising its jurisdiction over such a person.

The Appeals Chamber has yet to issue any decision specifically on this issue.

In relation to trials *in absentia*, complete agreement on its use in cases where universal jurisdiction is invoked is also not present, with some systems rejecting the idea of trying a person when he or she is not present at the proceedings while others provide for that possibility.[68] One may also note Article 14(3)(d) of the International Covenant on Civil and Political Rights granting every person the right "to be tried in his pres-

---

[67] International Court of Justice, *Case Concerning the Arrest Warrant of 11 April 2000 (Democratic Republic of the Congo v. Belgium)*, Judgment, 14 February 2002, ICJ Reports 2002, para. 54, available at http://www.legal-tools.org/doc/c6bb20/.

[68] International Court of Justice, *Case Concerning the Arrest Warrant of 11 April 2000 (Democratic Republic of the Congo v. Belgium)*, Judgment, 14 February 2002, ICJ Reports 2002, Joint separate opinion of Judges Higgins, Kooijmans and Buergenthal, p. 79, para. 56, available at http://www.legal-tools.org/doc/23d1ec/; see A.U.-E.U. Expert Report, para. 10, *supra* note 2.

ence, and to defend himself in person or through legal assistance of his own choosing".[69]

Certain practical challenges may also arise in the exercise of universal jurisdiction.[70] In this respect, two practical difficulties have been highlighted. First, collecting evidence with regard to crimes committed abroad in particular when the State where the crimes are alleged to have taken place refuses to co-operate.[71] This can also be aggravated in situations where the crimes occurred a long time ago while, in addition, even in cases in which that State wishes to co-operate, such co-operation may require a treaty basis (under the law of the State exercising jurisdiction). The A.U.-E.U. Expert report states that "[a] second practical limitation is the awareness on the part of many prosecuting authorities and courts of the diplomatic sensitivities at stake when the conduct of a serving, and in some cases former, state official is involved".[72] This is of course related to the issue of immunities referred to above. It can also be very costly and technically very difficult to successfully prosecute cases of universal jurisdiction.

Another difficulty is that which arises in relation to co-operation between States in the event of extradition and co-operation requests. Differing national legislation can be problematic and raise obstacles to the fulfilment of such requests.[73] As found in the course of an expert meeting in The Hague in November 2011,

> [...] it was generally felt that there was, indeed, a [legal gap in the international legal framework concerning mutual legal assistance between States for the national adjudication of international crimes] and that a further exploration of the issue was necessary.[74]

---

[69] International Covenant on Civil and Political Rights, 19 December 1966, Article 14(3)(d), in *UNTS*, vol. 999, pp. 171, 177; see also Gabriel Bottini, "Universal Jurisdiction after the Creation of the International Criminal Court", in *Journal of International Law and Politics,* vol. 36, p. 523.

[70] A.U.-E.U. Expert Report, Annex, para. 25, see *supra* note 2.

[71] *Ibid.*, para. 25.

[72] *Ibid.*, para. 25.

[73] See also Hall, 2010, pp. 224 *et seq.*, see *supra* note 2.

[74] "A Legal Gap? Getting the evidence where it can be found: Investigating and prosecuting international crimes", Report of an expert meeting in The Hague, 22 November 2011, HIIL and Government of the Netherlands, p. 2.

The report found that although there had been 'impressive progress' in the last ten years in the criminalisation of crimes under the Rome Statute into domestic law,

> [...] the gap at the heart of the exploration conducted with the expert meeting relates to the procedural issues: international legal cooperation between States that want to prosecute nationally. International cooperation in criminal matters is paramount for effective national prosecutions relating to mass atrocities. As the highly experienced prosecutor, **Siri Frigaard**, said in her key-note address: "rarely, and if ever, will all witnesses and evidence be found in the state that is conducting the prosecution". It is therefore of the utmost importance that the international legal framework for cooperation in criminal matters in this domain facilitates and stimulates this aspect of complementarity.[75]

It was pointed out that "the prosecution of war crimes was an extremely resource intensive endeavour" and that "[k]ey to this is the legal assistance from other states".[76] It was also pointed out "that greater cooperation in international criminal matters from States would lead to fewer instances of impunity".[77] It was agreed "that the nature of the legal gap merits further exploration in light of the shared view that there should not be any safe havens in respect of international crimes and that the system to deal with these crimes should be as efficient and as effective as possible".[78] Three issues for further exploration were specifically identified: jurisdiction, mutual legal assistance and extradition. It was also agreed to continue working on the issue and to try to involve more States in the process.[79] A second meeting should be held in 2012.[80]

Another challenge arising out of differing national legislation or approaches to universal jurisdiction can be that in relation to double jeopardy. It has been said that "the risk of double jeopardy becomes even more acute with the exercise of universal jurisdiction, raising the spectre of an accused being hounded 'in one court after another until the victims

---

[75] *Ibid.*, p. 3.

[76] *Ibid.*, p. 4.

[77] *Ibid.*, p. 4.

[78] *Ibid.*, p. 5.

[79] *Ibid.*, pp. 5–6.

[80] *Ibid.*, p. 6.

are satisfied that justice has been done'", or where the State most concerned with the crimes committed would not be satisfied with a trial elsewhere.[81] It was stated that,

> [...] the supposed cure of joining *ne bis in idem* with univer-
> sal jurisdiction would be worse than the disease. It would
> give the first court to hear the case the power to decide the
> fate of the accused and the whole world would have to defer
> to their possibly idiosyncratic judgment.[82]

The argument against this is that this "assumes a positive conflict of
jurisdiction between *fora* competing for the prosecution of international
crimes", ignoring the fact that actually "universal jurisdiction has been a
jurisdiction of last resort, a fail-safe solution called for by urgency and
necessity".[83]

Finally, as stated, the establishment of the ICTY, ICTR and ICC in
particular, represented innovative achievements in the pursuit of justice.
However, the exercise of jurisdiction, including universal jurisdiction, by
national jurisdictions over core international crimes, can only be positive
in the fight against impunity for the commission of these crimes. One
could argue that the ICC, with its principle of complementarity, will encourage States to exercise universal jurisdiction over core international
crimes; this would provide additional venues for the prosecution of these
crimes to those of the territorial or national State.[84] In addition, the ICC

---

[81] Abi-Saab, 2003, p. 599, see *supra* note 46, referring to a view by Fletcher, 2003, p.
580, see *supra* note 15, who himself refers to the cases of *Finta* and *Ariel Sharon*.

[82] Fletcher, 2003, p. 584, see *supra* note 15.

[83] Abi-Saab, 2003, p. 599, see *supra* note 46.

[84] AMICC, Questions & Answers on the ICC and Universal Jurisdiction:

> In some cases, the existence of the ICC may result in fewer uses of
> universal jurisdiction. States lacking necessary resources and suffi-
> ciently capable legal systems may be inclined to hand over cases to
> the ICC rather than try such cases in their own courts. However,
> the Court will increase awareness of atrocities and thus may stimu-
> late greater usage of universal jurisdiction. States with well devel-
> oped judiciaries and laws providing for universal jurisdiction may
> be encouraged to exercise their jurisdiction more frequently, pre-
> ferring to control the prosecutorial process rather than giving the
> task to the Court. Other states may be motivated to take the neces-
> sary steps to allow them to try cases within the ICC's jurisdiction
> and thus enact implementing legislation that incorporates aspects
> of the Rome Statute. Overall, the Court can provide an example

has a limited jurisdiction.[85] For example, its subject-matter jurisdiction is "limited to the most serious crimes of concern to the international community".[86] The crimes within the Court's jurisdiction are genocide, crimes against humanity, war crimes and aggression.[87] It is also limited in terms of time, in that it only has jurisdiction with respect to crimes committed after the entry into force of the Rome Statute,[88] which took place on 1 July 2002. And, it is also limited in terms of which persons it can prosecute, in that it only has jurisdiction when one of the crimes was committed on the territory of a State Party to the Rome Statute or by a national of a State Party, when a State accepted the Court's jurisdiction under Article 12(3) of the Statute or if the Security Council has referred a situation to the Court.[89] Contrary to this, national jurisdictions may have jurisdiction to prosecute all other crimes that do not fall within the jurisdiction of the ICC, for example those committed prior to the entry into force of the Rome Statute. Thus, even if the ICC does not have jurisdiction, individual States may still prosecute perpetrators of international crimes under domestic laws based on universal jurisdiction.[90]

Having considered some of the challenges in respect of the application of universal jurisdiction, it seems clear that its application in practice remains controversial. Further work to ensure its effective implementation will be welcomed. However, at present, the international community will continue fighting impunity in a genuine spirit of humanity.

---

and encouragement to states for their own exercise of jurisdiction to prosecute serious international crimes, and states will likely continue to exercise universal jurisdiction to prosecute cases not addressed by the Court.

[85] A.U.-E.U. Expert Report, Annex, para. 28, see *supra* note 2.

[86] Article 5 of the Rome Statute. See also Article 1.

[87] Articles 6–8*bis* of the Rome Statute respectively.

[88] Article 11 of the Rome Statute.

[89] Articles 12 and 13.

[90] AMICC, Questions & Answers on the ICC and Universal Jurisdiction:

Proponents of universal jurisdiction believe that both systems will serve international justice by providing states with more choices. In that way, the Court and universal jurisdiction, each operating where the other may not, may be said to be separate pieces of a comprehensive approach to ending impunity for perpetrators of serious international crimes.

8

The Connotation of Universal Jurisdiction and its Application in the Criminal Law of China

MA Chengyuan[*]

8.1. Introduction

Jurisdiction is one of the fundamental rights of a state.[1] It concerns the power of the state to affect people, property and circumstances and reflects the basic principles of state sovereignty, equality of states and non-interference in domestic affairs.[2] Jurisdiction can be divided into different categories on different bases and universal jurisdiction is one of them.

Universal jurisdiction is also called the 'principle of universal jurisdiction' or the 'universality principle'. Essentially, it is a jurisdiction exercised by state over criminal matters, though some scholars think there has existed now a so-called 'universal civil jurisdiction'.[3] Traditionally,

---

[*] MA Chengyuan is Professor of Law at China University of Political Science and Law, where he is the Assistant Dean of the Faculty of International Law. He holds a Doctor of Law and Master of Law from this University. He is a Member of the Council of the International Law Association of China. He was Visiting Scholar in the Law Center of Georgetown University U.S. from August 1993 to October 1994 and in the Law School of Nottingham University from January to June 2000.

[1] WANG Tieya, *International Law*, 1981, p. 93.

[2] Malcolm N. Shaw, *International Law*, fifth edition, Cambridge University Press, 2005, p. 572.

[3] Some scholars hold the opinion that universal jurisdiction contains both universal criminal jurisdiction and universal civil jurisdiction. *See* M.C. Bassiouni, *International Criminal Law*, second edition, Transnational Publishers, 1999, pp. 343–390; Luc Reydams, *Universal Jurisdiction: International and Municipal Legal Perspectives*, Oxford University Press, 2003, p. 2; Jane E. Stromseth, *Accountability for Atrocities: National and International Responses*, Transnational Publishers, 2003, p. 379; LIU Daqun, "Universal Jurisdiction in International Criminal Law", in *Peking University Comparative and International Law Review*, 2006, vol. 4, no. 2, p. 18; ZHU Lijiang, *Universal Jurisdiction over War Crimes in Non-International Armed Conflicts and International Law*, Law Press, Beijing, 2007, p. 4. The so-called universal civil jurisdiction refers mainly to the jurisdiction based on the Alien Tort Claims Act ('ATCA') (28 USC §1350) of the United States, which is also called the Alien Tort Statute ('ATS'). The ATCA was adopted in 1789 as part of the original Judiciary

the state relies on the 'territorial principle' or 'nationality principle' to exercise criminal jurisdiction over crimes committed either within its territory or by its citizens. However, as the time goes on, the state finds sometimes it is necessary to exercise jurisdiction over foreigners in respect of acts committed entirely abroad and without substantial connection with the state itself or its citizens. Thus, universal jurisdiction emerges as is required.

By textual research, the wording of 'universal jurisdiction' in English might appear in international legal instruments and literature only in 1920s,[4] but "historically, the thought of universal jurisdiction may be traced back to the European international and criminal law forerunner in the sixteenth or seventeenth century, even to the period of Roman Law".[5] Someone says, at the beginning of the seventeenth century, Hugo Grotius, the famous Dutch jurist, initiated and proved the principle of universal jurisdiction from the angle of the natural law.[6] But accurately speaking, in his book, The Law of War and Peace, published in 1625, Grotius only

---

Act, which reads: "The district courts shall have original jurisdiction of any civil action by an alien for a tort only, committed in violation of the law of nations or a treaty of the United States". This Act is notable for allowing U.S. courts to hear human rights cases brought by foreign citizens for conduct committed outside the U.S. From 1789 to 1980, the Act lay relatively dormant – only two courts based jurisdiction on it. But after 1980, several cases have been heard in the U.S. courts. Apart from the ATCA, the Torture Victim Protection Act of 1991 ('TVPA'; Pub. L., pp. 102–256, 12 March 1992, codified at 42 USCA §1350 note) is another U.S. act that allows victims of certain international law violations, or their representatives, to bring a civil action against those responsible in federal district court. Under the TVPA, "an individual who, under actual or apparent authority, or color of law, of any foreign nation, subjects an individual to: (1) torture will, in a civil action, be liable for damages to that individual; or (2) extrajudicial killing will, in a civil action, be liable for damages to the individual's legal representative, or to any person who may be a claimant in an action for wrongful death". But even these two Acts are positive in promoting the respect to human rights, the unilateral legislation and the limited judicial practice of the United States are impossible to make it a counterpart to universal jurisdiction in criminal matters.

[4] See ZHU Lijiang, *Universal Jurisdiction over War Crimes in Non-International Armed Conflicts and International Law*, Law Press, Beijing, 2007, p. 5.

[5] *Ibid.*, pp. 3–5.

[6] *See* CHEN Zhonglin, "The Principle of Universal Jurisdiction in the Criminal Law of China: Theoretical Interpretation of Article 9 of the Criminal Law", in *Journal of Huaiyin Teachers College*, 2004, vol. 4, p. 470.

---

expresses the view of *aut dedere aut punire*.[7] And some authors even doubt whether *aut dedere aut punire* is initiated by Grotius himself.[8]

In the *Law of War and Peace*, Grotius expounds the issue of returning of escaped criminals. He says:

> Since as a matter of fact states are not accustomed to permit other states to cross their borders with an armed force for the purpose of exacting punishment, and since such a course is inexpedient, it follows that the state in which he who has been found guilty dwells ought to do one of two things. When appealed to it should either punish the guilty person as he deserves, or it should entrust him to the discretion of the party making the appeal. The latter course is rendition, a procedure most frequently mentioned in historical narratives.[9]

Having analysed some of the examples, he points out that all the examples nevertheless must be interpreted in the sense that a people or king is not absolutely bound to surrender a culprit, but either to surrender or to punish him.[10] Finally, he points out:

> What we have said with regard to the surrender or punishment of guilty parties applies not merely to those who have always been subjects of the state in which they are at the

---

[7] See MA Chengyuan, *International Criminal Law*, China University of Political Science and Law Press, 2008, p. 221. But Bassiouni thinks that the expression of *aut dedere aut punire* is inconsistent with the principle of legality, and suggests that it shall be changed to *aut dedere aut judicare*. See M.C. Bassiouni, "Human Rights in the Context of Criminal Justice", in *Duke Journal of Comparative and International Law*, 1973, vol. 3, p. 235.

[8] The sixteenth-century Spanish author Covarruvias studied the practice of the medieval Italian city-states which generally recognised the jurisdiction of the criminal courts of both the *locus delicti* and the place of domicile of the offender. In Chapter II of his book *Practicorum Quaestionalen*, Covarruvias defended the proposition that the *judex deprehensionis* had a duty either to punish or extradite all dangerous criminals "*judex requisitus vel remittere tenetur, vel delinquentem ipsum punire*". G. Guillaume, the judge of the International Court of Justice, points out that the paternity of the maxim *aut dedere aut judicare* (extradite or try) comes to Covarruvias and not to Grotius as common opinion holds. *See* Reydams, 2003, *supra* note 3, p. 29.

[9] Hugo Grotius, *The Law of War and Peace*, 1925, Claredon Press, Oxford, p. 527, translated by Francis W. Kelsey.

[10] See *ibid.* p. 528.

> time found, but also to those who after having committed a crime have fled to another state for refuge.[11]

Following Grotius, the famous Swiss jurist Vattel also regards extradition as a way of avoiding state responsibility for the acts of private individuals. He expresses as follows:

> Since the sovereign should not permit his subjects to trouble or injure the subjects of another state, much less be so bold as to offend a foreign power, he should force the offender to repair the evil, if that can be done, or punish him as an example to others, or finally, according to the nature and circumstance3 of the case, deliver him up to the injured state, so that it may inflict due punishment upon him [...]. A sovereign who refuses to repair the evil done by one of his subjects, or to punish the criminal, or, finally to deliver him up, makes himself in a way an accessory to the deed, and becomes responsible for it.[12]

Piracy is the first crime that was brought under universal jurisdiction.[13] Malcolm N. Shaw points out: "universal jurisdiction over piracy has been accepted under international law for many centuries and constitutes a long-established principle of the world community".[14] Since piracy constituted a threat against the safety of ships navigating at sea, as well as persons and property on board, states started to enact domestic laws on the punishment of piracy from a long time ago, and the 1536 Offenses at Sea Act made by the United Kingdom is one of the earliest.[15] Article 1, Section 8 of the Constitution of the United States provides: "the Congress shall have power [...] to constitute tribunals inferior to the Supreme Court; to define and punish piracies and felonies committed on the high seas, and offenses against the law of nations".

On the basis of domestic legislation and judicial practice of states, there gradually formed the rule in modern international law to exercise

---

[11] *Ibid.* p. 529.

[12] M.C. Bassiouni, *Introduction to International Criminal Law*, Transnational Publisher, 2003, p. 341.

[13] MA, 2008, *supra* note 7, p. 221.

[14] Shaw, 2005, *supra* note 2, p. 470.

[15] See Wikipedia, "Offences at Sea Act 1536", available at http://en.wikipedia.org/wiki/ Offences_at_Sea_Act_1536, last accessed on 15 July 2012.

universal jurisdiction over piracy. L. Oppenheim expresses his view as follows:

> A pirate and his vessel loss *ipso facto* by an act of piracy their national character and the protection of their flag state. Every maritime state has by a customary rule of the Law of Nations the right to punish pirates. And the vessels of all nations, whether men-of war, other public vessels, or merchantmen, can on the Open Sea chase, attack, seize, and bring the pirate home for trial and punishment by the courts of their own country.[16]

The U.S. jurist Henry Wheaton also says, "pirates are the enemy of the nations and it is the common sense of the nations to seize and punish them. The war ships of every nation can seize pirates at sea, bring them home and surrender them to their courts for trial".[17]

Slave-trading is another crime which was brought under universal jurisdiction in the period of modern international law. Since the twentieth century, especially after World War II, the mutual exchange and influence in politics, economy, law and culture among states have greatly increased, which has caused the progress towards the same direction. The international community has forged bit by bit the common interest and produced relatively consistent moral standards and the same value orientation. Because some international crimes are so serious that they have shocked the conscience of peoples of the world and caused great damage to the interest of the international community, they are regarded the crimes against human beings by states. These crimes have been brought under universal jurisdiction one after the other, and the punishment for them has become important content of *jus cogens*.[18]

Unlike the other jurisdiction principles, the purpose of universal jurisdiction is not to protect the well-being of a given state or its citizens, but that of international community. In the contemporary world, the maintenance of international peace and security, protection of fundamental human rights and freedom, and safeguard of international well-being and order constitute the common interest of the international community, and

---

[16] L. Oppenheim, *International Law: A Treatise*, Longmans, Green, and Co., New York, 1905, p. 330.

[17] Henry Wheaton, *Elements of International Law*, Sampson Low, London, 1864, p. 112 (translated by William M.P. Matin).

[18] See LIU, 2006, *supra* note 3, p. 14.

states have formed common sense on it. At the same time, because of rampant international crimes and the limitation of national criminal laws, characterised by the territoriality and nationality, universal jurisdiction emerges as times require.[19]

Although there are still a few states or scholars who hold a negative, even contrary opinion on universal jurisdiction,[20] the principle of universal jurisdiction has been well established in the theory of international law and the legislation and judicial practice of states.

However, the problem now is that because scholars in international law and criminal law have had different views on the connotation of universal jurisdiction, they cannot reach an agreement on the definition of universal jurisdiction. Professor ZHU Lijiang says, "[…] now the opinions on the definition of universal jurisdiction are so controversial that it must be clarified and unified in order not to make the arguments more complicated".[21] It appears that the present definitions of universal jurisdiction are made in its narrow, broad and broader sense.[22] Scholars usually give a general definition to universal jurisdiction and then divide it into different categories according to the extent or conditions of its application. Antonio Cassese, an Italian jurist and the first President of the ICTY, divides 'universal jurisdiction' into 'absolute universal jurisdiction' and 'conditioned universal jurisdiction'.[23] Luc Reydams separates it into three categories, namely, 'the co-operative general universal jurisdiction', 'the co-operative limited universal jurisdiction', and 'the unilateral limited universal jurisdiction'[24]; and Marc Henzelin makes it 'unilateral universal jurisdiction', 'representative universal jurisdiction' and 'absolute universal jurisdiction'.[25] Professor ZHU Lijiang also gives a general definition of 'universal jurisdiction', and then based on his study and analysis of the clauses, which reflect universal jurisdiction in the criminal laws of states, divides them into three categories: 'clauses of universal

---

[19] See MA, 2008, *supra* note 7, p. 219.

[20] See LIU, 2006, *supra* note 3, pp. 18–22.

[21] ZHU, 2007, *supra* note 4, p. 38.

[22] See ZHU, 2007, *supra* note 4, pp. 418–419; ZHANG Zhihui, *International Criminal Law*, 2009, p. 76.

[23] Antonio Cassese, *International Criminal Law*, Oxford University Press, 2003, p. 285.

[24] Reydams, 2003, *supra* note 3, pp. 28–42.

[25] ZHU, 2007, *supra* note 4, p. 11.

jurisdiction based on treaties', 'clauses of universal jurisdiction based on customary international law' and 'representative jurisdiction clauses'.[26]

It is the opinion of the author that the divided views among jurists of the definition and categories of universal jurisdiction lie in their divergent understandings of its extent of application, and that again stems from their divided opinions of its legal sources. On the basis of study and analysis of different views of scholars and provisions of both international treaties and domestic criminal laws, the author will first divide universal jurisdiction into three categories: (1) universal jurisdiction based on customary international law, (2) universal jurisdiction based on international treaty, and (3) universal jurisdiction based on domestic law, and then expound respectively the definition and characteristics of each of the categories. Finally, after a general definition of universal jurisdiction is offered, a brief exposition will be made on the application of the universality principle in the criminal law of China. It is the hope of this author that the elaboration of universal jurisdiction in this chapter will be academically beneficial to the study of this subject.

8.2. Universal Jurisdiction Based on Customary International Law

8.2.1. Definition

Universal jurisdiction based on customary international law is the criminal jurisdiction that every state can exercise over the crime in customary international law committed abroad by a foreigner[27] not against this state or its citizens.

Customary international law, or international custom, is one of the important sources of international law. Professor WANG Tieya says:

> International custom is the oldest and most original source of international law. There was international custom in history before international treaty was concluded. In a sense, it could be regarded as the most important source of international law.[28]

Article 38(1)(b) of the Statute of the International Court of Justice provides that: "international custom, as evidence of a general practice ac-

---

[26] *Ibid.*, pp. 30–37.

[27] Note that the word 'foreigners' in this paper includes stateless persons.

[28] See WANG, 1981, *supra* note 1, p. 13.

cepted as law". In accordance with this provision, international custom has two elements, that is: (1) material element, and (2) psychological element. The material element refers to the actual behaviour of state, and the psychological element means that such behaviour is accepted as law by states.

> The formation of international custom has had a gradual process, because it not only needs states to repeat similar behaviour, but also that they think the repeat of such behaviour is out of legal obligations.[29]

International custom as a source of international law has been broadly accepted by states. To fulfil the obligations originating from international custom, many states provide in their constitutions or constitutional instruments that international custom constitutes a part of national law.[30] For example, after the ratification of the Rome Statute of the International Criminal Court ('Rome Statute'), the Parliament of the Republic of South Africa enacted the Implementation of the Rome Statute of the International Criminal Court Act 2002. Article 2 of the Act provides that:

> In addition to the Constitution and the law, any competent court in the Republic hearing any matter from the application of this Act must also consider and, where, appropriate, may apply:
>
> (a) Conventional international law, and in particular the Statute;
>
> (b) Customary international law; and
>
> (c) Comparable foreign law.

This provision is consistent with Article 21(1) of the Rome Statute, which stipulates that the applicable law of the International Criminal Court includes customary principles and rules of international law.

---

[29] *Ibid.*, p. 14.

[30] See Robert Jennings and Arthur Watts (eds.), *Oppenheim's International Law*, vol. I, 1995, pp. 32–45, translated by WANG Tieya *et al.*; ZHOU Zhonghai *et al.*, *International Law Review*, Law Press, 2001, pp. 111–121. But the states newly getting independence in the movement of decolonisation take a sceptical view towards customary international law, because they were not involved in the forming process. Their constitutions seldom contain provisions about the position of international custom in domestic legal systems. Before 1990s, the former Soviet Union and the other socialist countries in Eastern Europe took the same attitude. See BAI Guimei, *International Law*, 2006, pp. 73–74.

But up to now, neither the Constitutional Law nor the Criminal Law of China contains any provision as to the position or application of international custom in Chinese laws. At the same time, Chinese authors have held different views on it.[31]

8.2.2. Characteristics

Universal jurisdiction based on customary international law possesses the following characteristics.

8.2.2.1. The Subject of this Jurisdiction is Every State

Because of the universal application of international custom, the subject of universal jurisdiction based on customary international law is each and every state. Judge LIU Daqun of the ICTY points out that universal jurisdiction means every state has the jurisdiction over the person alleged to have committed an international crime, without regard to where the crime was committed, the nationality of the alleged or the victim, even without regard to whether the alleged is present in the territory of the state exercising such jurisdiction or not.[32] Here the universal jurisdiction referred to by Judge LIU is obviously universal jurisdiction based on customary international law, because its subject is "every state".

The provision on the jurisdiction over piracy in the United Nations Convention on the Law of the Sea clearly reflects this characteristic. Article 105 of the Convention provides as follows:

> On the high seas, or in any other place outside the jurisdiction of any state, every state may seize a pirate ship or aircraft, or a ship taken by piracy and under the control of pi-

---

[31] ZHANG Zhihui holds the argument that international treaty is the only source of international criminal law. Since international custom cannot meet the requirement of the principle of legality, it cannot be a source of international criminal law. *See* ZHANG, 2009, *supra* note 22, pp. 23–25. This argument confuses the relationship of international treaty and international custom, as well as the relationship of international law and domestic law. In fact, neither international treaty, nor international custom can be applied in municipal law without being combined with it by either transformation or incorporation. Although Article 9 of the Criminal Law of China requires the application of the law to crimes provided in the treaties ratified by China, practically, the Chinese court can hardly exercise criminal jurisdiction over some of the crimes because they have not been provided as crimes in the Criminal Law of China.

[32] LIU, 2006, *supra* note 3, p. 12.

> rates, and arrest the persons and seize the property on board.
> The courts of the state which carried out the seizure may de-
> cide upon the penalties to be imposed, and may also deter-
> mine the action to be taken with regard to the ships, aircraft
> or property, subject to the rights of third parties acting in
> good faith.

In this article, the Convention emphasises that 'every state' has the right to fight against piracy instead of 'states parties'. This has fully illustrated that piracy is one of the crimes in customary international law, and all the states are authorised to exercise criminal jurisdiction over it.

However, although the subject of universal jurisdiction – based on customary international law – is every state, before the adoption of the Rome Statute, there were only a few states which incorporated such a clause in their domestic legislation.[33] Israel and Belgium are typical among them. Israel enacted the Nazis and Nazi Collaborators (Punishment) Act in 1950 for the purpose of punishing Nazi war criminals[34], although as a state, Israel did not exist during World War II. The Belgian parliament passed the Act concerning the Punishment of Grave Breaches of International Humanitarian Law in 1993, and made amendment to it in 1999 after ratifying the Rome Statute. Article 7 of the Act provides:

> The Belgian courts shall be competent to deal with breaches
> provided for in the present Act, irrespective of where such
> breaches have been committed.

> In respect of breaches committed abroad by a Belgian na-
> tional against a foreigner, no filing of complaint by the for-
> eigner or his family or official notice by the authority of the
> country in which the breach was committed shall be re-
> quired.

According to Professor ZHU Lijiang, this Article embodies universal jurisdiction based on customary international law.[35] But it is worth noting that after the conclusion of the Rome Statute, many contracting states have made their domestic legislation containing articles of universal jurisdiction based on customary international law.

---

[33] ZHU, 2007, *supra* note 4, p. 31.

[34] MA, 2008, *supra* note 7, p. 225.

[35] ZHU, 2007, *supra* note 4, at 125.

In judicial practice, the 1961 trial of Eichmann,[36] the 1993 trial of Demjanjuk in Israel and the 2001 trial of the Rwandan nuns in Belgium[37] are famous cases in applying this kind of universal jurisdiction.[38]

8.2.2.2. This Jurisdiction Applies to Crimes in Customary International Law

The crimes over which universal jurisdiction is exercised are crimes in customary international law. But since international custom is unwritten law, sometimes it is hard to tell which crimes are crimes in customary international law. Professor WANG Tieya says that international custom is formed in diplomatic relations of states, the practice of international organisations and organs and internal activities of states. They indicate the wills and practice of states and constitute evidence of international custom.[39] So, in order to find out which crimes are crimes in customary international law, much research has to be done. Based on the two elements of international custom – if the general practice and *opinio juris* of states and international organisations indicate that an act constitutes an international crime, and there is no such practice or *opinio juris* to the contrary – it would be identified as a crime under universal jurisdiction based on customary international law.

The 'universal jurisdiction' defined in the Princeton Principles on Universal Jurisdiction[40] forged by the Princeton Project on Universal ju-

---

[36] See MA, 2008, *supra* note 7, pp. 226–229.

[37] See David A. Tallman, "Universal Jurisdiction: Lessons from Belgium's Experience", in Jane E. Stromseth (ed.), *Accountability for Atrocities: National and International Responses*, Transnational Publisher, 2003, pp. 386–388.

[38] See more cases in *supra* note 4, pp. 114–215.

[39] See WANG, 1981, *supra* note 1, p. 15.

[40] The "Princeton Principles on Universal Jurisdiction" document was prepared by the Princeton Project on Universal jurisdiction sponsored by Princeton University's Program in Law and Public Affairs and the Woodrow Wilson School of Public and International Affairs, the International Commission of Jurists, the American Association for the International Commission of Jurist, the Urban Morgan Institute for Human Rights, and the Netherland Institute of Human Rights. The Project convened at Princeton University in January 2001 an assembly of scholars and jurists from around the world. On 27 January 2001, those assembled arrived at a final text, the "Princeton Principles on Universal Jurisdiction". It can be said to be an important civil codification on the principle of universal jurisdiction. See Stephen Macedo (ed.), *Universal*

risdiction is the universal jurisdiction based on customary international law.[41] Principle I of the Princeton Principles on Universal Jurisdiction provides:

> For purpose of these Principles, universal jurisdiction is criminal jurisdiction based solely on the nature of the crime, without regard to where the crime was committed, the nationality of the alleged or convicted perpetrator, the nationality of the victim, or any other connection to the state exercising such jurisdiction.

According to Principle II of the Princeton Principles on Universal Jurisdiction, serious crimes under international law include: (1) piracy; (2) slavery; (3) war crimes; (4) crimes against peace; (5) crimes against humanity; (6) genocide; and (7) torture.

The late Judge Cassese of the ICTY argued that 'international crimes' are the actions which violate customary international law rules. Those rules are aimed at protecting the interest of the international community as a whole and thus have binding force on all states and individuals.[42] In his opinion, international crimes include piracy, war crimes, crimes against humanity (especially genocide), torture, aggression and crimes of terrorism.[43]

Compared with the crimes enumerated in the Princeton Principles on Universal Jurisdiction, Judge Cassese's list of crimes in customary international law does not include slavery, but adds crimes of terrorism. It is worth noting that in both material and psychological elements, originating from slave trading, slavery has undoubtedly become one of the crimes in customary international law. As to crimes of terrorism, since there are always widely divided opinions among states, international organisations and scholars on its definition and contents, it is still hard to prove that it has become a crime in customary international law. In the Princeton Principles on Universal Jurisdiction, the list of serious crimes is explicitly il-

---

Jurisdiction: National Courts and the Prosecution of Serious Crimes under International Law, University of Pennsylvania Press, 2004, pp. 18–25.

[41] See Macedo, *ibid.*, p. 26.

[42] Antonio Cassese, *International Law*, Oxford University Press, 2001, p. 246.

[43] *Ibid.*, pp. 246–247.

lustrative, not exhaustive, and terrorism, apartheid and drug crimes are listed as candidates of serious crimes for future inclusion.[44]

In brief, piracy, slavery, aggression, war crimes, crimes against humanity, genocide and torture have acquired material and psychological elements as international custom. States and international organisations, including the United Nations, consistently condemn these crimes and international legal systems have been established to prevent and punish them. Undoubtedly, they have become crimes in customary international law. With the progress of the international community and the development of international criminal law, more crimes will be included in the future.

8.2.2.3. This Jurisdiction Applies to Crimes Committed by Foreigners Abroad not Against this State or its Citizens

Universal jurisdiction based on customary international law serves as a complement to territorial, nationality and protective jurisdiction of states. It is aimed at crimes in customary international law committed by foreigners abroad, not against the state exercising jurisdiction or its citizens. Professor WANG Tieya defines universal jurisdiction as this:

> According to the provisions of international law, because some international crimes injure universally the international peace and security and interest of mankind, every state has the right to exercise jurisdiction over them, no matter where the crime is committed and what nationality the criminal has.[45]

Except a few[46], most Chinese scholars have also incorporated "no matter where the crime is committed and what nationality the criminal has" or similar expressions as part of their definitions of universal jurisdiction.[47]

---

[44] See Macedo, *supra* note 40, p. 31.

[45] See WANG, 1981, *supra* note 1, p. 94.

[46] See HAN Depei, *Contemporary International Law*, 1992, p. 123; ZHU, 2007, *supra* note 4, p. 14.

[47] See ZHU Qiwu, *The Theory and Practice of International Law in China*, Law Press, Beijing, 1998, p. 85; SHAO Jing (ed.), *International Law*, 2000, p. 44; DUAN Muzheng (ed.), *International Law*, Peking University Press, 2000, p. 73; LIANG Shuying (ed.), *International Law*, China University of Political Science and Law Press, 2011, p. 62; GAO Mingxuan and ZHAO Bingzhi (eds.), *Criminal Law of China*, vol. I,

But as to this author's opinion, such an expression is not accurate or appropriate, because "no matter where the crime is committed and what nationality the criminal has" must include the situation that the crime is committed within the territory of the state claiming criminal jurisdiction or the criminal is the citizen of that state. However, what must be clarified is that, even for an international crime, if it is committed within the territory of the state exercising jurisdiction or the criminal is the citizen of that state, the jurisdiction that this state exercises over the crime is that of territorial or nationality jurisdiction rather than universal jurisdiction. So universal jurisdiction based on customary international law is only directed against the foreigner who has committed the international crime abroad, which produces no substantial impact on the interest of the state exercising criminal jurisdiction or that of its citizens. It is not against the international crime committed within the territory of the state or the crime committed by its citizen.

8.2.2.4. This Jurisdiction can be Exercised *in absentia*

Generally, the prerequisite for a state to exercise criminal jurisdiction is that the suspect or defendant is within the territory of that state. But in exercising universal jurisdiction based on customary international law, the state may sometimes claim jurisdiction over a foreign suspect not present in its territory. This is so-called 'universal jurisdiction *in absentia*' and it has been provided in the domestic laws of some states.

After the ratification of the Rome Statute, New Zealand enacted its International Crimes and International Criminal Court Act in 2000. Section 8 of the Act is as follows:

> Jurisdiction in respect of international crimes
>
> (1)   Proceedings may be brought for an offense [...]
>
> > (c)   against section 9 (genocide) or section 10 (crimes against humanity)or section 11 (war crimes) regardless of
> >
> > > (i)   the nationality or citizenship of the person accused; or

---

1998, Law Press, p. 48; ZHAO Bingzhi *et al.* (eds.), *International Criminal Law*, 2004, p. 57; ZHANG Zhihui, *International Criminal Law*, 2009, pp. 76–77; JIA Yu, *International Criminal Law*, 2004, p. 59; among others. This sort of expression is also popular in definitions given by foreign authors.

(ii) whether or not any act forming part of the offense occurred in New Zealand; or

(iii) whether or not the person accused was in New Zealand at the time that the act constituting the offense occurred or at the time a decision was made to charge the person with an offense.

Universal jurisdiction based on customary international law is also provided in domestic laws of other states, including Germany. But viewing it as a whole, most states only exercise criminal jurisdiction over international crimes when the suspects are present in their territories.[48]

Belgium's prosecution of Ariel Sharon, the former Prime Minister of Israel, and the arrest warrant issued against Abdoulaye Yerodia Ndombasi, the Foreign Minister of the Democratic Republic of the Congo, are very famous cases claiming universal jurisdiction *in absentia* over crimes in customary international law.[49] Because of the arrest warrant issued against its Foreign Minister, the Democratic Republic of the Congo instituted proceedings against Belgium before the International Court of Justice ('ICJ') asking for the annulment of the warrant. On 14 February 2002, the ICJ delivered its judgment unfavourable to Belgium.[50] There are such cases in the courts of France and other states as well.[51]

8.2.2.5. Statutory Limitations are not Applicable when Exercising this Jurisdiction

Unlike the general situation, in contemporary international criminal law, the statutory limitation provided in domestic laws is not applicable when exercising universal jurisdiction based on customary international law to prosecute international crimes. On 26 November 1968, the Assembly of the United Nations adopted the Convention on the Non-applicability of Statutory Limitations to War Crimes and Crimes against Humanity. Arti-

---

[48] See ZHU, 2007, *supra* note 4, p. 231. What Professor ZHU studies is universal jurisdiction *in absentia* over war crimes in civil war; but for other crimes in customary international law, the situation is roughly the same.

[49] See David A. Tallman, 2003, *supra* note 37, pp. 389–394.

[50] See Arrest Warrant of 11 April 2000 (*Democratic Republic of the Congo v. Belgium*), Judgment of 14 February 2002, available at http://www.legal-tools.org/doc/c6bb20/.

[51] *Ibid.*

cle 1 of the Convention declares that no statutory limitations shall apply to war crimes (particularly the "grave breaches" enumerated in the Geneva Conventions of 12 August 1949 for the protection of war victims), crimes against humanity and genocide, irrespective of the date of their commission. Then Article 3 has the following provision:

> The State Parties to the present Convention undertake to adopt, in accordance with their respective constitutional processes, any legislative or other measures necessary to ensure that statutory or other limitations shall not apply to the prosecution and punishment of the crimes referred to in Articles 1 and 2 of the Convention and that, where they exist, such limitations shall be abolished.

The Council of Europe adopted the European Convention on the Non-applicability of Statutory Limitations to Crimes against Humanity and War Crimes on 25 January 1974. It contains similar provisions to those of the U.N. Convention.

On 5 June 2000, the United Nation Transitional Administration in East Timor promulgated Regulation No. 2000/15 on the Establishment of Panels with Exclusive Jurisdiction over Serious Criminal Offenses. Articles 4 to 7 define crimes under the jurisdiction of the panels. They are genocide, crimes against humanity, war crimes and torture. Then in Article 17(1), it provides that the serious criminal offenses defined in the present regulation shall not be subject to any statute of limitations.[52]

8.2.2.6. International Crimes can be Prosecuted Retroactively when Applying this Jurisdiction

'Non-retroactivity of law' is a well-established legal principle. But because of the seriousness of the crimes in customary international law, states can enact their domestic laws and prosecute these crimes retroactively. In 1950, Israel passed the Nazis and Nazi collaborators (Punishment) Act for the purpose of punishing Nazi war criminals. This act applies retroactively to crimes against Jewish people, crimes against humanity and war crimes committed during the period of the Nazi regime in an enemy country. A person who has committed these crimes is liable to se-

---

[52] Regulation on the Establishment of Panels with Exclusive Jurisdiction over Serious Criminal Offenses, UNTAET/REG/2000/15, 6 June 2000, available at http://www.un.org, last accessed on 27 August 2012.

vere punishment. In fact, after World War II, many Allied countries adapted their domestic laws to prosecute and punish war criminals of the Axis states. China also promulgated its Judicial Regulations on War Crimes and brought Japanese war criminals to trial according to Chinese laws and regulations, as well as international treaties acceded to by China.

In the 1980s, considering that some persons who committed serious war crimes in Europe during World War II might have entered their territories and become citizens or residents, the United Kingdom, Canada, Australia, the Netherlands and some other countries amended their original legislation or enacted new laws and applied them retroactively to crimes committed by Nazi war criminals. For example, Australia enacted the War Crimes Act in 1945 and promulgated the War Crimes Amendment Act in 1988. According to Article 9 of the Amendment Act, "a person who on or after 1 September 1939 and on or before 8 May 1945 and whether as an individual or as a member of an organization committed a war crime is guilty of an indictable offense against this Act". But Article 11 of the Act provides that a person shall not be charged with an offense against this Act unless he or she is an Australian citizen or a resident of Australia or of an external territory.

8.3. Universal Jurisdiction Based on International Treaty

8.3.1. Definition

'Universal jurisdiction based on international treaty' is the criminal jurisdiction that a contracting state of a treaty can exercise over the international crime defined in that treaty, which is committed abroad by a foreigner not against this state or its citizens.

International treaty is the other important source of international law. Professor LI Haopei points out: "treaty is the consensus of expression of at least two states in which they intend to create, amend or abolish each other's rights and obligations according to international law".[53] In the period of modern international law, the major source of international law is international custom. But because treaty is written law and its conclusion is comparatively faster, it can to a certain extent avoid disputes between or among states and thus meets better the needs of international relations. From the twentieth century, the number of international treaties

---

[53] LI Haopei, *Introduction to the Law of Treaties*, Law Press, 1987, p. 1.

concluded has increased greatly. Treaties have become more and more important among the sources of international law.

Pacta sunt servanda is a significant legal principle and the basis of binding force of treaties as well. A treaty is the consensus of the free wills of states parties, as Professor LI Haopei says: "for a treaty concluded legally, in the period of validity, the states parties are obliged to perform the obligations in good faith. This is called *pacta sunt servanda*, or Sanctity of Treaties in international law. *Pacta sunt servanda* is the most important fundamental principle in the law of treaties".[54]

The international treaties that seek to prevent and punish international crimes are usually called "conventions of international criminal law". Generally, this kind of conventions will: (1) define what the criminal activity is, (2) request the contracting states to make it a crime in domestic law, (3) provide their jurisdiction over the crime, and (4) impose the obligations upon them to co-operate in investigation, prosecution and punishment of the crime. Due to the fact that, in some circumstances, these conventions permit contracting states to exercise jurisdiction over the defined crimes committed by foreigners abroad not against the state exercising jurisdiction or its citizens, such a jurisdiction is provided with the character of universality. For example, Article 6(5) of the International Convention for the Suppression of Terrorist Bombings of 1998 provides: "this Convention does not exclude the exercise of any criminal jurisdiction established by a State Party in accordance with its domestic law".

8.3.2. Characteristics

'Universal jurisdiction based on international treaty' possesses the following characteristics.

8.3.2.1. The Subject of this Jurisdiction is the States Parties of a Treaty

Different from "universal jurisdiction based on customary international law", the subject of universal jurisdiction based on international treaty is the contracting states, instead of every state. This is determined by the principle of *pacta tertiis nec nocent nec prosunt*. Since a treaty is con-

---

[54] *Ibid.*, p. 329.

cluded by contracting states in accordance with international law to define their rights and obligations, it can only have binding force for states parties, producing no effects for third states.[55] The origin of the principle of *pacta tertiis nec nocent nec prosunt* can be traced back to Roman Law.[56] In contemporary international law, it embodies the fundamental principle of equality of state sovereignty. Article 34 of the Vienna Convention on the Law of Treaties has also confirmed the principle of *pacta tertiis nec nocent nec prosunt*: "A treaty does not create either obligations or rights for a third State without its consent".

To fulfil the purpose of prevention and punishment of international crimes, all conventions of international criminal law have explicitly stipulated jurisdiction of the contracting states. For example, Article 9 of the International Convention for the Suppression of Acts of Nuclear Terrorism (2005) provides respectively the criminal jurisdiction that the states parties 'shall' or 'may' exercise:

1. Each state party shall take such measures as may be necessary to establish its jurisdiction over the offenses set forth in article 2, when:

   (a) The offense is committed in the territory of that State; or

   (b) The offense is committed on board a vessel flying the flag of that State or an aircraft which is registered under the laws of that State at the time the offense is committed; or

   (c) The offense is committed by a national of that State.

2. A State Party may also establish its jurisdiction over any such offense when:

   (a) The offense is committed against a national of that State; or

   (b) The offense is committed against a State or government facility of that State abroad, including an embassy or other diplomatic or consular premises of that State; or

---

55 See ZHOU Zhonghai (ed.), *International Law*, 2008, p. 246.
56 See SHAO Jing (ed.), *International Law*, 2000, p. 341.

> (c) The offense is committed by a stateless person who has his or her habitual residence in the territory of that State; or
>
> (d) The offense is committed in an attempt to compel that State to do or abstain from doing any act; or
>
> (e) The offense is committed on board an aircraft which is operated by the Government of that State.

In fact, the jurisdiction set forth in Article 9(1) and (2) of the Convention is actually the defined jurisdiction, which is claimed to be exercised only by those states parties that have some substantial connection with the crime. However, Article 9(5) provides the possibility for other states parties to exercise criminal jurisdiction over the crime. It reads, "[…] this Convention does not exclude the exercise of any criminal jurisdiction established by a State Party in accordance with its national law".

8.3.2.2. The Manifestation of this Jurisdiction is the Clause or Principle of *Aut Dedere Aut Judicare*

It is generally acknowledged that the principle of *aut dedere aut judicare* ('extradite or prosecute') in contemporary international criminal law originates from the idea of *aut dedere aut punire* initiated by Grotius in the Law of War and Peace.[57] For the first time, the clause of *aut dedere aut judicare* is explicitly stipulated in the Convention for the Suppression of Unlawful Seizure of Aircraft of 1970 ('The Hague Convention'). Article 7 of the Convention reads as follows:

> The Contracting State in the territory of which the alleged offender is found shall, if it does not extradite him, be obliged, without exception whatsoever and whether or not the offense was committed in its territory, to submit the case to its competent authorities for the purpose of prosecution. Those authorities shall take their decision in the same manner as in the case of any ordinary offense of a serious nature under the law of that State.

Hereafter, the same or similar expression of *aut dedere aut judicare* has been incorporated in many conventions of international criminal

---

[57] See MA, 2008, *supra* note 7, p. 221.

law.[58] It seems that now *aut dedere aut judicare* has become a regular clause in this category of international conventions. Article 11(1) of the newly concluded International Convention for the Suppression of Acts of Nuclear Terrorism also stipulates:

> The State Party in the territory of which the alleged offender is present shall, in case to which article 9 applies, if it does not extradite that person, be obliged, without exception whatsoever and whether or not the offense was committed in its territory, to submit the case without undue delay to its competent authorities for the purpose of prosecution, through proceedings in accordance with the laws of that State. Those authorities shall take their decision in the same manner as in the case of any other offense of a grave nature under the law of that State.

The scholars in different states hold divided opinions on the issue whether *aut dedere aut judicare* is a rule of customary international law or that of conventional law. But undoubtedly, it imposes such an explicit obligation upon the states parties: the state in whose territory the suspect is present can only choose to extradite him to other contracting states or prosecute him by itself.[59] If the state chooses to prosecute him and the crime he committed has no connection either of territory or nationality with this state, the jurisdiction it exercises surely has the character of universality.

---

[58] Article 7 of the Convention for the Suppression of Unlawful Acts against the Safety of Civil Aviation (1971); Article 7 of the Convention on the Prevention and Punishment of Crimes against Internationally Protected Persons, including Diplomatic Agents (1973); Article 8(1) of the International Convention against the Taking of Hostages (1979); Article 9 of the Convention on the Physical Protection of Nuclear Materials (1980); Article 7(1) of the Convention against Torture and Other Cruel, Inhuman or Degrading Treatment or Punishment (1984); Article 10(1) of the Convention for the Suppression of Unlawful Acts against the Safety of Maritime Navigation (1988); Article 3(4) of the Protocol for the Suppression of Unlawful Acts against the Safety of Fixed Platforms Located on the Continental Shelf (1988); Article 4(2) of the Convention against Illicit Traffic in Narcotic Drugs and Psychotropic Substances (1988); Article 8(1) of the International Convention for the Suppression of Terrorist Bombings (1998); Article 10(1) of the International Convention for the Suppression of Financing Terrorism (1999); Article 16(10) of the United Nations Convention against Transnational Organized Crime (2000).

[59] See ZHU, 2007, *supra* note 4, pp. 26–27.

Professor ZHU Lijiang points out that most of the Continental law states stipulate the clause of universal jurisdiction based on international treaty in their criminal laws. The clause usually provides that if a valid international treaty requires the criminal law of the state be applied to the defined act, the criminal law of the state should apply to it regardless of whether the criminal act has any connection (such as territory, nationality or state interest) with it or not. The purpose of the provision is to conform to the trend that more and more conventions of international criminal law have contained the clause of *aut dedere aut judicare* which reflects the character of universal jurisdiction.[60]

Article 689(1) of the French Code of Criminal Procedure provides as follows:

> In accordance with the international Conventions quoted in the following articles, a person guilty of committing any of the offences listed by these provisions outside the territory of the Republic and who happens to be in France may be prosecuted and tried by French courts. The provisions of the present article apply to attempts to commit these offences, in every case where attempt is punishable.

Article 4(2) of the Criminal Code of Japan stipulates:

> In addition to the provisions of Article 2 through the preceding Article, this Code shall also apply to anyone who commits outside the territory of Japan those crimes prescribed under Part II which are governed by a treaty even if committed outside the territory of Japan.

The Criminal Law of China contains the clause of universal jurisdiction based on international treaty too. Article 9 of the Criminal Law reads as follows:

> This Law is applicable to the crimes prescribed in the international treaties concluded or acceded to by the People's Republic of China and over which the People's Republic of China has criminal jurisdiction within its obligation in accordance with the treaties.

Lastly, and most importantly, all the conventions of international criminal law with the clause of *aut dedere aut judicare* also contain such a clause as mentioned above in the International Convention for the Sup-

---

[60] *Ibid.* p. 32.

pression of Acts of Nuclear Terrorism: "This Convention does not exclude the exercise of any criminal jurisdiction established by a State Party in accordance with its national law". This kind of clause also manifests the quality of universal jurisdiction in addition to the clause of *aut dedere aut judicare*.

8.3.2.3. This Jurisdiction Applies to the Crimes Defined in International Treaties

Universal jurisdiction based on international treaty applies to crimes defined in conventions of international criminal law. As to what kind of convention is an international criminal law convention, Professor Bassiouni's opinion is that there are ten penal characteristics which, if found, even singularly, in any convention, is sufficient to make it an international criminal law convention. These penal characteristics are as follows:

1. explicit or implicit recognition of proscribed conduct as constituting an international crime, or a crime under international law, or a crime;
2. implicit recognition of the penal nature of the act by establishing a duty to prohibit, prevent, prosecute, punish, or the like;
3. criminalisation of the proscribed conduct;
4. duty or right to prosecute;
5. duty or right to punish the proscribed conduct;
6. duty or right to extradite;
7. duty or right to co-operate in prosecution, punishment (including judicial assistance);
8. establishment of a criminal jurisdiction basis;
9. reference to the establishment of an international criminal court or international tribunal with penal characteristics;
10. no defence of superior order.[61]

Having analysed 281 conventions of international criminal law up to then, Bassiouni induces 28 international crimes. They are (1) aggression; (2) genocide; (3) crimes against humanity; (4) war crimes; (5) unlawful possession, use or emplacement of weapons; (6) theft of nuclear

---

[61] M.C. Bassiouni, *Introduction to International Criminal Law*, Transnational Publisher, 2003, p. 115.

materials; (7) mercenarism; (8) apartheid; (9) slavery and slave-related practices; (10) torture and other forms of cruel, inhuman or degrading treatment; (11) unlawful human experimentation; (12) piracy; (13) aircraft hijacking and unlawful acts against international air safety; (14) unlawful acts against the safety of maritime navigation and the safety of platforms on the high seas; (15) threat and use of force against internationally protected persons; (16) crimes against United Nations and associated personnel; (17) taking of civilian hostages; (18) unlawful use of the mail; (19) attacks with explosives; (20) financing of terrorism; (21) unlawful traffic of drugs and related drug offenses; (22) organised crime; (23) destruction and/or theft of national treasures; (24) unlawful acts against certain internationally protected elements of the environment; (25) international traffic in obscene materials; (26) falsification and counterfeiting; (27) unlawful interference with submarine cables; and (28) bribery of foreign public officials.[62]

According to the study of this author, there are 27 crimes in the conventions of international criminal law,[63] plus the crime of acts of nuclear terrorism based on the International Convention for the Suppression of Acts of Nuclear Terrorism. Of all the crimes stipulated in the conventions of international criminal law, some belong to the crimes in customary international law. In this case, the provisions of conventions may be regarded as important evidence of the existence of international custom. Jurisdiction over these crimes cannot only be exercised by states parties in accordance with the conventions, but also non-States Parties according to customary international law.

8.3.2.4. This Jurisdiction cannot be Exercised *in absentia*

Unlike universal jurisdiction based on customary international law, jurisdiction based on international treaty cannot be exercised *in absentia*. Generally, the conventions of international criminal law require that the prerequisite for a State Party to claim jurisdiction over a crime is the presence of the suspect in its territory. The clause of *aut dedere aut judicare* has proved this too, because if the suspect is not present within the territory of the State Party, there is not such a problem of extradition or prosecution. Article 9(2) of the International Convention for the Suppression of

---

[62]   *Ibid.*, pp. 116–117.

[63]   See MA, 2008, *supra* note 5, p. 271.

the Financing of Terrorism provides: "upon being satisfied that the circumstances so warrant, the State Party in whose territory the offender or
alleged offender is present shall take the appropriate measures under its
domestic law so as to ensure that person's presence for the purpose of
prosecution or extradition". Article 10(1) of the Convention has the provision as follows:

> The State Party in the territory of which the alleged offender
> is present shall, in case to which article 7 applies, if it does
> not extradite that person, be obliged, without exception
> whatsoever and whether or not the offense was committed in
> its territory, to submit the case without undue delay to its
> competent authorities for the purpose of prosecution, through
> proceedings in accordance with the laws of that State. Those
> authorities shall take their decision in the same manner as in
> the case of any other offense of a grave nature under the law
> of that State.

Because of the requirement of the conventions of international
criminal law, the states which have accepted universal jurisdiction based
on international treaty, including China, usually stipulate in their legislation that the pre-condition to exercise jurisdiction over crimes defined in
international conventions is the presence of the suspect within their territories.[64] Professor GAO Mingxuan says:

> In accordance with Article 9 of the Criminal Law of China,
> for the crime stipulated in an international treaty concluded
> or acceded to by China, provided the alleged offender is
> found in China, China will exercise the criminal jurisdiction
> within its obligation in accordance with the treaty, without
> regard to whether the alleged offender is a Chinese citizen or
> not, and whether the crime was committed within the terri-
> tory of China or not. It means that the Criminal Law of
> China has established universal jurisdiction over the crimes
> defined in international treaties.[65]

8.3.2.5. This Jurisdiction cannot be Exercised Retroactively

Different from universal jurisdiction based on customary international
law, universal jurisdiction based on international treaty cannot be retroac-

---

[64] See ZHU, 2007, *supra* note 4, p. 231.
[65] GAO and ZHAO (eds.), 1998, *supra* note 47, p. 53.

tively exercised over crimes committed before the treaty concerned comes into force. This is determined by the principle of "non-retroactivity of law". Professor WEI Min points out:

> Generally, a treaty starts to apply from the date when it goes into effect. In principle, a treaty has no retroactive effect. That is to say, for any acts or facts done before the date of the treaty's coming into force, the provisions of the treaty do not have binding force to the states parties. Of course, some treaties explicitly provide that they apply to situations that previously existed. This is an exceptional issue.[66]

Article 28 of the Vienna Convention on the Law of Treaties thus provides the principle of non-retroactivity of treaties:

> [U]nless a different intention appears from the treaty or is otherwise established, its provisions do not bind a party in relation to any act or fact which took place or any situation which ceased to exist before the date of the entry into force of the treaty with respect to that party.

Professor BAI Guimei regards Article 9 of the Convention as the application of inter-temporal law in international treaties.[67]

In accordance with the principle of non-retroactivity of law, neither can a State Party of an international treaty exercise jurisdiction over the crime committed before the treaty's entry into force, nor can it exercise jurisdiction over the crime committed before its ratification of or accession to the treaty, unless there are exceptional provisions otherwise.

8.4. Universal Jurisdiction Based on Domestic Law

8.4.1. Definition

Universal jurisdiction based on domestic law is the criminal jurisdiction that a state exercises over the crime committed abroad by a foreigner not against this state or its citizens, in case he is found in the state and extradition is not available.

The legal source of this jurisdiction is the legislation of some states, specifically, the clause of representative jurisdiction in criminal laws of

---

[66] WANG, 1981, *supra* note 1, p. 240.
[67] See BAI, 2006, *supra* note 30, p. 177.

Germany and some other states in north and middle-east Europe.[68] Section 7(2) of the German Criminal Code provides as follows:

> German criminal law shall apply to other offenses committed abroad if the act is a criminal offense at the locality of its commission or if that locality is not subject to any criminal jurisdiction, and if the offender:
>
> 1) was German at the time of the offense or became German after the commission; or
>
> 2) was a foreigner at the time of the offense, is discovered in Germany and, although the Extradition Act would permit extradition for such an offense, is not extradited because a request for extradition within a reasonable period of time is not made, is rejected, or the extradition is not feasible.

The Criminal Code of the Republic of Turkey stipulates representative jurisdiction clause too. Article 12(1) and (2) provide respectively the situations that a foreigner found in Turkey committed a crime in a foreign country causing injury to Turkey and to a Turkish citizen or a legal entity, and Article 12(3)–(4) is the situation causing injury to another foreigner. The provision reads as follows:

> (3) If the aggrieved party is a foreigner, he is tried upon request of the Ministry of Justice in case of existence of the following conditions;
>
> 1) Where the offense requires punishment with a minimum limit of less than three years imprisonment according to the Turkish Laws;
>
> 2) Where there is no extradition agreement or the demand of extradition is rejected by the nation where the crime is committed or the person accused of a crime holds citizenship.
>
> (4) A foreigner who is convicted of an offence in a foreign country within the scope of first subsection, or the action filed against him is extinguished or the punishment is abated, or the offence committed is not qualified for

---

[68] See ZHU, 2007, *supra* note 2, p. 33. But as for universal jurisdiction based on domestic law, Chinese scholars hold divided opinion. See HAN, 1992, *supra* note 46, p. 122; LIU, 2006, *supra* note 3 pp. 9–10; LIN Xin and LI Qiongying, *International Criminal Law*, 2005, pp. 53–55.

the prosecution, then a new trial can be filed in Turkey
upon request of the Ministry of Justice.

Universal jurisdiction based on domestic law stems from two theories of criminal law. One is the theory of continued offense, and the other
is the universal theory of crime. The first theory means that a thief continues his offense wherever he takes the stolen object, so he could be punished according to the law of the place where he is detained.[69] In accordance with the second theory, since a crime is invariably an injury to the
community, no matter where it is committed or what nationality the
criminal possesses, every state has the right to exercise jurisdiction over it
and suppress it.[70] The famous Italian jurist Beccaria expresses his idea as
follows:

> There are always those who think, that an act of cruelty
> committed, for example, at Constantinople may be punished
> at Paris, for this abstracted reason, that he who offends hu-
> manity should have enemies in all mankind, and be the ob-
> ject of universal execration, as if judges were to be the
> knights errant of human nature in general, rather than
> guardians on particular conventions between men.[71]

Although in the light of Professor Bassiouni's understanding Beccaria
himself does not endorse this position,[72] he does believe that an extremely
effective measure to prevent crimes is to give offenders no place to escape
to.[73]

Generally speaking, universal jurisdiction based on domestic law
shows an idealistic thought of universal criminal law, or a kind of thought
'to hold justice for God' as is said in Chinese. The applicability of this
jurisdiction is extensive. Actually, it covers the contents of the two categories of universal jurisdiction discussed above. But if a state claims jurisdiction over all the crimes, including international or domestic, committed abroad by foreigners, it will invariably conflict with the jurisdiction, even sovereignty of other states. Meanwhile, the investigation,
prosecution and interrogation of the state claiming jurisdiction over these

---

[69] See Luc Reydams, 2003, *supra* note 3, p. 29.

[70] See HAN, 1992, *supra* note 46, p. 122.

[71] Cesare Beccaria-Bonesana, *An essay on Crimes and Punishments*, 2005, p. 76, translated by HUANG Feng.

[72] See M.C. Bassiouni, 2003, *supra* note 61, p. 336.

[73] See *supra* note 71, p. 76.

crimes will invariably have difficulties in international criminal co-operation, as well as problems of judicial cost or efficiency. As Professor ZHU Lijiang says, this kind of universal jurisdiction is the distinctive practice of some continental law states in north and middle-east Europe with Germany as the centre. Since its application demands some essential conditions, it has not been generally accepted in either treaties or customary international law.

8.4.2. Characteristics

8.4.2.1. The Object of this Jurisdiction is the Foreign Suspect Found in the State

The object of universal jurisdiction based on domestic law is the foreign suspect who committed a crime in a foreign state, but is discovered in the state exercising jurisdiction. Neither a foreign suspect not present within the territory of the state, nor a citizen of the state who committed a crime abroad and escaped back thereafter, is the object of this jurisdiction. Some scholars hold the opinion that the principle of representative jurisdiction applies not only to a foreign suspect found in the state, but also to a citizen of this state who escaped back after the commission of a crime abroad. On the request of the foreign state concerned, the state should bring him before its court for trial.[74]

It should be pointed out that this interpretation of representative jurisdiction is different from the concept of universal jurisdiction based on domestic laws of some states, more accurately, based on the clause of representative jurisdiction in the criminal laws of some states. First, the object of universal jurisdiction based on domestic law is the foreign suspect found in the state-claiming jurisdiction, not the citizen of that state who committed a crime abroad and escaped back. Second, the jurisdiction exercised by a state over its citizen who committed a crime abroad is nationality jurisdiction, not universal jurisdiction based on domestic law. Lastly, the exercise of universal jurisdiction based on domestic law does not need a request from the foreign state concerned as the prerequisite.

Universal jurisdiction based on domestic law is different from the transfer of criminal proceedings too. As one of the forms of penal co-

---

[74] See LIN Xin and LIU Nanlai (eds.), *Study of International Criminal Law Issues*, 2000, p. 235; LIN Xin and LI Qiong Ying, *International Criminal Law*, 2005, p. 54.

operation in contemporary international criminal law, the transfer of criminal proceedings generally means when a person committed a crime abroad and escaped to his native state, on the request of the state where the crime was committed, the court of the native state exercises criminal jurisdictions over the crime in accordance with the international agreement concluded between them.[75] Actually, because the state where the crime was committed cannot get the suspect extradited due to the principle of non-extradition of nationals, it has to give up its territorial jurisdiction and request the native state of the suspect to exercise nationality jurisdiction over the crime. Since the suspect is the citizen of the state exercising jurisdiction and the transfer of proceedings is carried out on the basis of international agreement, the transfer of criminal proceedings is a different concept from that of universal jurisdiction based on domestic law or the clause of preventative jurisdiction.

8.4.2.2. This Jurisdiction Requires Inability to Extradite

Before exercising universal jurisdiction based on domestic law over the crime done by the foreign suspect, the state claiming jurisdiction must seek to extradite him to other states which may have jurisdiction over the crime according to the territorial, nationality or protective principle. Only when extradition is not available, can the state exercise criminal jurisdiction. The situations which make the extradition not available include that no state has made the request of extradition; the requesting state has not concluded an extradition treaty with the requested state, and the latter can only extradite to the states with which it has concluded extradition treaties; and the request of extradition has been rejected due to the dissatisfaction of conditions able to be extradited.

8.4.2.3. This Jurisdiction Applies to All Crimes Able
to be Extradited

Unlike universal jurisdiction based on customary international law and international treaty which only apply to international crimes, the crimes to which universal jurisdiction based on domestic law is applied are extensive. "It is not limited to a few international crimes. In fact, it applies to

---

[75] *See* ZHAO Bingzhi *et al.* (eds.), *Punishment of Transnational and Transregional Crimes*, China Gangzheng Press, 1999, p. 20.

all the crimes able to be extradited, including common crimes".[76] In international practice the extradition treaties and laws of states have provided the crimes able to be extradited. Generally speaking, they are serious crimes. For example, Article 7 of the Extradition Law of China stipulates as follows:

> Request for extradition made by a foreign state to the People's Republic of China may be granted only when it meets the following conditions;
>
> (1) the conduct indicated in the request for extradition constitutes an offence according to the laws of both the People's Republic of China and the Requesting State; and
>
> (2) where the request for extradition is made for the purpose of instituting criminal proceedings, the offence indicated in the request for extradition is, under the laws of both the People's Republic of China and the Requesting State, punishable by a fixed term of imprisonment for one year or more or by any other heavier criminal penalty; where the request for extradition is made for the purpose of executing a criminal penalty, the period of sentence that remains to be served by the person sought is at least six months at the time when the request is made.

8.4.2.4. This Jurisdiction has to Conform to the Principle of Double Criminality

Double criminality is an important principle in extradition, and one of the conditions for extradition too. Double criminality means that extradition could only be granted when the act as the reason of extradition constitutes a crime by the laws of both the requesting and requested states. "It is the manifestation of the principle of legality in the field of international criminal cooperation".[77]

When a state exercises universal jurisdiction based on domestic law over the crime committed abroad by a foreigner found in the territory of this state, it should also conform to the principle of double criminality. If

---

[76] See ZHU, 2007, *supra* note 4, p. 35.

[77] HUANG Feng, *Rules and Practices of International Judicial Cooperation in Criminal Matters*, 2008, p. 7.

the alleged act does not constitute a crime by either the law of the state in whose territory the foreigner is found, or by the law of the state in whose territory the act was carried out, the state could not claim criminal jurisdiction over it.

8.5. Application of Universal Jurisdiction in the Criminal Law of China

8.5.1. Universal Jurisdiction in the Criminal Law of China

The principle of universal jurisdiction is a long-established principle in international law. But after 1949, because the People's Republic of China was relatively closed to the outside world and for ideological reasons, the Chinese government basically took a sceptical, even negative, attitude towards the principle. The first Criminal Law of China promulgated in 1979 contains no provision of universal jurisdiction either. Professor ZHU Lijiang points out that before the end of the 1980s, even the beginning of the 1990s, almost all Chinese scholars were against the concept of universal jurisdiction, regarding it as the manifestation of imperialism and hegemonism, as well as an infringement of state sovereignty.[78] But this conclusion might not be so objective because even at that time, many Chinese scholars in international law still made an objective introduction to and appreciation of the principle of universal jurisdiction.[79]

On 10 September 1980, China acceded to the Convention for the Suppression of Unlawful Seizure of Aircraft and the Convention for the Suppression of Unlawful Acts against the Safety of Civil Aviation. After that, China acceded to a succession of conventions of international criminal law, including the International Convention on the Elimination of All Forms of Racial Discrimination, the International Convention on the Suppression and Punishment of the Crime of Apartheid, the Single Convention on Narcotic Drugs (1961), and the Convention on Psychotropic Substances (1971).

---

[78] See ZHU, 2007, supra note 4, pp. 343–344.

[79] See WANG, 1981, supra note 1, p. 94; ZHOU Gengsheng, International Law, vol. II, Commercial Press, 1981, pp. 493–496; ZHU Lisong, International Law, 1985, pp. 175–177; WEI Min and LUO Xiangwen (eds.), Law of the Sea, 1987, pp. 210–215; ZHOU Zhonghai, International Law of the Sea, 1987, pp. 145–146; BAI Guimei et al., International Law, 1988, p. 66; HUANG Huikang, A Course in International Law, 1989, p. 39.

In order to fulfil the obligations arising from these conventions, especially from the clause of *aut dedere aut judicare*, on 23 June 1987, the Standing Committee of the National People's Congress of China passed the Decision on the Exercise of Criminal Jurisdiction over the Crimes Prescribed in the International Treaties Concluded or Acceded to by the People's Republic of China, which provides:

> For the crimes prescribed in the international treaties concluded or acceded to by the People's Republic of China, the People's Republic of China shall exercise criminal jurisdiction within its obligation in accordance with the treaties.

This decision fills in the gap of universal jurisdiction in the Criminal Law of China promulgated in 1979 and provides the legal basis for the application of universal jurisdiction in China's domestic law.[80]

After the promulgation of this decision, satirically, "Almost all the Chinese scholars change their mind to support universal jurisdiction".[81] For some persons in China, the so-called 'political correctness' is much more important than academic study and to echo the government is undoubtedly safe and politically correct.

On 28 December 1990, the Standing Committee of the National People's Congress of China promulgated the Decision on the Prohibition against Narcotic Drugs. Article 13(2) of the Decision provides that the Chinese judicial organs shall have jurisdiction over foreigners who committed the crimes of smuggling, trafficking, transporting or manufacturing narcotic drugs outside the territory of China, unless they are extradited pursuant to the international conventions or bilateral treaties which China has acceded to or concluded. In order to bring the criminal legislation in line with the international obligations assumed, Article 9 was added to the Criminal Law of China as amended on 14 March 1997, stipulating that:

> This Law is applicable to the crimes prescribed in the international treaties concluded or acceded to by the People's Republic of China and over which the People's Republic of China has criminal jurisdiction within its obligation in accordance with the treaties.

---

[80] GAO Mingxuan and WANG Xiumei, "Pondering of the Characteristics of Universal Jurisdiction and its Localization", in *Journal of Rule of Law and Social Development*, 2001, vol. 6, p. 23.

[81] ZHU, 2007, *supra* note 4, p. 344.

"This provision has put an end to the situation that the application of universal jurisdiction has no explicit basis in the Criminal Law of China, and makes the process of localization of universal jurisdiction tend to perfection".[82] Professor GAO Mingxuan says that in accordance with this provision, China should exercise criminal jurisdiction over all the crimes prescribed in the international treaties concluded or acceded to by China, within its obligation undertaken according to the treaties – in case the criminal is found in China, no matter whether the crime was committed within the territory of China or not, or whether the criminal is a Chinese citizen or not.[83]

The universal jurisdiction in the Criminal Law of China possesses the following characteristics:

1. It belongs to the universal jurisdiction based on international treaty.

2. The precondition of its exercise is that the Chinese court cannot exercise criminal jurisdiction based on the territorial, nationality or protective principles prescribed respectively in Articles 6, 7 and 8 of the Criminal Law of China.

3. It applies to the crimes prescribed in the international treaties concluded or acceded to by China.

4. China exercises criminal jurisdiction over the crimes within its obligation in accordance with the treaties. It means that, on the one hand, the reservations to conventions of international criminal law made by China are not applicable; on the other hand, China should take the legislative, administrative and judicial measures necessary to fulfil the obligations originating from the conventions, particularly the obligation of *aut dedere aut judicare*.

5. As regards procedure, the prerequisite of the exercise of universal jurisdiction is that the suspect is present in the territory of China and his extradition is not available.

8.5.2. Problems in Application of Universal Jurisdiction in China

Although universal jurisdiction has been stipulated in Article 9 of the Criminal Law of China, China has had some problems in its application which should not be ignored and need to be elaborated here.

---

[82] GAO and WANG, 2001, *supra* note 80, p. 23.
[83] GAO and ZHAO, 1998, *supra* note 65, p. 53.

8.5.2.1. Universal Jurisdiction Based on Customary International Law is Not Incorporated in the Criminal Law of China

As discussed above, international custom is one of the sources of international law, and many states in their constitutional laws or other legislation have defined its position and validity in the domestic legal system. However, although Chinese scholars generally recognise both international custom and international treaty as sources of international law and international criminal law, there is no definite provision in the Constitutional Law of China or other laws on the concept of international custom or its validity in the Chinese legal system. Consequently, some hold the view that international custom is not a source of international criminal law, for it does not conform to the principle of legality.[84]

Since there is no provision on international custom in the legislation, it means that universal jurisdiction based on customary international law is not accepted in the domestic laws of China. If a crime in customary international law has not been stipulated in the international treaties concluded or acceded to by China, no matter how serious it is, China has no jurisdiction over it. For example, because China does not accede to the international conventions which provide for crimes against humanity and aggression, it is impossible for China to exercise criminal jurisdiction over them. But for those crimes in customary international law which are incorporated in the treaties China has acceded to, such as piracy, genocide and torture, there is at least the possibility for China to claim jurisdiction in accordance with Article 9 of the Criminal Law. It is necessary to accept universal jurisdiction based on customary international law in the Criminal Law, but it is hard to achieve now.

8.5.2.2. China Violates its International Obligation by Not Transforming Crimes in International Treaties into its Criminal Law

As a basic obligation of contracting states, conventions of international criminal law usually request states parties to stipulate the crimes defined in the conventions in their criminal laws and impose appropriate penalties to them. For example, Article 5 of the International Convention for the Suppression of the Acts of Nuclear Terrorism prescribes as follows:

---

[84] *See* ZHANG, 2009, *supra* note 22, pp. 23–25.

> Each State Party shall adopt such measures as may be necessary:
>
> (a) To establish as criminal offences under its national law the offence set forth in article 2;
>
> (b) To make those offences punishable by appropriate penalties which take into account the grave nature of these offences.[85]

At the same time, Article 9 of the Criminal Law of China also stipulates that China shall exercise criminal jurisdiction over the crimes defined within its obligation in accordance with the treaties. It is doubtless that to prescribe the crimes set forth in conventions of international criminal law as criminal offences under the Criminal Law of China is within its obligations according to the conventions, because the clauses defining international crimes concern the object and purpose of the treaties, and pursuant to Article 19(3) of the Vienna Convention on the Law of Treaties, states parties are not permitted to make reservation to such clauses. So it is clear that China has the obligation to act as the conventions request.

But unfortunately, although the Criminal Law of China has provided or embodied some international crimes, such as sabotaging means of transport, hijacking of aircraft, organising, leading or participating in terror organisations, smuggling, trafficking, transporting or producing narcotic drugs, illegal holding of narcotic drugs, corruption, bribery, money laundering, *et cetera*, most of the crimes prescribed in conventions of international criminal law concluded or acceded to by China have not been incorporated in its Criminal Law yet. They include war crimes, genocide, crimes of racial discrimination, apartheid, torture, crimes against internationally protected persons, crimes against the safety of United Nations and associated personnel, piracy, crimes against the safety of maritime navigation, crimes against the safety of fixed platforms on the continental shelf, *et cetera*. For instance, although China ratified the United Nations Convention on the Law of the Sea in 1996 and committed itself to suppress piracy on the high seas, by now there is no crime of piracy in its Criminal Law, which has caused confusion in the judicial practice.

---

[85] United Nations, *International Convention for the Suppression of the Acts of Nuclear Terrorism*, available at http://www.legal-tools.org/doc/5891b5/.

In brief, China has not incorporated most of the crimes prescribed in the conventions of international criminal law it has concluded or acceded to into its Criminal Law. It is the most conspicuous problem in the application of universal jurisdiction in China. This situation does not only violate the principle of *pacta sunt servanda*, but also the obligations assumed by China in accordance with the international conventions. Professor CHEN Zhonglin has expressed that if China cannot change the crimes prescribed in the international treaties that it has concluded or acceded to in the provisions of its Criminal Law, it is impossible for the judicial organs to exercise universal jurisdiction pursuant to the Criminal Law. In such a situation, China cannot fulfil its international obligations to suppress international crimes either.[86]

8.5.3.3. Universal Jurisdiction Prescribed in Article 9 Conflicts with the Principle of Legality in Article 3

The principle of legality is another basic principle in criminal law. It is composed of three concrete principles: (1) no crime without a law (*nullum crimen sine lege*), (2) no penalty without a law (*nulla poena sine lege*), and (3) non-retroactivity of application of laws (no *ex post facto* application of laws).[87] The principle of legality is a very important principle and it is universally observed by civilised states with the significance to prevent the abuse of judicial powers and to protect fundamental freedom and human rights. Article 3 of the Criminal Law of China stipulates this principle as follows: "[f]or acts that are explicitly defined as criminal act in law, the offenders shall be convicted and punished in accordance with law; otherwise, they shall not be convicted or punished".

As discussed above, since most of the crimes prescribed in conventions of international criminal law concluded or acceded to by China have not been transformed into the Criminal Law, Article 9 of the Criminal Law can be understood as China having taken the attitude to incorporate the conventions of international criminal law in its domestic legal system. The Chinese courts can prosecute international crimes, even though there are no such crimes in its Criminal Law. But by doing this, it obviously

---

[86] CHEN, 2004, *supra* note 6, p. 473.

[87] CHEN Weizuo, *Latin-Chinese Dictionary of Legal Terms and Maxims*, Law Press, 2009, p. 237; Editorial Group, *An English-Chinese Dictionary of Law*, Zhongguo shangye chu ban she, 1985, p. 569.

---

violates the principle of legality. To prosecute a crime in accordance with the convention of international criminal law which is not prescribed in criminal law constitutes a violation of the principle of *nullum crimen sine lege*. Even if China could prosecute the crime prescribed in the convention, because such a convention provides only the criminal act without penalty, to impose the penalty according the Criminal Law of China constitutes a violation of the principle of *nulla poena sine lege*.

8.5.3.4. Prosecution of International Crime with Other Classification in the Criminal Law Violates the Principle of Prohibition of Analogy

If the judicial organs prosecute the crimes in the conventions of international criminal law which are not prescribed in the Criminal Law of China, they violate the principle of *nullum crimen sine lege*. In practice sometimes judicial organs substitute crimes in the Criminal Law for international crimes which have not been listed in it, and institute proceedings against the offenders. For example, because there is no crime of piracy in the Criminal Law, the foreign offender is accused of intentional homicide, intentional injury, sabotaging means of transport, robbery or unlawful detention. Although the purpose of punishing the offenders can be achieved in this way, it seriously violates the principle of 'prohibition of analogy'.

The principle of 'prohibition of analogy' originates from the inherent connotation of the principle of *nullum crimen sine lege*. If analogy is permitted when an act has not been prescribed as a crime in criminal law, the principle of *nullum crimen sine lege* will lose its significance completely. Besides, it is ridiculous to replace piracy by intentional homicide, intentional injury, sabotaging means of transport, robbery or unlawful detention. In accordance with the United Nations Convention on the Law of the Sea, as a State Party, China definitely has the right to exercise jurisdiction over piracy, even though the crime is committed by foreigners on the high seas and not against the state, the citizens or ships of China. But China has no jurisdiction at all over the crimes such as intentional homicide, intentional injury, sabotaging means of transport, robbery or unlawful detention which are committed by foreigners on the high seas without any substantial connection with the state, the citizens or ships of China. For these crimes, only when they are carried out within the territory of China, the offenders are Chinese citizens or they cause injury to the state or citizens of China, can China claim criminal jurisdiction over them. In a word, there is no legal basis for China to exercise criminal jurisdiction over international crimes prescribed in the treaties concluded or acceded to by China by analogising them to the crimes in the Criminal Law of China.

8.6. Conclusion

Jurisdiction is one of the fundamental rights of the state, by which the state administers and disposes of people, property and circumstances in accordance with its sovereignty. Based on its character, jurisdiction of state can be divided into legislative, administrative and judicial jurisdiction. As for judicial jurisdiction, it is composed of civil and criminal jurisdiction.[88]

Traditionally, the state exercises mainly territorial and nationality jurisdiction over crimes carried out within its territory or by its citizens. But with the lapse of time, it is sometimes necessary for the state to break the restriction of territorial and nationality principle to exercise criminal jurisdiction over some crimes committed by foreigners abroad. At the beginning, it is because the crime is committed in a place outside the jurisdiction of any state, or to make it more accurate, in a place where the state cannot perform its power effectively.[89] Later, it is because certain crimes possess a grave nature and infringe the common interest of the international community. The definition of 'universal jurisdiction' given by Principle I of the Princeton Principles on Universal Jurisdiction makes it

---

[88] *See* MA Chengyuan and LI Juqian (eds.), *International Law*, China University of Political Science and Law Press, 2008, p. 56.

[89] When people talk about universal jurisdiction, they often take piracy as an example and say that historically it takes place on the high seas, which is the place outside the jurisdiction of any state. After Columbus discovered the New Continent in 1492, in 1493, Pope Alexander VI distributed the oceans of the world to Spain and Portugal approximately along the meridian line in the Atlantic Ocean. From that time to the establishment of traditional law of the sea in the nineteenth century, there are lots of controversies on the legal status of the sea and Grotius published his other famous book *Mare Liberum*. The practices of states are confused too. Before the nineteenth century there was no such division of territorial sea and open sea. It was not correct to say that piracy was the crime committed in the open sea or in a place outside the jurisdiction of any state. See *ibid.,* p. 132.

clear.[90] This signifies the progress of the international community and international law.

Although universal jurisdiction has been fully established both theoretically and practically, there are still controversies on the definition and categories of universal jurisdiction. The major reason is that scholars have divergent views on the scope of application of universal jurisdiction, which again originates from their different understanding of its legal sources. This author's opinion is to divide universal jurisdiction into three categories in accordance with the different legal sources. They are: (1) universal jurisdiction based on customary international law, (2) universal jurisdiction based on international treaty, and (3) universal jurisdiction based on domestic law.

Universal jurisdiction based on customary international law is the criminal jurisdiction that every state can exercise over the crime in customary international law committed abroad by a foreigner not against this state or its citizens. This jurisdiction applies to crimes in customary international law. Though it is generally exercised when the accused is present within the territory of the state claiming jurisdiction, sometimes it can also be exercised *in absentia*.

Universal jurisdiction based on international treaty is the criminal jurisdiction that a contracting state of a treaty can exercise over the international crime defined in that treaty, which is committed abroad by a foreigner not against this state or its citizens. The object of this jurisdiction is the crimes defined in international criminal conventions, and the major manifestation of this jurisdiction in international treaties is the clause or principle of *aut dedere aut judicare*.

Universal jurisdiction based on domestic law is the criminal jurisdiction that a state exercises over the crime committed abroad by a foreigner not against this state or its citizens, in case he is found in the state and extradition is not available. This category of universal jurisdiction is adopted by Germany and some other European counties and its legal source is the representative jurisdiction clause in the criminal law. The prerequisite to exercise this jurisdiction is that the accused is present in

---

[90] For the purpose of these Principles, universal jurisdiction is criminal jurisdiction based solely on the nature of the crime, without regard to where the crime was committed, the nationality of the alleged or convicted perpetrator, the nationality of the victim, or any other connection to the state exercising such jurisdiction.

the territory of the state and it is unable to extradite him to another state. The crimes applicable are crimes able to be extradited, including both international and common crimes. Up to now, it has not been generally accepted in either international treaties or customary international law. Besides, the transfer of criminal proceedings is not the same as universal jurisdiction based on domestic law.

By summarising the common elements of the three definitions of universal jurisdiction, it is the view of this author that universal jurisdiction is the criminal jurisdiction that a state can exercise over a crime committed abroad by a foreigner not against this state or its citizens in accordance with international law or domestic criminal law. This can be seen as a general definition of universal jurisdiction.

Universal jurisdiction is provided for the first time in Article 9 of the Criminal Law of the People's Republic of China in 1997. According to this Provision, universal jurisdiction in the Criminal Law of China is universal jurisdiction based on international treaty, which applies only to crimes defined in the conventions of international criminal law concluded or acceded to by China. It is a serious problem that China has not transformed most of the crimes in these conventions into its Criminal Law. This doubtlessly violates the principle of *pacta sunt servanda* and the obligations arising from the conventions. Since the Criminal law of China does not contain the same classifications as the conventions do, Chinese judicial organs sometimes have to use other classifications in the Criminal Law than the international crimes proscribed in conventions for the purpose of prosecution. This constitutes a violation of both the principle of *nullum crimen sine lege* and the principle of *nulla poena sine lege*, as well as the principle of prohibition of analogy.

9

Universal Jurisdiction Before the United Nations General Assembly: Seeking Common Understanding under International Law[*]

ZHU Lijiang[**]

9.1. Introduction

After heated debates for over a decade, the issue of universal jurisdiction ('U.J.') eventually came to the front of the General Assembly of the United Nations ('UNGA'), the largest and authoritative international forum of States in the world. On 18 September 2009, the sixty-fourth UNGA listed the item of 'The Scope and Application of the Principle of Universal Jurisdiction' in its agenda,[1] and allocated it to the Sixth Committee.[2] This means that the UNGA is seized of this thorny and controversial issue in international law on criminal jurisdiction of States. It was not beyond my expectation, because, as early as 2006, in my Ph.D. dissertation at Peking University Law School, I proposed that, as a formal means, States could raise the issue of U.J. before the UNGA for discussion, which is conducive to clarifying the scope and application of U.J.[3]

Two and a half years since the listing of this issue in the agenda of the UNGA, it is time to look at what has been achieved in the discussion of this issue in the UNGA. This is the main purpose of this chapter, which

---

[*] This chapter is a part of the project sponsored by the Chinese National Social Science Foundation for young scholars, Project No. 11CFX068.

[**] **ZHU Lijiang**, Associate Professor in International Law, Faculty of International Law, China University of Political Science and Law ('CUPL'); Researcher, the Research Center for International Criminal Law and International Humanitarian Law ('RCICL'), CUPL, Beijing, People's Republic of China.

[1] "Item 84: The scope and application of the principle of universal jurisdiction", A/64/251, p. 7.

[2] A/64/252, p. 16.

[3] ZHU Lijiang, *Universal Jurisdiction over War Crimes in Non-International Armed Conflicts and International Law* (Dui Guonei Zhanzhengzui de Pubian Guanxia yu Guojifa), Law Press, Beijing, 2007, p. 411.

---

seeks to identify the result of the discussion on the principle of U.J. in the UNGA up to now, or, in the terms of Mr. Ulibarri, Chair of the Working Group on the scope and application of the principle of U.J. in the Sixth Committee of the UNGA, the "common understanding that was achievable on the scale between the minimalist and maximalist positions".[4] For this purpose, the chapter will first introduce the way to the UNGA with a view to telling how this issue was referred to the Assembly. Then, in the second part, the chapter will introduce the on-going discussions in the UNGA from the perspective of procedure. In the third part, it attempts to identify what has been achieved in international law in the UNGA in terms of the merits of this issue. The last part contains some concluding remarks.

9.2. The Way to New York

Historically speaking, U.J. is not a new form of criminal jurisdiction of States permitted under international law. But before World War II, U.J. was usually considered by traditional international lawyers to be only against piracy committed on the high seas, an area not subject to jurisdiction of any sovereign State. Immediately after World War II, some international lawyers began to argue that certain international crimes, such as genocide, crimes against humanity and war crimes, are similar to piracy in nature, and that they should also be subject to U.J. of any sovereign State, though this category of international crimes was different from piracy in that they were usually committed within the territory of sovereign States.[5] But in reality during the Cold War only a couple of cases related to genocide, crimes against humanity and war crimes were tried on the basis of the principle of U.J. by some States. The most famous was the *Eichmann* case before the Israeli courts.[6] Interestingly, the Israeli representative before the Sixth Committee of the sixty-fourth UNGA specially pointed out

---

[4] A/C.6/66/SR.17, para. 25.

[5] Willard B. Cowles, "Universality of Jurisdiction Over War Crimes", in *California Law Review*, 1945, vol. 33, pp. 177–194.

[6] *Attorney General of Israel v. Eichmann*, District Court of Jerusalem, 12 December 1961; Supreme Court of Israel, 29 May 1962, in *International Law Review*, vol. 36, p. 5.

that even in the *Eichmann* case Israel has some kind of 'jurisdictional links' with it.[7]

The exercise of U.J. by western European States in the period from the termination of the Cold War to the end of the twentieth century mainly resulted from the influence of the establishment of the first *ad hoc* international criminal tribunal by the U.N. Security Council, the ICTY, in May 1993.[8]

Judicial practices on exercise of U.J. emerged in States such as Germany[9], Switzerland[10], Austria[11], Denmark[12], France[13], Finland[14] and the Netherlands[15].

---

[7] A/C.6/64/SR.13, para. 20.

[8] Gérard Dive, "The Belgian Law Relating to the Repression of Grave Violations of International Humanitarian Law and the Implementation of the Rome Statute", in Matthias Neuner (ed.), *National Legislation Incorporating International Crimes: Approaches of Civil and Common Law Countries*, Berliner Wissenschafts-Verlag GmbH, 2003, p. 165.

[9] *Prosecutor v. Tadić*, Bundesgerichtshof, 13 February 1994; *Prosecutor v. Djajić*, Bayerisches Oberstes Landesgericht, 23 May 1997; *X v. SB and DB*, Bundesgerichtshof, 11 December 1998; *Prosecutor v. Jorgić*, Oberstes Landes-gericht Düsseldorf, 26 September 1997; *Prosecutor v. Sokolović*, Bundesgerichtshof, 21 February 2001. With regard to the judicial practice in this regard in Germany, see also, Luc Reydams, *Universal Jurisdiction: International and Municipal Legal Perspectives*, Oxford University Press, Oxford, 2003, pp. 149–156; *see also* Ruth Rissing-van Saan, "The German Federal Supreme Court and the Prosecution of International Crimes Committed in Former Yugoslavia", in *Journal of International Criminal Justice*, 2005, vol. 3, pp. 381–399.

[10] *Military Prosecutor v. Gabrež*, Tribunal Militaire, Division I, Lausanne, 18 April 1997; *see also* Andreas R. Ziegler, "In re G", in *American Journal of International Law*, 1998, vol. 92, pp. 78–82.

[11] *Republic of Austria v. Cvjetković*, Landesgericht, Salzburg, 31 May 1995, available at http://www.redress.org/documents/annex.html, last accessed on 7 September 2012.

[12] *Prosecutor v. Sarić*, Østre Landsret, 25 November 1994 (Trial Judgment); Højesteret, 15 August 1995 (Appeal Judgment), reprinted in *Ugeskrift for Retsvæsen* 1995, 838H. See also, *Yearbook of International Humanitarian Law*, 1998, vol. 1, p. 431.

[13] *Javor et al. v. X*, Tribunal de Grande Instance de Paris (examining magistrate), 6 May 1994; Cour d'Appel de Paris, 24 October 1994; Cour de Cassation (chambre criminelle), 26 March 1995. *See also* Brigitte Stern, "In re *Javor;* In re *Munyeshyaka*", in *American Journal of International Law*, 1999, vol. 93, p. 527; Brigitte Stern, "La compétence universelle en France: Le cas des crimes commis en ex-Yugoslavie et au Rwanda", in *German Yearbook of International Law*, 1997, vol. 40, p. 280; Rafaëlle Maison, "Les premiers cas d'applications des dispositions pénales des Conventions de

Some features appeared in the exercise of U.J. by these States. First, legislatively speaking, in this period the criminal codes or criminal procedural codes of these States often contained the so-called 'treaty-based U.J. article'[16] or representative jurisdiction article[17]. A few States incorporated the absolute, genuine, pure or unconditional U.J. into their criminal law. Second, judicially speaking, in this period, the crimes which were subject to treaty-based U.J. or representative jurisdiction in these States were mainly the crime of murder or other ordinary crimes in their criminal codes, rather than genocide, crimes against humanity or war crimes because only a few western European States had these core international crimes in their criminal law. Third, all the exercise of U.J. in this period by these western European States was not successful. In the limited available cases, the accused was set free due to lack of the provision of genocide, crimes against humanity or war crimes in their criminal codes. Finally, in this period, the accused who were charged or tried on basis of U.J. were predominantly from former Yugoslavia.

Then, at the turn of the century, nationals of other States, in particular those of former colonies, became the target of the exercise of U.J. by

---

Genève par les jurisdictions internes", in *European Journal of International Law*, 1995, vol. 6, pp. 260–273.

[14] Ari-Matti Nuutila, "Implementation of the Rome Statute in Finnish Law", in Matthias Neuner (ed.), *National Legislation Incorporating International Crimes: Approaches of Civil and Common Law Countries* Berliner Wissenschafts-Verlag GmbH, 2003, p. 87.

[15] *Prosecutor v. Knesević*, Examining Magistrate, 1 December 1995; Hoge Raad der Niederlanden, 11 November 1997; *see also Yearbook of International Humanitarian Law*, 1998, vol. 1, p. 601.

[16] The so-called 'treaty-based U.J. article' is usually a provision in the criminal law of a country in which the State exercises criminal jurisdiction over a case on the basis of an international treaty ratified by that country, even if the case has no any link with that State in territory, nationality or special State interest. Quite a number of States have such a U.J. provision in their criminal codes or criminal procedure codes.

[17] The representative article is usually an article in the criminal law of a State in which the State exercises criminal jurisdiction over a foreign suspect present in its territory on the condition that no request to extradition has been made by any foreign State or such request has been rejected, even if the case has no link with that State in territory, nationality or special State interest. As a representative article, a ratified international treaty is not required to be present. A number of European States, in particular the central and eastern European States or Nordic States have such a provision in their criminal law.

---

western European States. Quite a number of African nationals were targeted by the exercise of U.J. by their former European colonial powers. Among them were some political figures of African States. This gave rise to diplomatic disputes between them. Among others, three disputes have been referred to the International Court of Justice ('ICJ') in The Hague.

The first dispute is the well-known *Arrest Warrant* case, in which originally the Democratic Republic of the Congo ('DRC') requested the Court to adjudicate, *inter alia*, the legality of the exercise of U.J. over the then Congolese Foreign Minister by Belgium on basis of the Belgian Act on Punishment of Grave Breaches of International Humanitarian Law, which empowered the Belgian courts to exercise criminal jurisdiction over any grave breaches of IHL, regardless of where they were committed. Unfortunately, the DRC abandoned the request during the oral submissions so the ICJ did not deliver an answer in its judgment in 2002, although quite a number of judges expressed their views on the Belgian style of U.J. legislative provision in their separate or dissenting opinions.[18]

In the second case, just after the delivery of the judgment in the *Arrest Warrant* case, the Democratic Republic of the Congo ('DRC') requested the ICJ to adjudicate that the investigation and prosecution by the French authorities against the President and other political leaders of the DRC for alleged crimes against humanity and torture on basis of the treaty-based U.J. article in the French Criminal Procedural Code was illegal. Regrettably, the ICJ removed the case from the list on the request of the DRC,[19] thus losing another golden opportunity to examine the legality of the French style treaty-based U.J. in this case.

Unlike the previous two cases in which both plaintiffs were former colonies of both defendants respectively, the third case was filed by a former colonial power, namely Belgium, against a former French colonial, the Republic of Senegal. Belgium seemingly wishes to compel Senegal to exercise treaty-based U.J. over Mr. Hissène Habré, former President of Chad who has been living in Senegal for over a decade, for the

---

[18] ICJ, *Arrest Warrant of 11 April 2000* (*Democratic Republic of the Congo v. Belgium*), available at http://www.legal-tools.org/doc/c6bb20.

[19] ICJ, *Order of 16 November 2010* (*Republic of the Congo v. France: Case Concerning Certain Criminal Proceedings in France*), available at http://www.legal-tools.org/doc/422994/.

alleged crimes of torture and crimes against humanity in Chad, by requesting the Court to adjudicate and declare that Senegal violates its obligations under the Convention against Torture and customary international law. On 20 July 2012, the Court declared that Senegal must, without further delay, submit the case of Mr. Hissène Habré to its competent authorities for the purpose of prosecution, if it does not extradite him.[20]

Another couple of incidents in relation to U.J. eventually annoyed Rwanda, which pushed forward collective action of African States. In November 2006, a French investigating judge in Paris issued an arrest warrant against nine Rwandan citizens, including Rose Kabuye, the then Chief of Protocol of the Rwandan President, for allegedly being involved in the shooting down of an airplane carrying Rwanda's former President, Juvenal Habyarimana and Burundi's former President, Cyprien Ntayamira in 1994, which sparked the massacre that claimed the lives of 800,000 to 1,000,000 persons.[21] The issuance of the arrest warrant was criticised by the Rwandan government as "baseless and unfounded".[22] Rwanda then severed diplomatic relations with France. In February 2008, a Spanish investigating judge also issued an indictment charging 40 current or former high-ranking Rwandan military officials with serious crimes including genocide, crimes against humanity, war crimes and terrorism, perpetrated over a period of 12 years, from 1990 to 2002, against the civilian population, and primarily against members of the Hutu ethnic group. While the investigations were initially based on complaints from families of nine Spaniards who were killed, harmed or disappeared during the period at issue, the indictment was subsequently expanded to include crimes committed against Rwandan and Congolese victims, based on the U.J. doctrine.[23]

---

[20] ICJ (*Belgium v. Senegal: Questions relating to the Obligation to Prosecute or Extradite*), available at http://www.icj-cij.org/docket/index.php?p1=3&p2=3&code=bs&case=144&k=5e, last accessed on 7 September 2012.

[21] The full-text of the arrest warrant is available at http://rud-urunana.org/documenta tion%5CBruguiereArrestWarrants.pdf, last accessed on 13 October 2012.

[22] Available at http://www.minaffet.gov.rw/index.php?id=886&tx_ttnews%5Btt_news %5D=55&cHash= a1600843ce217f5052270a5209cfdd24, last accessed on 7 September 2012.

[23] "The Spanish Indictment of High-ranking Rwandan Officials", in *Journal of International Criminal Justice*, 2008, vol. 6. pp. 1003–1011.

In response to these incidents, in April 2008, a conference of African Union ('A.U.') Ministers of Justice and Attorneys-General was held in Addis Ababa at the A.U.'s Headquarters. The Conference requested the Commission of the A.U. to undertake a study on the application and scope of the principle of U.J. The report was prepared and presented to the eleventh Assembly of the A.U. through its Executive Council in July 2008, in Sharm El-Sheikh, Egypt. The eleventh Assembly adopted a decision on the report, putting it plainly that the "political nature and abuse of the principle of universal jurisdiction by judges from some non-African States against African leaders, particularly Rwanda, is a clear violation of the sovereignty and territorial integrity of these States". The decision pointed out that "there is need for establishment of an international regulatory body with competence to review and/or appeals arising out of abuse of the principle of universal jurisdiction by individual States". It requested the Chairperson of the A.U. to table the matter before the U.N. Security Council and the U.N. General Assembly for consideration, further requested the Chairperson of the A.U. to urgently facilitate a meeting between the A.U. and E.U. to discuss the matter with a view to finding a lasting solution to this problem and in particular to ensuring that those warrants are withdrawn and are not executable in any country.[24]

In accordance with the decision, the A.U. began to discuss the issue of U.J. with the E.U. On 16 September 2008, the tenth meeting of the A.U.-E.U. Ministerial Troika was held in Brussels.[25] Nevertheless, irrespective of the request by the A.U. that no warrant on the basis of U.J. be executed in any country, in particular E.U. States, and irrespective of the meeting being held between the A.U. and E.U., on 9 November 2008, the German authorities arrested Mrs. Rose Kabuye, Chief of Protocol to the Rwandan President in Frankfurt while she was traveling on business, executing the arrest warrant of a French investigating judge. After the arrest, Rwanda expelled the German ambassador and ordered his envoy in Berlin

---

[24] Decision on the Report of the Commission on the Abuse of the Principle of Universal Jurisdiction, Assembly/AU/Dec.199 (XI), available at http://www.africa-union.org/root/au/conferences/2008/june/summit/dec/ASSEMBLY%20DECISIONS%20193%20-%20207%20(XI).pdf, last accessed on 7 September 2012.

[25] The eleventh meeting was held in Addis Ababa and the A.U.-E.U. expert report on the principle of U.J. was delivered in April 2009, Council of the European Union, the A.U.-E.U. Export on the Principle of Universal Jurisdiction, Doc. 8672/1/09 REV 1, 16 April 2009.

to return to Kigali for consultations. Furthermore, the Rwandan Prime Minister managed to bring together all African ministers of justice in Kigali and called for "a unified stand to fight neo-colonialism spearheaded by foreign judges hiding under international law".[26]

This incident further put incentives to the determination of the A.U. to refer the issue of U.J. to the U.N. On 21 January 2009, the Permanent Representative of Tanzania to the U.N. addressed the Secretary-General ('UNSG') in his capacity as the Chair of the A.U. requesting that an additional item – "Abuse of the Principle of Universal Jurisdiction" – be included in the agenda of the sixty-third UNGA. The request was made on behalf of the Group of the African States.[27] Annexed to the request was an explanatory memorandum which set out the reasons for such a request, that is, "the extent of the application of [the principle of universal jurisdiction] has never been discussed at the level of the United Nations", and that "there is no widespread state practice".[28] It recognised that "the African Union fully subscribes to and supports the principle of universal jurisdiction within the context of fighting impunity as well as the need to punish perpetrators of genocide, crimes against humanity and war crimes, it is however opposed to the selective and abusive application of the principle against African leaders". It further underlined that "any continued abuse of this principle could potentially endanger not only the respect for international law and the conduct of international relations, but also threaten the political, economic and socio-economic development of African States".[29]

On 1–3 February 2009, the twelfth Assembly of the A.U. was held in Addis Ababa. The Assembly adopted a decision on the implementation of its decision on the abuse of the principle of the U.J. The decision underscored that an A.U. speaking with one voice is the appropriate collective response to counter the exercise of power by strong States over weak States, and requested the Chairperson of the A.U. to follow up on this

---

[26] E. Musoni, *AU Justice Ministers Protest Abuse of Universal Jurisdiction*, New York Times, 5 November 2008, available at http://allafrica.com/stories/200811050742.html, last accessed on 7 September 2012.

[27] A/63/237, 3 February 2009, p. 1.

[28] *Ibid.*, p. 2, para. 4.

[29] *Ibid.*, p. 2, para. 5.

matter with a view to ensuring that it is exhaustively discussed at the level of the U.N. Security Council and General Assembly.[30]

Then, during the meeting of the General Committee held on 18 February 2009, Tanzania requested the postponement of the discussion on the proposed item because some delegations raised concerns about the title of the proposed item. Following extensive consultations and agreement with concerned delegations, on 29 June 2009, Tanzania requested the inclusion in the agenda of the sixty-third UNGA of an additional item entitled "The Scope and Application of the Principle of Universal Jurisdiction".[31] In contrast with the request of 21 January 2009, the request of 29 June 2009 further explained in the explanatory memorandum that the purpose of referring the issue of U.J. for discussion in the UNGA is to establish "regulatory provisions for its application".[32] On 10 September 2009, Tanzania, on behalf of the States members of the U.N. that are members of the Group of African States, formally submitted a draft decision entitled 'The Scope and Application of the Principle of Universal Jurisdiction' to the sixty-third UNGA. The draft decision reads,

> [t]he General Assembly decides to include in the agenda of its sixty-fourth session the item entitled "Scope and application of the principle of universal jurisdiction" and recommends that it be considered by the Sixth Committee at that session.[33]

At the 105th plenary meeting of the sixty-third UNGA on 14 September 2009, a draft decision was adopted by consensus. This entailed that the UNGA was seized of the issue of U.J. for the first time. The discussion of U.J. was thus to be made at the level of the UN. The representative of Rwanda stated after the adoption of the decision that "it is therefore imperative that a clear universal mechanism be established to ensure the impartial and appropriate application of the principle of universal jurisdiction".[34] The representative of Sweden explained after the adoption of the decision on behalf of the E.U. that "the discussion about universal

---

[30]   Assembly/AU/Dec. 213 (XII).

[31]   A/63/237/Rev.1, 23 July 2009, p. 1.

[32]   *Ibid.*, p. 2, para. 6.

[33]   "Item 158: The scope and application of the principle of universal jurisdiction", A/63/L.100, 10 September 2009.

[34]   A/63/PV.105, 14 September 2009, p. 10.

jurisdiction is, first and foremost, a legal subject that rightly belongs in the Sixth Committee".[35] On 18 September 2009, the sixty-fourth UNGA listed the item of "The Scope and Application of the Principle of Universal Jurisdiction" in its agenda,[36] and allocated it to the Sixth Committee.[37]

9.3. Procedural Progress in New York

The Sixth Committee considered the item at its twelfth, thirteenth and twenty-fifth meetings, on 20 and 21 October and on 12 November 2009. At its twelfth meeting on 20 October 2009, the representatives of 27 States and State groups made statements, including Australia (on behalf of CANZ), Tunisia (on behalf of Group of African States), Mexico (on behalf of Rio Group), Iran (on behalf of MNACs), Switzerland, El Salvador, Costa Rica, Swaziland, South Africa, China, the Democratic Republic of the Congo, Guatemala, Kenya, Slovakia, Thailand, Peru, Norway, Tanzania, France, Austria, Germany, Finland, Sudan, Slovenia, Belgium, Libya and Lebanon.[38] At its thirteenth meeting on 21 October 2009, the representatives from 17 States joined the statements, including Indonesia, the United Kingdom, Algeria, Spain, Russia, Israel, Burkina Faso, the United States, Liechtenstein, Rwanda, Togo, Malaysia, Senegal, Nigeria, Italy, Ethiopia and Argentina.[39] At its twenty-fifth meeting on 12 November 2009, the representative of Rwanda introduced a draft resolution entitled "The scope and application of the principle of universal jurisdiction". The draft resolution:

> 1. Requests the Secretary-General to invite Member States to submit, before 30 April 2010, information and observations on the scope and application of the principle of universal jurisdiction, including information on the relevant applicable international treaties, their domestic legal rules and judicial practice, and to prepare and submit to the General Assembly, at its sixty-fifth session, a report based on such information and observations;

---

[35] *Ibid.*

[36] "Item 84: The scope and application of the principle of universal jurisdiction", A/64/251, p. 7.

[37] A/64/252, p. 16.

[38] A/C.6/64/SR.12.

[39] A/C.6/64/SR.13.

2. Decides that the Sixth Committee shall continue its consideration of the scope and application of the principle of universal jurisdiction, without prejudice to the consideration of related issues in other forums of the United Nations;

3. Decides to include in the provisional agenda of its sixty-fifth session the item entitled "The scope and application of the principle of universal jurisdiction".[40]

The draft resolution was adopted by the Committee without a vote.[41] It was further adopted in the plenary meeting of the sixty-fourth U.N. General Assembly on 16 December 2009.[42]

On 29 July 2010, the U.N. Secretary-General submitted his report in accordance with the above Resolution of the UNGA.[43] The report indicated that responses were received from 44 States, including: Armenia, Australia, Austria, Azerbaijan, Belarus, Belgium, Bolivia, Bulgaria, Cameroon, Chile, China, Costa Rica, Cuba, Cyprus, the Czech Republic, Denmark, El Salvador, Estonia, Ethiopia, Finland, France, Germany, Iraq, Israel, Italy, Kenya, Kuwait, Lebanon, Malaysia, Malta, Mauritius, the Netherlands, New Zealand, Norway, Peru, Portugal, South Korea, Rwanda, Slovenia, South Africa, Sweden, Switzerland, Tunisia and the United States.[44] At its second plenary meeting on 17 September 2010, the sixty-fifth U.N. General Assembly, on the recommendation of the General Committee, decided to include the item of the scope and application of U.J. in its agenda and to allocate it to the Sixth Committee. The Sixth Committee considered the item at its tenth, eleventh, twelfth, twenty-seventh and twenty-eighth meetings, on 13, 14 and 15 October, as well as on 5 and 11 November 2010, respectively. At its tenth meeting on 13 October 2010, representatives of eight States and State groups made statements, including Iran (on behalf of MNACs), Chile (on behalf of Rio Group), Malawi (on behalf of Group of African States), Canada (on behalf of CANZ), Egypt, Guatemala, Belarus and Peru.[45] At its eleventh

---

[40] A/C.6/64/L.18.

[41] A/64/452.

[42] A/64/PV.64; A/64/117.

[43] A/65/181.

[44] The responses from these States are available at http://www.un.org/en/ga/sixth/65/ScopeAppUniJuri.shtml, last accessed on 7 September 2012.

[45] A/C.6/65/SR.10.

meeting on 14 October 2010, representatives of 27 States made statements, including Libya, Rwanda, Norway, Thailand, South Korea, the Czech Republic, Senegal, Spain, Slovenia, China, Algeria, Argentina, the Democratic Republic of the Congo, Cuba, the United States, Belgium, Tanzania, Lebanon, Viet Nam, Finland, Russia, the Netherlands, Ghana, Tunisia, Ethiopia, El Salvador, Germany and South Africa.[46] At its twelfth meeting on 15 October 2010, representatives of 13 States and observers made statements, including Iran, Chile, Israel, Brazil, Sweden, Venezuela, Sudan, Malaysia, the United Kingdom, India, Liechtenstein, Lesotho, Nigeria and the ICRC.[47] On 3 November 2010, Ghana introduced a draft resolution.[48] In contrast with the previous Resolution drafted by Rwanda and adopted in the sixty-fourth UNGA and its Legal Committee, this draft resolution contained some new developments, as explained by the representative of Ghana in the twenty-seventh meeting of the Legal Committee on 5 November 2010, of which two points are notable in the preamble: first, the preamble recognised the diversity of views expressed by States and the need for further consideration towards a better understanding of the topic; second, the preamble noted the view expressed by States that the legitimacy and credibility of the use of universal jurisdiction were best ensured by its responsible and judicious application consistent with international law. In the operative part, paragraph 2 included a decision to establish a working group of the Committee at the forthcoming session. It was understood that the Secretariat would prepare a compilation of treaties and decisions of international tribunals that were relevant to the activities of the working group. In accordance with paragraph 3, the invitation to submit information to the Secretary-General, which had previously been extended to Member States, now included "relevant observers, as appropriate". The phrase should be understood to include Palestine, the Holy See, the ICRC and INTERPOL.[49] This draft resolution was adopted at the twenty-eighth meeting of the Legal Committee of the sixty-fifth UNGA on 11 November 2010,[50] further

---

[46] A/C.6/65/SR.11.

[47] A/C.6/65/SR.12.

[48] A/C.6/65/L.18.

[49] A/C.6/65/SR.27, paras. 37–38.

[50] A/C.6/65/SR.28.

adopted in the fifty-seventh plenary meeting of the sixty-fifth UNGA on 6 December 2010.[51]

On 20 June 2011, the U.N. Secretary-General submitted a second report on the scope and application of the principle of U.J. in accordance with the UNGA Resolution. The report indicated that responses were received from 17 States, including Argentina, Azerbaijan, Bosnia and Herzegovina, Botswana, Colombia, Cyprus, El Salvador, Lebanon, Lithuania, Paraguay, the Philippines, Slovenia, Spain, Sweden, Switzerland and the United Kingdom.[52] Responses were also received from the following observers: the A.U., the Council of Europe, the ILO, the IMO, the Organization for the Prohibition of Chemical Weapons, and the ICRC.[53] The Sixth Committee considered the item at its twelfth, thirteenth, seventeenth and twenty-ninth meetings, on 12 and 21 October, as well as 9 November 2011 respectively. At its twelfth meeting on 12 October 2011, representatives of 28 States and State groups made statements, including Iran (on behalf of MNACs), Chile (on behalf of Rio Group), Australia (on behalf of CANZ), Qatar (on behalf of Arab Group), Kenya (on behalf of Group of African States), Egypt, Switzerland, Norway, Guatemala, Colombia, El Salvador, Peru, Cuba, Sudan, Ethiopia, Russia, the Democratic Republic of the Congo, Swaziland, Belgium, Zambia, Venezuela, Malaysia, Algeria, Senegal, Rwanda, Argentina, Israel and the Czech Republic.[54] At its thirteenth meeting on 12 October 2011, representatives of 20 States and observers made statements, including Sri Lanka, China, South Africa, Sweden, Indonesia, Greece, Chile, the United Kingdom, Finland, Burkina Faso, Kenya, Spain, Ireland, Iran, the Netherlands, the United States, Brazil, Tunisia, Mozambique, South Korea and ICRC.[55] At its seventeenth meeting on 21 October 2011, the Chair of the Working Group on the scope and application of the principle of the U.J. (established at its first meeting on 3 October 2011 by the Sixth Committee) from Costa Rica introduced its work to the Committee. The Working Group had held three meetings, on 13, 14 and

---

[51] A/65/33.

[52] The responses from these States are available at http://www.un.org/en/ga/ sixth/66/ScopeAppUniJuri.shtml, last accessed on 13 October 2012.

[53] A/66/93.

[54] A/C.6/66/SR.12.

[55] A/C.6/66/SR.13.

20 October 2011, conducting its work in the framework of informal con-sultations against the backdrop of the plenary debate at the twelfth and thirteenth meetings of the Sixth Committee on 12 October 2011.[56]

At the twenty-ninth meeting, on 9 November 2011, the representative of the Democratic Republic of the Congo introduced a draft resolution.[57] Operative paragraph 4 was orally revised to read as follows: "4. *Decides* that the Working Group shall be open to all Member States and that relevant observers to the General Assembly will be invited to participate in the work of the Working Group". At the same meeting, the Committee adopted the draft resolution, as orally revised, without a vote. Under the draft resolution, the UNGA would invite Member States and relevant observers, as appropriate, to submit information and observations before 30 April 2012 on the scope and application of U.J., including, where appropriate, information on the relevant applicable international treaties, their domestic legal rules and judicial practice; and would further request the UNGA to prepare and submit to the UNGA, at its sixty-seventh session, a report based on such information and observations. The Assembly would moreover decide that the Sixth Committee shall continue its consideration of the item, without prejudice to the consideration of the topic and related issues in other forums of the UN. For this purpose, a working group of the Sixth Committee would be established at the sixth-seventh session to continue to undertake a thorough discussion of the scope and application of universal jurisdiction. The Assembly would decide that the working group shall be open to all Member States and that relevant observers to the General Assembly be invited to participate in the work of the working group. The draft resolution was adopted by the UNGA on 9 December 2011.[58]

9.4. Common Understanding in the UNGA

The ICJ pointed out in *Nuclear Weapons* case that,

> General Assembly resolutions, even if they are not binding, may sometimes have normative value. They can, in certain circumstances, provide evidence important for establishing the existence of a rule or the emergence of an *opinio juris.*

---

[56] A/C.6/66/SR.17, para. 15.

[57] A/C.6/66/L.19.

[58] A/RES/66/103.

To establish whether this is true of a given General Assembly resolution, it is necessary to look at its content and the conditions of its adoption; it is also necessary to see whether an *opinio juris* exists as to its normative character. Or a series of resolutions may show the gradual evolution of the *opinio juris* required for the establishment of a new rule.[59]

As regards the scope and application of the principle of U.J., the UNGA only adopted three resolutions on this issue in three years 2009–2011.[60] In terms of the content of these three resolutions, no clear and specific merits on the scope and application of the principle of U.J. have been stated in them. Rather, the UNGA simply, on the one hand, "reaffirmed its commitment to the purposes and principles of the Charter of the UN, to international law and to an international order based on the *rule of law*, which is essential for peaceful coexistence and cooperation among States",[61] and on the other hand, "reiterated its commitment to *fighting impunity*, and noting the views expressed by States that the legitimacy and credibility of the use of universal jurisdiction are best ensured by its responsible and judicious application consistent with international law".[62] In terms of the process of adoption of these three resolutions, all three were adopted without vote in the UNGA. Accordingly, it is premature and difficult to see any *opinio juris* on the scope and application of the principle of U.J. from these three resolutions of the UNGA.

Nevertheless, this *status quo* in the resolutions of the UNGA does not prejudice the identification of possible rules in customary international law in this regard. The statements made by States before the Sixth Committee of the UNGA are a good source to know the *opinio juris* of States with regard to such possible rules, and the description of legislative and judicial practices in their responses is an important window to state practice. The ICJ Statute defines customary international law as the rules constituted by "a general practice accepted as law".[63] In the *Nicaragua* case, the ICJ confirmed that a custom is constituted by two elements, the objective one of "a general practice", and the subjective one "accepted as

---

[59] ICJ, *Legality of the Threat or Use of Nuclear Weapons*, Advisory Opinion of 8 July 1996, para. 70.

[60] A/RES/64/117; A/RES/65/33; A/RES/66/103.

[61] A/RES/64/117; A/RES/65/33; A/RES/66/103.

[62] A/RES/65/33; A/RES/66/103.

[63] Statute of the International Court of Justice, in *UNTS*, vol. 33, p. 993.

law", or the so-called *'opinio juris'*.[64] To prove the existence of an international custom both elements must be simultaneously present.

9.4.1. *Opinio Juris*

As far as *opinio juris* is concerned, the statements made before the Sixth Committee is its main evidence. According to my statistics, 74 States have expressed their views on the scope and application of the principle of U.J. through the statements made before the Sixth Committee, covering not only both A.U. and E.U. States, but also States from other continents. As seen from these statements, it is a common denominator that U.J., as a principle of international law on national criminal jurisdiction, is not controversial *per se*. This can be illustrated by the Decision of the A.U. on this principle. The preamble of this decision recognised that "universal jurisdiction is a principle of international law whose purpose is to ensure that individuals who commit grave offences such as war crimes and crimes against humanity do not do so with impunity and are brought to justice, which is in line with Article 4(h) of the Constitutive Act of the African Union".[65] The Explanatory Memorandum of Tanzania on the request to list the issue of U.J. on the agenda of the UNGA also stated that the "principle of universal jurisdiction is well established in international law".[66] The Chair of the Working Group in the Sixth Committee on this issue also pointed out that "no delegation had rejected the concept of universal jurisdiction".[67] He further noted that, "a wide majority of delegations had acknowledged the importance of universal jurisdiction as a tool in the fight against impunity for the most serious crimes against humanity".[68] However, he also underlined that, "the approaches to its meaning, scope and application had been many and varied".[69] This is also reflected

---

[64] ICJ (*Nicaragua v. USA: Military and Paramilitary Activities in and against Nicaragua*), Judgment of 27 June 1986, para. 184, available at http://www.legal-tools.org/doc/046698/.

[65] Decision on the Report of the Commission on the Abuse of the Principle of Universal Jurisdiction, Assembly/AU/Dec.199 (XI), available http://www.africa-union.org/root/au/conferences/2008/june/summit/dec/ASSEMBLY%20DECISIONS%20193%20-%20207%20(XI).pdf, last accessed on 7 September 2012.

[66] A/63/237/Rev.1, Annex, para. 1.

[67] A/C.6/66/SR.17, para. 18.

[68] *Ibid.*

[69] *Ibid.*

---

in the preamble of the resolutions of the UNGA in 2010 and 2011. Both recognised "diversity of views expressed by States and the need for further consideration towards a better understanding of the scope and application of universal jurisdiction".[70] Nevertheless, it is still possible to examine each point involving U.J. which have been made by delegates of States, State groups or observers one by one.

9.4.1.1. Definition of Universal Jurisdiction

Of the 74 States that have made statements on the scope and application of principle of U.J. before the Sixth Committee, 49 States did not make a statement on the definition of U.J.; four States said that there is no well-recognised definition of U.J.;[71] and 21 States expressed their understandings of definition of U.J. Of these 21 States, 19 said that U.J. is a form of criminal jurisdiction that can be exercised even if the forum State has no link in territory (place of crime), nationality (of suspect or victim), or special state interest with the crimes concerned.[72] Only the U.S. and the Democratic Republic of the Congo pointed out that U.J. is based on the presence of the suspect in the territory of the forum State, although they agreed that the forum State does not need to have a link of territory (place of crime), nationality (of suspect or victim), or special state interest with the crimes concerned.[73] It can therefore be said that the common under-

---

[70]   A/RES/65/33; A/RES/66/103.

[71]   Those four States and State groups which stated that there is no well-recognised definition of U.J. included France (A/C.6/64/SR.12, para. 76), Malawi (on behalf of Group of African States) (A/C.6/65/SR.10, para. 60), Norway (A/C.6/65/SR.11, para. 7), and Ethiopia (A/C.6/66/SR.12, para. 39).

[72]   Australia (on behalf of CANS) (A/C.6/64/SR.12, para. 10; A/C.6/66/SR.12, para. 6); Switzerland (A/C.6/64/SR.12, para. 22); El Salvador (A/C.6/64/SR.12, para. 25); South Africa (A/C.6/64/SR.12, para. 39); Austria (A/C.6/64/SR.12, para. 79); Malaysia (A/C.6/64/SR.13, para. 37); Canada (on behalf of CANS) (A/C.6/65/SR.10, para. 63); Belarus (A/C.6/65/SR.10, para. 74); South Korea (A/C.6/65/SR.11, para. 13); Belgium (A/C.6/65/SR.11, para. 41); Russia (A/C.6/65/SR.11, para. 56; A/C.6/66/SR.12, para. 41); Venezuela (A/C.6/65/SR.12, para. 19; A/C.6/66/SR.12, para. 57); U.K. (A/C.6/65/SR.12, para. 30; A/C.6/66/SR.13, para. 24); Lesotho (A/C.6/65/SR.12, para. 38); Colombia (A/C.6/66/SR.12, para. 26); Greece (A/C.6/66/SR.13, para. 16); Burkina Faso (A/C.6/66/SR.13, para. 30); Ireland (A/C.6/66/SR.13, para. 40); Mozambique (A/C.6/66/SR.13, para. 57).

[73]   U.S. (A/C.6/64/SR.13, para. 24; A/C.6/65/SR.11, para. 37; A/C.6/66/SR.13, para. 48); the Democratic Republic of the Congo (A/C.6/65/SR.11, para. 29).

standing or maximum common denominator of definition of U.J. among those 21 States is that the forum State does not need any link of territory (place of crime), nationality (of suspect or victim), or special state interest with the crimes concerned.

In order to further clarify the definition of U.J., the following points have been made in the discussions of the Sixth Committee. First, with regard to the nature of U.J., a couple of States said that U.J. could play a role in both criminal and civil law,[74] but more States considered U.J. as a form of jurisdiction in criminal law, or requested to focus the discussion in the Sixth Committee on criminal law.[75]

Second, with regard to the relationship between U.J. and jurisdiction of international criminal courts or tribunals, a few States said that U.J. is also a form of jurisdiction of international criminal courts or tribunals, in particular the International Criminal Court ('ICC'),[76] but many more States said that U.J. shall not be confused with the jurisdiction of international criminal courts or tribunals, including the ICC.[77]

Third, with regard to the relationship between U.J. and *aut dedere aut judicare* (or the obligation to extradite or prosecute), a diversity of views has been presented. Some States said that U.J. shall not be confused with *aut dedere aut judicare* because they are different from each other.[78]

---

[74] Costa Rica (A/C.6/64/SR.12, para. 29).

[75] Austria (A/C.6/64/SR.12, para. 80); U.S. (A/C.6/64/SR.13, para. 24; A/C.6/64/SR.13, para. 37; A/C.6/66/SR.13, para. 48); Peru (A/C.6/65/SR.10, para. 80; *cf.* A/C.6/66/SR.12, para. 33).

[76] El Salvador (A/C.6/64/SR.12, para. 26); Ghana (A/C.6/65/SR.11, para. 65).

[77] Australia (on behalf of CANZ) (A/C.6/64/SR.12, para. 9); Mexico (A/C.6/64/SR.12, para. 18); South Africa (A/C.6/64/SR.12, para. 39); Kenya (A/C.6/64/SR.12, para. 62); Slovakia (A/C.6/64/SR.12, para. 64); Thailand (A/C.6/64/SR.12, para. 68; A/C.6/65/SR.11, para. 11); Peru (A/C.6/64/SR.12, para. 69; A/C.6/65/SR.10, para. 78); France (A/C.6/64/SR.12, para. 78); Austria (A/C.6/64/SR.12, para. 80); Finland (A/C.6/64/SR.12, para. 89; A/C.6/65/SR.11, para. 51); Slovenia (A/C.6/64/SR.12, para. 97); U.K. (A/C.6/64/SR.13, para. 6; A/C.6/65/SR.12, para. 30); Liechtenstein (A/C.6/64/SR.13, para. 29; A/C.6/65/SR.12, para. 37); Rwanda (A/C.6/64/SR.13, para. 31); Togo (A/C.6/64/SR.13, para. 35); Chile (on behalf of Rio Group) (A/C.6/65/SR.10, para. 57; A/C.6/66/SR.12, para. 4); Guatemala (A/C.6/65/SR.10, para. 71); Colombia (A/C.6/66/SR.12, para. 27); Cuba (A/C.6/66/SR.12, para. 34); Russia (A/C.6/66/SR.12, para. 42); Venezuela (A/C.6/66/SR.12, para. 59).

[78] China (A/C.6/64/SR.12, para. 48; A/C.6/65/SR.11, para. 25; A/C.6/66/SR.13, para. 5); Austria (A/C.6/64/SR.12, para. 82); Malaysia (A/C.6/64/SR.13, para. 37); Chile (A/C.6/65/SR.10, para. 57); Peru (A/C.6/65/SR.10, para. 78); Thailand (A/C.6/65/

They even explained how they differ. For example, China said (*aut dedere aut judicare*) is a treaty obligation applicable only to States Parties to the instrument in question. Such treaties always set out the specific conditions under which the obligation applied, and those conditions differed from one treaty to another.[79] Thailand said U.J. is a basis for jurisdiction only and did not itself imply an obligation to submit a case for potential prosecution. In that sense, universal jurisdiction was quite distinct from the obligation to extradite or prosecute, which is primarily a treaty obligation whose implementation is subject to conditions and limitations set out in a particular treaty containing the obligation. Any attempt to exercise treaty-based criminal jurisdiction against a non-State Party would therefore have no legal basis.[80] Israel said that the existence in an international treaty of an obligation to extradite or prosecute does not imply that a given offence amounts to a serious crime under international law that is necessarily subject to U.J.[81] Australia (on behalf of CANZ) said that the obligation to extradite or prosecute is usually a mandatory one, imposed by convention, whereas U.J. functions as an entitlement.[82] Malaysia said that *aut dedere aut judicare* does not in itself establish U.J. for a treaty-based offence any more than the inclusion of such a provision in domestic extradition legislation or bilateral extradition treaties would do.[83] While some States admitted that U.J. is different from *aut dedere aut judicare*, they highlighted that they a have mutual link or partly overlap.[84] For example, South Korea observed that if a State is a signatory to treaties containing the obligation to prosecute or extradite, it might exercise jurisdic-

SR.11, para. 10); South Korea (A/C.6/65/SR.11, para. 14; A/C.6/66/SR.13, para. 58); Sweden (A/C.6/65/SR.12, para. 15); Venezuela (A/C.6/65/SR.12, para. 19; A/C.6/66/SR.12, para. 59); Argentina (A/C.6/65/SR.11, para. 27; A/C.6/66/SR.12, para. 72); Malaysia (A/C.6/65/SR.12, para. 29; A/C.6/66/SR.12, para. 62); U.K. (A/C.6/65/SR.12, para. 30); India (A/C.6/65/SR.12, para. 34); Chile (on behalf of Rio Group) (A/C.6/66/SR.12, para. 4); Australia (on behalf of CANZ) (A/C.6/66/SR.12, para. 7); Colombia (A/C.6/ 66/SR.12, para. 27); Cuba (A/C.6/66/SR.12, para. 34); Israel (A/C.6/66/SR.12, para. 75).

[79] A/C.6/64/SR.12, para. 48; A/C.6/65/SR.11, para. 25; A/C.6/66/SR.13, para. 5.

[80] A/C.6/65/SR.11, para. 10.

[81] A/C.6/65/SR.12, para. 9; A/C.6/66/SR.12, para. 75.

[82] A/C.6/66/SR.12, para. 7; see also Colombia (A/C.6/ 66/SR.12, para. 27).

[83] A/C.6/65/SR.12, para. 29; A/C.6/66/SR.12, para. 62.

[84] Thailand (A/C.6/64/SR.12, para. 66); Finland (A/C.6/64/SR.12, para. 90); Czech Republic (A/C.6/65/SR.11, para. 17).

tion over a crime otherwise entirely unrelated to it.[85] Argentina stated that the two principles are not identical, but there is some overlap where a State unconnected with an offence other than through the mere presence of the offender in its territory decides, in accordance with the *aut dedere aut judicare* principle, not to grant extradition but to prosecute solely on the basis of U.J.[86] Sweden said that states would not have that an obligation if they lacked jurisdiction, and the obligation is therefore inextricably linked with U.J.[87] There were also a few States which simply said that the relationship between U.J. and *aut dedere aut judicare* needs to be carefully considered.[88]

9.4.1.2. Rationale of Universal Jurisdiction

Many States made statements on the rationale of U.J. The absolute majority of these States held the view that U.J. is valuable for the international community in the fight against impunity.[89] Some States highlighted that it

---

[85] A/C.6/65/SR.11, para. 14; A/C.6/66/SR.13, para. 58.

[86] A/C.6/66/SR.12, para. 72.

[87] A/C.6/66/SR.13, para. 11.

[88] Indonesia (A/C.6/64/SR.13, para.1); Russia (A/C.6/64/SR.13, para. 16); Israel (A/C.6/64/SR.13, para. 18); Guatemala (A/C.6/65/SR.10, para. 73).

[89] Australia (on behalf of CANZ) (A/C.6/64/SR.12, para. 10; A/C.6/66/SR.12, para. 6); Switzerland (A/C.6/64/SR.12, para. 22; A/C.6/66/SR.12, para. 16); El Salvador (A/C.6/64/SR.12, para. 25; A/C.6/65/SR.11, para. 72); Costa Rica (A/C.6/64/SR.12, para. 27); South Africa (A/C.6/64/SR.12, para. 38; A/C.6/66/SR 13, para. 8); Democratic Republic of the Congo (A/C.6/64/SR.12, para. 52; A/C.6/65/SR.11, para. 29; A/C.6/66/SR.12, para. 46); Guatemala (A/C.6/64/SR.12, para. 58; A/C.6/66/SR.12, para. 22); Kenya (A/C.6/64/SR.12, para. 61; A/C.6/66/SR.12, para. 13; A/C.6/66/SR.13, para. 34); Slovakia (A/C.6/64/SR.12, para. 64); Thailand (A/C.6/64/SR.12, para. 66); Peru (A/C.6/64/SR.12, para. 69; A/C.6/65/SR.10, para. 78; A/C.6/66/SR.12, para. 33); Norway (A/C.6/64/SR.12, para. 72; A/C.6/65/SR.11, para. 6; A/C.6/66/SR.12, para. 19); France (A/C.6/64/SR.12, para. 76); Austria (A/C.6/64/SR.12, para. 81); Germany (A/C.6/64/SR.12, para. 85; A/C.6/65/SR.11, para. 73); Finland (A/C.6/64/SR.12, para. 89; A/C.6/65/SR.11, para. 54; A/C.6/66/SR.13, para. 29); Slovenia (A/C.6/64/SR.12, para. 97; A/C.6/65/SR.11, para. 24); Tunisia (A/C.6/64/SR.12, para. 99; A/C.6/65/SR.11, para. 69; A/C.6/66/SR.13, para. 54); Belgium (A/C.6/64/SR.12, para. 102; A/C.6/65/SR.11, para. 41; A/C.6/66/SR.12, para. 52); Libya (A/C.6/64/SR.12, para. 105; A/C.6/65/SR.11, para. 1); Indonesia (A/C.6/64/SR.13, para. 1; A/C.6/66/SR.13, para. 10); Iran (A/C.6/64/SR.13, para. 5); U.K. (A/C.6/64/SR.13, para. 7; A/C.6/66/SR.13, para. 24); Algeria (A/C.6/64/SR.13, para. 8; A/C.6/65/SR.11, para. 26); Spain (A/C.6/64/SR.13, para. 9; A/C.6/66/SR.13, para. 37); Russia (A/C.6/64/SR.13, para. 14; A/C.6/65/SR.11, para. 57; A/C.6/66/SR.12, para. 41); Liechtens-

is the heinous nature of the crimes concerned that make U.J. acceptable under international law.[90] There were also some States which said that U.J. is also conducive to redressing the plight of victims of those heinous crimes.[91] Therefore, the benefit to the fight against impunity could be considered a common understanding of the rationale of U.J. among the States that have made statements before the Sixth Committee.

tein (A/C.6/64/SR.13, para. 26; A/C.6/65/SR.12, para. 35); Rwanda (A/C.6/64/SR.13, para. 32; A/C.6/65/SR.11, para. 4; A/C.6/66/SR.12, para. 69); Togo (A/C.6/64/SR.13, para. 35); Malaysia (A/C.6/64/SR.13, para. 37); Italy (A/C.6/64/SR.13, para. 46); Ethiopia (A/C.6/64/SR.13, para. 47; A/C.6/66/SR.12, para. 38); Chile (on behalf of Rio Group) (A/C.6/65/SR.10, para. 57; A/C.6/66/SR.12, para. 4); Malawi (on behalf of Group of African States) (A/C.6/65/SR.10, para. 61); Canada (on behalf of CANZ) (A/C.6/65/SR.10, para. 63); Egypt (A/C.6/65/SR.10, para. 69; A/C.6/66/SR.12, para. 15); Guatemala (A/C.6/65/SR.10, para. 70); Belarus (A/C.6/65/SR.10, para. 74); South Korea (A/C.6/65/SR.11, para. 13; A/C.6/66/SR.13, para. 58); the Czech Republic (A/C.6/65/SR.11, para. 16); Argentina (A/C.6/65/SR.11, para. 27; A/C.6/66/ SR.12, para. 76); Viet Nam (A/C.6/65/SR.11, para. 46); Ghana (A/C.6/65/SR.11, para. 63); Chile (A/C.6/65/SR.12, para. 6; A/C.6/66/SR.13, para. 21); India (A/C.6/65/ SR.12, para. 34); Lesotho (A/C.6/65/SR.12, para. 38); Nigeria (A/C.6/65/SR.12, para. 40); Iran (on behalf of MNACs) (A/C.6/66/SR.12, para. 2); Qatar (A/C.6/66/SR.12, para. 10); Sudan (A/C.6/66/SR.12, para. 35); Zambia (A/C.6/66/SR.12, para. 54); Senegal (A/C.6/66/SR.12, para. 67); Sweden (A/C.6/66/SR.13, para. 10); Greece (A/C. 6/66/SR.13, para. 16); Burkina Faso (A/C.6/66/SR.13, para. 31); Ireland (A/C.6/66/ SR.13, para. 41); the Netherlands (A/C.6/66/SR.13, para. 46); Brazil (A/C.6/66/SR. 13, para. 49); Mozambique (A/C.6/66/SR.13, para. 57); the ICRC (A/C.6/66/SR.13, para. 64).

[90] Australia (on behalf of CANZ) (A/C.6/64/SR.12, para. 10); Mexico (on behalf of the Rio Group) (A/C.6/64/SR.12, para. 18); Switzerland (A/C.6/64/SR.12, para. 22); El Salvador (A/C.6/64/SR.12, para. 25); Kenya (A/C.6/64/SR.12, para. 61); Thailand (A/C.6/64/SR.12, para. 66); Norway (A/C.6/64/SR.12, para. 72; A/C.6/65/SR.11, para. 6); France (A/C.6/64/SR.12, para. 76); Germany (A/C.6/64/SR.12, para. 85); Slovenia (A/C.6/64/SR.12, para. 97; A/C.6/65/SR.11, para. 24); Mexico (A/C.6/64/ SR.13, para. 12); Liechtenstein (A/C.6/64/SR.13, para. 26); Egypt (A/C.6/65/SR.10, para. 69; A/C.6/66/SR.12, para. 15); Belarus (A/C.6/65/SR.10, para. 74); Venezuela (A/C.6/65/SR.12, para. 19); Malaysia (A/C.6/66/SR.12, para. 61); Indonesia (A/C.6/ 66/SR.13, para. 10); Brazil (A/C.6/66/SR.13, para. 49).

[91] Slovenia (A/C.6/64/SR.12, para. 97; A/C.6/65/SR.11, para. 24); Germany (A/C.6/64/ SR.12, para. 85); Belgium (A/C.6/64/SR.12, para. 102); Sweden (A/C.6/66/SR.13, para. 10).

9.4.1.3. Crimes Subject to Universal Jurisdiction

Determining which crimes are subject to U.J. has been one of the most controversial issues. Many of the States that have made statements on scope and application of U.J. have expressed their views on which crimes can be subject to U.J. As of the sixty-sixth UNGA session, 41 States, State groups and observers have expressed their views on the crimes subject to U.J. The following table was made to list the crimes which those States, State groups and observers said fall within the scope of U.J.

No.	States	Piracy	Slavery	Genocide	CAH	War Crimes	Torture	Terrorism	Hijacking	Aggression	Source
1.	Australia (CANZ)	X	X	X	X	X	X				A/C.6/64/SR. 12, para. 10
2.	Costa Rica			X	X	X	X				A/C.6/64/SR. 12, para. 29
3.	South Africa	X	X	X	X	X					A/C.6/64/SR. 12, para. 43
4.	China	X									A/C.6/64/SR. 12, para. 48
5.	DRC			X	X	X	X				A/C.6/64/SR. 12, para. 54
6.	Kenya	X		X	X	X					A/C.6/64/SR. 12, para. 61
7.	Slovakia	X	X	X	X	X	X				A/C.6/64/SR. 12, para. 64
8.	Thailand	X	X						X		A/C.6/64/SR. 12, para. 67
9.	Austria	X		X	X	X	X				A/C.6/64/SR. 12, para. 81

10.	Germany			X	X	X			A/C.6/64/SR. 12, para. 85
11.	Sudan	X	X						A/C.6/64/SR. 12, para. 95;
12.	Slovenia	X	X	X	X	X	X		A/C.6/64/SR. 12, para. 96
13.	Belgium			X	X	X	X		A/C.6/64/SR. 12, para. 102
14.	Burkina Faso	X	X						A/C.6/64/SR. 13, para. 23
15.	U.S.	X		X			X	X	A/C.6/64/SR. 13, para. 25
16.	Liechtenstein			X	X	X	X		A/C.6/64/SR. 13, para. 26
17.	Senegal	X			X	X	X		A/C.6/64/SR. 13, para. 38
18.	Malawi (GAS)	X	X						A/C.6/65/SR. 10, para. 60
19.	Egypt			X	X	X	X		A/C.6/65/SR. 10, para. 68
20.	Belarus	X	X	X	X	X		X	A/C.6/65/SR. 10, para. 75
21.	Cuba					X			A/C.6/65/SR. 11, para. 35
22.	Russia	X		X		X			A/C.6/65/SR. 11, para. 56
23.	Ghana	X	X						A/C.6/65/SR. 11, para. 62

24.	El Salvador	X		X	X	X		A/C.6/65/SR. 11, para. 71
25.	Chile	X		X	X	X		A/C.6/65/SR. 12, para. 6
26.	Sweden			X	X	X	X	A/C.6/65/SR. 12, para. 15
27.	Malaysia	X				X		A/C.6/65/SR. 12, para. 27
28.	U.K.	X				X		A/C.6/65/SR. 12, para. 31
29.	Lesotho			X	X	X		A/C.6/65/SR. 12, para. 38
30.	ICRC					X		A/C.6/65/SR. 12, para. 42
31.	Kenya (GAS)			X	X	X		A/C.6/66/SR. 12, para. 12
32.	Colombia			X	X	X		A/C.6/66/SR. 12, para. 27
33.	Zambia			X		X	X	A/C.6/66/SR. 12, para. 54
34.	Algeria	X	X	X	X	X	X	A/C.6/66/SR. 12, para. 66
35.	Sri Lanka	X		X	X	X	X	A/C.6/66/SR. 13, para. 1
36.	Indonesia	X						A/C.6/66/SR. 13, para. 14
37.	Greece	X						A/C.6/66/SR. 13, para. 16

38.	Ireland				X	X				A/C.6/66/SR. 13, para. 40
39.	Iran	X									A/C.6/66/SR. 13, para. 42
40.	Mozambique			X	X	X					A/C.6/66/SR. 13, para. 57
41.	South Korea	X				X					A/C.6/66/SR. 13, para. 58
		26	11	25	23	31	16	1	1	1	

Note: CAH = crimes against humanity; CANZ = Canada, Australia, and New Zealand; GAS = Group of African States; ICRC = International Committee of the Red Cross.

The table shows that the most well-recognised crimes subject to U.J. by the 41 States, State groups and observers are war crimes (31), piracy (26), genocide (25), and crimes against humanity (23). Since piracy is an international crime that has been unanimously accepted by the international community as falling within the scope of U.J., I assume the States, State groups and observers which did not mention piracy in their statements also accept piracy. Several States or State groups only mentioned piracy and did not mention genocide, crimes against humanity and war crimes. They pointed out that genocide, crimes against humanity and war crimes do not fall within the scope of U.J. For example, China said that apart from piracy there is no unanimity among States and therefore no established customary law about which crimes are subject to universal jurisdiction.[92] Ghana observed that there is a growing corpus of international standards aimed at combating impunity for such offences as torture, human trafficking, crimes against humanity, war crimes and genocide, and that some has wrongly interpreted that welcome trend as justifying the exercise under customary law of universal jurisdiction over those crimes.[93] Sudan stated that there is a misconception that if States are sig-

---

[92] A/C.6/65/SR.11, para. 25.
[93] A/C.6/65/SR.11, para. 63.

natories to the Universal Declaration of Human Rights and parties to the Convention on the Prevention and Punishment of the Crime of Genocide and the Convention against Torture and Other Cruel, Inhuman or Degrading Treatment or Punishment, their citizens are automatically subject to the principle of universal jurisdiction. Not only is that contention academically and intellectually false, it also ignores the noble intentions of the drafters of those instruments who had believed that they were stating general principles rather than enacting laws that would be enforced by national courts against the citizens of other States.[94]

Against this background, it can be safely deduced from the statements made by the 41 States, State groups and observers that piracy falls within the scope of U.J., and that there is disagreement among these States as to whether genocide, crimes against humanity and war crimes also fall within the scope of U.J.

9.4.1.4. Preconditions to the Exercise of Universal Jurisdiction

Several preconditions to the exercise of U.J. have been discussed before the Sixth Committee of the UNGA since 2009. The first precondition is whether it is necessary for the suspect of the crimes concerned to be present in the territory of the forum State in order to exercise U.J. In this regard, 15 States and State groups said that the suspect must be present in order to exercise U.J.[95] Costa Rica even said that so-called 'absolute universal jurisdiction', whereby trials are conducted in the absence of the accused, and imposition of the death penalty should be prohibited.[96] No State or State groups clearly said that the suspect does not need to be present. While the Netherlands said she also requires the presence of the suspect in her territory in order to exercise U.J., further research could be

---

[94] A/C.6/64/SR.12, para. 95.

[95] Australia (on behalf of CANZ) (A/C.6/64/SR.12, para. 11); Switzerland (A/C.6/64/SR.12, para. 23); Costa Rica (A/C.6/64/SR.12, para. 27); Peru (A/C.6/64/SR.12, para. 70); France (A/C.6/64/SR.12, para. 77); Iran (A/C.6/64/SR.13, para. 4; A/C.6/65/SR.12, para. 5; A/C.6/66/SR.13, para. 43); Israel (A/C.6/64/SR.13, para. 21; A/C.6/65/SR.12, para. 10; A/C.6/66/SR.12, para. 75); U.S. (A/C.6/64/SR.13, para. 24); Canada (on behalf of CANZ) (A/C.6/65/SR.10, para. 66); Egypt (A/C.6/65/SR.11, para. 14); Spain (A/C.6/65/SR.11, para. 21); the Democratic Republic of the Congo (A/C.6/65/SR.11, para. 29); the Netherlands (A/C.6/65/SR.11, para. 60; A/C.6/66/SR.13, para. 46); Ethiopia (A/C.6/66/SR.12, para. 40); Greece (A/C.6/66/SR.13, para. 17).

[96] A/C.6/64/SR.12, para. 27.

---

done on this point.[97] Considering the very limited number of States and State groups that has expressed a position on this point and its importance it is still too early to say that there has up to now been a common understanding on this point among the 74 States, State groups and observers before the Sixth Committee.

The second precondition is whether the exercise of U.J. shall be subsidiary, complementary or residual to criminal jurisdiction of other States, including territorial jurisdiction of the State where the crimes concerned have been committed, active personality jurisdiction of the State whose national is a suspect of the crimes concerned, or passive personality jurisdiction of the State whose national is a victim of the crimes concerned, as well as even the ICC. In this regard, 35 States, State groups and observers made statements in the affirmative.[98] No State, State groups or observers object to the principle of subsidiary or complementarity. Accordingly, it can be said that to observe this principle is almost one of common understandings of the 74 States, State groups and observers which made statements on scope and application of U.J. before the Sixth Committee.

---

[97] A/C.6/65/SR.11, para. 60; A/C.6/66/SR.13, para. 46.

[98] Australia (on behalf of CANZ) (A/C.6/64/SR.12, para. 11; A/C.6/66/SR.12, para. 6); Costa Rica (A/C.6/64/SR.12, para. 29); Kenya (A/C.6/64/SR.12, para. 61; A/C.6/66/SR.13, para. 34); Germany (A/C.6/64/SR.12, para. 86); Belgium (A/C.6/64/SR.12, para. 102); the United Kingdom (A/C.6/64/SR.13, para. 6; A/C.6/65/SR.12, para. 32); Algeria (A/C.6/64/SR.13, para. 8); Spain (A/C.6/64/SR.13, para. 10); Liechtenstein (A/C.6/64/SR.13, para. 26; A/C.6/65/SR.12, para. 35); Canada (on behalf of CANZ) (A/C.6/65/SR.10, para. 64); Egypt (A/C.6/65/SR.10, para. 68); Guatemala (A/C.6/65/SR.10, para. 70); Peru (A/C.6/65/SR.10, para. 78; A/C.6/66/SR.12, para. 33); Norway (A/C.6/65/SR.11, para. 6); Slovenia (A/C.6/65/SR.11, para. 23); Algeria (A/C.6/65/SR.11, para. 26; A/C.6/66/SR.12, para. 65); Cuba (A/C.6/65/SR.11, para. 36); Viet Nam (A/C.6/65/SR.11, para. 46); Tunisia (A/C.6/65/SR.11, para. 69); Chile (A/C.6/65/SR.12, para. 7; A/C.6/66/SR.13, para. 20); Israel (A/C.6/65/SR.12, para. 10; A/C.6/66/SR.12, para. 75); the ICRC (A/C.6/65/SR.12, para. 42; A/C.6/66/SR.13, para. 64); Qatar (on behalf of Arab Group) (A/C.6/66/SR.12, para. 9); Colombia (A/C.6/66/SR.12, para. 26); El Salvador (A/C.6/66/SR.12, para. 31); Sudan (A/C.6/66/SR.12, para. 36); Ethiopia (A/C.6/66/SR.12, para. 38); Argentina (A/C.6/66/SR.12, para. 71); Sri Lanka (A/C.6/66/SR.13, para. 3); Indonesia (A/C.6/66/SR.13, para. 13); Greece (A/C.6/66/SR.13, para. 17); Finland (A/C.6/66/SR.13, para. 27); Iran (A/C.6/66/SR. 13, para. 43); Brazil (A/C.6/66/SR.13, para. 49).

The third precondition issue is whether the exercise of U.J. shall not violate fundamental principles of international law, including the equality of State sovereignty, the non-intervention in the internal affairs of other States, and the immunity of high officials from foreign criminal jurisdictions. Thirty-seven States and State groups said that the fundamental principles including equality of State sovereignty and non-intervention in internal affairs shall not be ignored in the exercise of U.J., almost all of them are from Africa, Asia and Latin America.[99] No State, State groups or observers said that such fundamental principles can be violated. With regard to the specific rule of immunity of high officials, 32 States and State groups said that the immunity of high officials from foreign criminal jurisdiction shall be respected in the exercise of U.J., almost all are from Africa, Asia and Latin America.[100] While seven States and State groups

---

[99] Tunisia (on behalf of Group of African States) (A/C.6/64/SR.12, para. 14); Iran (on behalf of Movement of Non-Alignment Countries) (A/C.6/64/SR.12, para. 20; A/C.6/65/SR.10, para. 55; A/C.6/66/SR.12, para. 1); Sudan (A/C.6/64/SR.12, para. 93; A/C.6/66/SR.12, para. 35); Tunisia (A/C.6/64/SR.12, para. 101; A/C.6/65/SR.11, para. 69; A/C.6/66/SR.13, para. 54); Lebanon (A/C.6/64/SR.12, para. 104); Indonesia (A/C.6/64/SR.13, para. 1); Iran (A/C.6/64/SR.13, para. 2); Algeria (A/C.6/64/SR.13, para. 8; A/C.6/66/SR.12, para. 65); Russia (A/C.6/64/SR.13, para. 14; A/C.6/65/SR.11, para. 57); Togo (A/C.6/64/SR.13, para. 35); Senegal (A/C.6/64/SR.13, para. 40; A/C.6/65/SR.11, para. 19); Ethiopia (A/C.6/64/SR.13, para. 47; A/C.6/66/SR.12, para. 38); Malawi (on behalf of Group of African States) (A/C.6/65/SR.10, para. 59); Egypt (A/C.6/65/SR.10, para. 69); Belarus (A/C.6/65/SR.10, para. 76); Libya (A/C.6/65/SR.11, para. 1); China (A/C.6/65/SR.11, para. 25); Cuba (A/C.6/65/SR.11, para. 34); Viet Nam (A/C.6/65/SR.11, para. 46); Iran (A/C.6/65/SR.12, para. 4; A/C.6/66/SR.13, para. 44); Venezuela (A/C.6/65/SR.12, para. 18; A/C.6/66/SR.12, para. 57); Qatar (on behalf of Arab Group) (A/C.6/66/SR.12, para. 11); Kenya (on behalf of Group of African States) (A/C.6/66/SR.12, para. 12); Egypt (A/C.6/66/SR.12, para. 15); Colombia (A/C.6/66/SR.12, para. 28); Swaziland (A/C.6/66/SR.12, para. 49); Zambia (A/C.6/66/SR.12, para. 55); Malaysia (A/C.6/66/SR.12, para. 63); Senegal (A/C.6/66/SR.12, para. 68); Argentina (A/C.6/66/SR.12, para. 71); Sri Lanka (A/C.6/66/SR.13, para. 1); South Africa (A/C.6/66/SR.13, para. 8); Greece (A/C.6/66/SR.13, para. 17); Burkina Faso (A/C.6/66/SR.13, para. 30); Kenya (A/C.6/66/SR.13, para. 35); Brazil (A/C.6/66/SR.13, para. 49); Mozambique (A/C.6/66/SR.13, para. 56).

[100] Tunisia (on behalf of Group of African States) (A/C.6/64/SR.12, para. 14); Iran (on behalf of MNACs) (A/C.6/64/SR.12, para. 20; A/C.6/65/SR.10, para. 55; A/C.6/66/SR.12, para. 1); China (A/C.6/64/SR.12, para. 48; A/C.6/65/SR.11, para. 25; A/C.6/66/SR.13, para. 5); South Africa (A/C.6/64/SR.12, para. 55; A/C.6/66/SR.13, para. 8); Sudan (A/C.6/64/SR.12, para. 94; A/C.6/65/SR.12, para. 22; A/C.6/66/SR.12, para. 37); Tunisia (A/C.6/64/SR.12, para. 101); Lebanon (A/C.6/64/SR.12, para. 104); Indonesia (A/C.6/64/SR.13, para. 1); Iran (A/C.6/64/SR.13, para. 5; A/C.6/65/SR.12,

said that the issue of immunity is a separate issue which has been and shall be dealt with by the International Law Commission in Geneva, though they agreed that it should be respected.[101] In such a situation, it can be said that it is a common understanding that national courts, while exercising U.J., shall respect the immunity of high officials from jurisdiction under international law, regardless of whether the immunity issue is separate from U.J.

9.4.1.5. Establishment of an International Regulatory Body

The proposal to establish an international regulatory body was put forward by the eleventh Assembly of A.U. in 2008, and was introduced to the UNGA by Tanzania on behalf of Group of African States on 29 June 2009.[102] As of 2011, five States expressed their consent to such a proposal, most of them are African States.[103] However, this proposal was rejected by nine European States on the grounds that it will jeopardise the principle of the independence of the judiciary. They prefer to settle disputes arising from the exercise of U.J. through the present institutions,

---

para. 4; A/C.6/66/SR.13, para. 45); Spain (A/C.6/64/SR.13, para. 9); Russia (A/C. 6/64/SR.13, para. 14; A/C.6/66/SR.12, para. 43); Togo (A/C.6/64/SR.13, para. 35); Senegal (A/C.6/64/SR.13, para. 39; A/C.6/65/SR.11, para. 19; A/C.6/66/SR.12, para. 68); Ethiopia (A/C.6/64/SR.13, para. 47; A/C.6/66/SR.12, para. 40); Malawi (on behalf of Group of African States) (A/C.6/65/SR.10, para. 59); Egypt (A/C.6/65/SR.10, para. 69); Belarus (A/C.6/65/SR.10, para. 76); Libya (A/C.6/65/SR.11, para. 1); Algeria (A/C.6/65/SR.11, para. 26; A/C.6/66/SR.12, para. 65); the Democratic Republic of the Congo (A/C.6/65/SR.11, para. 32); Cuba (A/C.6/65/SR.11, para. 34; A/C.6/66/SR.12, para. 34); Viet Nam (A/C.6/65/SR.11, para. 46); Ghana (A/C.6/65/SR.11, para. 66); Venezuela (A/C.6/65/SR.12, para. 20; A/C.6/66/SR.12, para. 59); Kenya (on behalf of Group of African States) (A/C.6/66/SR.12, para. 12); Colombia (A/C.6/66/SR.12, para. 29); Peru (A/C.6/66/SR.12, para. 33); Swaziland (A/C.6/66/SR.12, para. 51); Zambia (A/C.6/66/SR.12, para. 56); Sri Lanka (A/C.6/66/SR.13, para. 1); Brazil (A/C.6/66/SR.13, para. 51); Mozambique (A/C.6/66/SR.13, para. 56).

[101] France (A/C.6/64/SR.12, para. 78); Austria (A/C.6/64/SR.12, para. 82); Finland (A/C. 6/64/SR.12, para. 90); Canada (on behalf of CANZ)(A/C.6/65/SR.10, para. 67); Norway (A/C.6/65/SR.11, para. 8; A/C.6/66/SR.12, para. 21); Belgium (A/C.6/65/SR.11, para. 42; A/C.6/66/SR.12, para. 53); Sweden (A/C.6/65/SR.12, para. 17).

[102] See Section 9.2.

[103] Swaziland (A/C.6/64/SR.12, para. 34); Sudan (A/C.6/64/SR.12, para. 95); Rwanda (A/C.6/65/SR.11, para. 5); Algeria (A/C.6/65/SR.11, para. 26; A/C.6/66/SR.66); Chile (A/C.6/65/SR.12, para. 8; A/C.6/66/SR.13, para. 23).

such as the ICJ.[104] Therefore, it seems that this proposal is one of the most controversial points, especially between African and European States. In such a situation, it can be said that there was no common understanding on whether it is necessary to establish such a body.

9.4.2. State Practice

Even if arguably *opinio juris* on the definition, scope and application of U.J. has been formalised from the available materials provided by the States, State groups or observers in the Sixth Committee, a customary rule of international law could not be found without the support of state practice. As the ICJ put in the *Nicaragua* case,

> [t]he mere fact that States declare their recognition of certain rules is not sufficient for the Court to consider these as being part of customary international law [...] Bound as it is by Article 38 of its Statute [...] the Court must satisfy itself that the existence of the rule in the *opinio iuris* of States is confirmed by practice.[105]

As far as U.J. is concerned, the most important state practice is the legislative and judicial practices of States. In terms of legislative or prescriptive practice, among about 90 States that have responded to the UNSG, the majority provides for so-called treaty-based U.J. in their domestic law. As summarised by the UNSG in his first report,

> [i]t was noted, at least in one case, by a Government that its courts had universal jurisdiction over any crime falling within the category of international or cross-border crimes, such as genocide, war crimes, crimes against humanity, torture, money-laundering, piracy and drug trafficking (Rwanda). In another instance, it was noted that universal jurisdiction was not enshrined in the law, while observing further that domestic legal rules and judicial practice had not adopted the principle (Lebanon). In most cases, however, references were made to penal or criminal codes, codes of

---

[104] Slovakia (A/C.6/64/SR.12, para. 65); Finland (A/C.6/64/SR.12, para. 92; A/C.6/66/SR.13, para. 29); Belgium (A/C.6/64/SR.12, para. 103; A/C.6/65/SR.11, para. 43); Liechtenstein (A/C.6/64/SR.13, para. 28; A/C.6/65/SR.12, para. 37); Italy (A/C.6/64/SR.13, para. 45); the Czech Republic (A/C.6/65/SR.11, para. 16; A/C.6/66/SR.77); the Netherlands (A/C.6/65/SR.11, para. 60; A/C.6/66/SR.13, para. 46); the United Kingdom (A/C.6/66/SR.13, para. 25); Ireland (A/C.6/66/SR.13, para. 41);

[105] ICJ (*Nicaragua v. U.S.*), Judgment of 27 June 1986, para. 184, *supra* note 64.

criminal procedure and specific legislation which had given
effect to international obligations, as providing the basis for
the exercise of universal jurisdiction.[106]

In other words, U.J. legislation or prescription with no treaty basis
is exceptionally rare at the present stage. What is worse, if the legislative
or prescriptive practice of States is mainly treaty-based U.J. provisions,
judicial practice implementing such provisions is more rare among the
States that have responded to the UNSG. As summarised from the responses by the UNSG in his first report,

> [i]n some instances, it was noted that there had been no cases
> of application of universal jurisdiction (e.g., Armenia, Bo-
> livia, Chile, the Czech Republic, El Salvador, Estonia,
> Kenya, Malta, Peru, Slovenia), that no prosecutions had been
> pursued under legislation providing for universal jurisdiction
> (e.g., New Zealand), that the courts rarely exercised it (e.g.,
> Republic of Korea), or that no one had been convicted since
> the legislation containing crimes for which universal juris-
> diction would be asserted entered into force (e.g., Azerbai-
> jan, the Netherlands). It was also noted that there had been
> no cases in which extradition had been requested on the basis
> of universal jurisdiction (e.g., Peru).[107]

The number of States that reported cases in relation to U.J. to the
UNSG is very limited, including Peru, Belgium, China, Denmark, France,
Rwanda, the Netherlands, South Korea and Switzerland. It should be
noted that in the very few judicial cases reported by these States, often
one or two mainly relate to the execution of treaty-based U.J. provisions
in domestic law.

9.5. Concluding Remarks

In my observation, outside the context of the relevant treaties in relation
to the fight against international crimes, what can be safely said at the
present stage is that the principle of universal jurisdiction may have crys-
tallised in customary international law as a whole, but it is hard to say that
its definition, scope and application are clear in customary international
law. Perhaps this reflects the common understanding of the issue of universal jurisdiction among States in the U.N. General Assembly at the pre-

---

[106] A/65/181, para. 34.
[107] A/65/181, para. 55.

sent stage. Many arguments are simply publicists' teachings, staying at the level of legal doctrine in international law. In this matter, we should be prudent and cautious, not confusing *lex lata* with *lex ferenda*. Whether, and how, to make such principles a reality in customary international law depends on the will and actual practice of States. In this regard, it is hoped that more States will express their views or submit their legislative or judicial information to the Sixth Committee of the U.N. General Assembly.

Nevertheless, it should be noted that the international community has woken up during the past decade. With the emergence of a common understanding of universal jurisdiction in the U.N. General Assembly and a growing practice of universal jurisdiction, new customary international law on its definition, scope and application could be formalised in a relatively short period.

10

The International Criminal Court
and Immunities under International Law
for States Not Party to the Court's Statute

Claus Kreß[*]

10.1.   Introduction

The international law of immunities is *en vogue*. It has been at the heart of two recent judgments of the International Court of Justice ('ICJ')[1], has been the subject of two recent resolutions adopted by the *Institut de Droit International* ('IDI')[2], and is one of the topics to which the International

---

[*]   **Claus Kreß** (Dr. jur. Cologne; LL.M. Cantab.) is Professor for Criminal Law and Public International Law. He holds the Chair for German and International Criminal Law and he is Director of the Institute of International Peace and Security Law at the University of Cologne while he rejected calls to the University Regensburg and the Max-Planck-Institute for International, European and Regulatory Procedural Law in Luxembourg. His prior practice was in the German Federal Ministry of Justice on matters of criminal law and international law. Since 1998 he has been representing Germany in the negotiations regarding the International Criminal Court. He was member of the Expert Group on the German Code of Crimes under International Law (2000/2001) and he acted as War Crimes Expert for the Prosecutor General for East Timor (2001), as Head of the ICC's Drafting Committee for the Regulations of the Court (2004) and as a sub-coordinator in the negotiations on the crime of aggression. Claus Kreß is co-editor of several law journals, including the Journal of International Criminal Justice. He is Life Member of Clare Hall College at the University of Cambridge and Member of the Academy of Sciences and Arts of Northrhine-Westfalia.

[1]   International Court of Justice, *Jurisdictional Immunities of the State (Germany v. Italy: Greece Intervening)*, Judgment, 3 February 2012, available at http://www.legal-tools.org/doc/674187/; ICJ, *Case Concerning the Arrest Warrant of 11 April 2000 (Democratic Republic of the Congo v. Belgium)*, Judgment, 14 February 2002, ICJ Reports 2002, p. 3, available at http://www.legal-tools.org/doc/c6bb20/; the international law of immunities was also touched upon in International Court of Justice *(Djibouti v. France: Case Concerning Certain Questions of Mutual Assistance in Criminal Matters)*, Judgment, 4 June 2008, ICJ Reports 2008, p. 177, available at http://www.legal-tools.org/doc/7b6a80/.

[2]   Institut de droit international, *Resolution on the Immunity from Jurisdiction of the State and of Persons Who Act on Behalf of the State in case of International Crimes,*

Law Commission ('ILC') is currently addressing its attention.[3] All of these developments have sparked, as one would suspect, a considerable amount of scholarly writing.[4]

Napoli Session 2009, Third Commission, available at http://www.idi-iil.org/idiE/resolutionsE/2009_naples_01_en.pdf, last accessed on 17 July 2012; Institut de droit international, *Les immunités de juridiction et d'exécution du chef d'Etat et de gouvernement en droit international*, Vancouver Session 2001, Thirteenth Commission, available at http://www.idi-iil.org/idiF/resolutionsF/2001_van_02_fr.PDF, last accessed on 17 July 2012.

[3] For a summary of the work, see International Law Commission, *Report on the Work of its sixty-third session*, A/66/10, paras. 102–203 (Chapter VII – Immunity of State officials from foreign criminal jurisdiction); for the first three reports of Special Rapporteur Roman Anatolevich Kolodkin, see International Law Commission, *Third Report on immunity of State officials from foreign criminal jurisdiction*, 24 May 2011, A/CN.4/646; *Second report on immunity of State officials from foreign criminal jurisdiction*, 10 June 2010, A/CN.4/631; *Preliminary report on immunity of State officials from foreign criminal jurisdiction*, 29 May 2008, A/CN.4/601; for a voluminous memorandum prepared by the Secretariat at the request of the ILC, see International Law Commission, Immunity of State officials from foreign criminal jurisdiction, 31 March 2008, A/CN.4/596.

[4] The following is a selection of more recent publications; for a leading treatise of the subject as a whole, see Lady Hazel Fox, *The Law of State Immunity*, second ed., Oxford University Press, Oxford, 2009; for a most thorough monograph on international immunity rights and international criminal law, see Helmut Kreicker, *Völkerrechtliche Exemtionen. Grundlagen und Grenzen völkerrechtlicher Immunitäten und ihre Wirkungen im Strafrecht* (two volumes), Duncker and Humblot, Berlin, 2007; for two other recent monographs, see Rosanne van Alebeek, *The Immunity of States and their Officials in International Criminal Law and International Human Rights Law*, Oxford University Press, Oxford, 2008; Ellen L. Lutz and Caitlin Reiger (eds.), *Prosecuting Heads of State*, Cambridge University Press, Cambridge, 2009; for another detailed study, see Advisory Committee on Issues of Public International Law, *Advisory Report on the Immunity of Foreign State Officials*, Advisory Report No. 20, 2011, available at http://www.rijksoverheid.nl/documenten-en-publicaties/rapporten/2011/10/19/advies-inzake-de-immuniteit-van-buitenlandse-ambtsdragers.html, last accessed on 17 July 2012; for some important shorter analyses, see Chimène I. Keitner, "Foreign Official Immunity and the 'Baseline' Problem", in *Fordham Law Review*, 2011–2012, vol. 80, p. 605; Joanne Foakes, "Immunity for International Crimes? Developments in the Law on Prosecuting Heads of States in Foreign Courts", in *Chatham House briefing paper*, IL BP 2011/02; Beth Stephens, "Abusing the Authority of the State: Denying Foreign Official Immunity for Egregious Human Rights Abuses", in *Vanderbilt Journal of Transnational Law*, 2011, vol. 44, p. 1163; Dapo Akande and Sangeeta Shah, "Immunities of State Officials, International Crimes, and Foreign Domestic Courts", in *European Journal of International Law*, 2010, vol. 21, p. 815; Mary Margaret Penrose, "The Emperor's Clothes: Evaluating Head of State Immunity Under

It would be pretentious to confront the subject as a whole within the limited scope of a chapter as this. I shall therefore narrowly confine my considerations to one single facet of the broad theme, and shall discuss two closely interrelated questions pertaining to international law immunity rights in proceedings before the International Criminal Court ('ICC').[5] The first question is whether international law immunities of States not party to the Statute of the ICC ('Statute') prevent the latter from exercising its jurisdiction over an incumbent Head of State, Head of Government, Foreign Minister and certain other holders of high-ranking office of such a State. Only if this first question is answered in the negative does the second question arise, which is whether such international law of im-

---

International Law", in *Santa Clara Journal of International Law*, 2009–2010, vol. 7, p. 85; Gionato Piero Buzzini, "Lights and Shadows of Immunities and Inviolability of State Officials in International Law: Some Comments on the *Djibouti v. France* Case", in *Leiden Journal of International Law*, 2009, vol. 22, p. 455; Mark A. Summers, "Diplomatic Immunity Ratione Personae: Did the International Court of Justice Create a New Customary Law Rule in *Congo v. Belgium*?", in *Michigan State Journal of International Law*, 2007–2008, vol. 16, p. 459; Natalino Ronzitti, "L'immunità funzionale degli organi stranieri dalla giurisdizione penale: Il caso Calipari", in *Rivista di diritto internatzionale*, vol. XCI, 2008, p. 1033; Sarah M. H. Nouwen, "The Special Court for Sierra Leone and the Immunity of Taylor: The *Arrest Warrant* Case Continued", in *Leiden Journal of International Law*, 2005, vol. 18, p. 645; Philippe Sands, "International Law Transformed? From Pinochet to Congo?", in *Leiden Journal of International Law*, 2003, vol. 16, p. 37; Antonio Cassese, "When May Senior State Officials be Tried for International Crimes? Some Comments on the Congo v. Belgium Case", in *European Journal of International Law*, 2002, vol. 18, p. 853; Steffen Wirth, "Immunity for Core Crimes? The ICJ's Judgment in the Congo v. Belgium Case", in *European Journal of International Law*, 2002, vol. 13, p. 877; Andrea Bianchi, "Immunity versus Human Rights: The Pinochet Case", in *European Journal of International Law*, 1999, vol. 10, p. 237; Christian Dominicé, "Quelques observations sur l'immunité de jurisdiction pénale de l'ancien Chef d'Etat", in *Révue Générale de Droit International Public*, 1999, vol. 103, p. 297.

5   Specifically on (aspects relating to) those questions, see Dapo Akande, "The Legal Nature of Security Council Referrals to the ICC and its Impact on Al Bashir's Immunities", in *Journal of International Criminal Justice*, 2009, vol. 7, p. 333; Paola Gaeta, "Does President Al Bashir Enjoy Immnuity from Arrest?", in *Journal of International Criminal Justice*, 2009, vol. 7, p. 315; Robert Uerpmann-Wittzack, "Immunität vor Internationalen Strafgerichtshöfen", in *Archiv des Völkerrechts*, 2006, vol. 44, p. 33; Dapo Akande, "International Law Immunities and the International Criminal Court", in *The American Journal of International Law*, 2004, vol. 98, p. 407; Vanessa Klingberg, "(Former) Heads of State Before International(ized) Criminal Courts: the Case of *Charles Taylor* Before the Special Court for Sierra Leone", in *German Yearbook of International Law*, 2003, vol. 46, p. 537.

munities precludes the ICC from requesting a State Party to arrest and surrender a suspect who falls into one the above-listed categories and who is sought by an arrest warrant issued by the Court.

Both questions have recently acquired, almost literally, burning practical relevance. On 4 March 2009, ICC Pre-Trial Chamber I decided that the Court is not prevented by Sudan's immunity under international law from exercising its jurisdiction over the incumbent President of this non-party State, Al Bashir.[6] More than two years later, on 12 and 13 December 2011, a differently composed Pre-Trial Chamber I specified (or, if this way to put it is preferred: added) in two decisions that the Court is also not precluded from requesting the States Parties of Chad and Malawi to arrest Al Bashir during his visit to their country and to surrender him to the Court.[7] Shortly thereafter, on 9 January 2012, the African Union Commission voiced its "deep regret" about, and its "total disagreement" with, the "ill-considered" and "self-serving" decisions of December 2011.[8]

---

[6] International Criminal Court, *The Prosecutor v. Omar Hassan Ahmad Al Bashir* ("*Omar Al Bashir*"), Decision on the Prosecution's Application for a Warrant of Arrest against Omar Hassan Ahmad Al Bashir, 4 March 2009, ICC-02/05-01/09-3, paras. 41–45, available at http://www.legal-tools.org/doc/e79f78/.

[7] Cour Pénal Internationale ('CPI'), Le Procureur International Criminal Court, *Le Procureur c. Omar Hassan Ahmad Al Bashir*, Décision rendue en application de l'article 87–7 du Statut de Rome concernant le refus de la République du Tchad d'accéder aux demandes de coopération délivrées par la Cour concernant l'arrestation et la remise d'Omar Hassan Ahmad Al Bashir, 13 December 2011, ICC-02/05-01/09-140, available at available at http://www.legal-tools.org/doc/c33d51/; International Criminal Court, *The Prosecutor v. Omar Hassan Ahmad Al Bashir*, Decision Pursuant to Article 87(7) of the Rome Statute on the Failure by the Republic of Malawi to Comply with the Cooperation Requests Issued by the Court with Respect to the Arrest and Surrender of Omar Hassan Ahmad Al Bashir, 12 December 2011, ICC-02/05-01/09-139, available at http://www.legal-tools.org/doc/476812/.

[8] Press Release of 9 January 2012 on the Decisions of Pre-Trial Chamber I of the International Criminal Court ('ICC') pursuant to Article 87(7) of the Rome Statute on the Alleged Failure by the Republic of Chad and the Republic of Malawi to Comply with the Cooperation Requests Issued by the Court with respect to the Arrest and Surrender of President Omar Hassan Al Bashir of the Republic of the Sudan; on file with the author.

10.2. The Decisions of 4 March 2009 and 12 December 2011 in the Case Against Al Bashir and the Dissent by the African Union Commission

In its decision of 4 March 2009, Pre-Trial Chamber I determined:

> [...] the current position of Omar Al Bashir as Head of a state which is not a party to the Statute, has no effect on the Court's jurisdiction over the present case.[9]

The Chamber advanced four considerations in support of this determination.[10] It referred, firstly, to the goal to end impunity, as referred to in the Statute's Preamble. Secondly, it quoted Article 27 of the Statute. Thirdly, it seemed to indicate that the sources of applicable law listed in Article 21(1)(a) of the Statute, if relied upon within the spirit of Articles 31 and 32 of the Vienna Convention on the Law of Treaties and Article 21(3) of the Statute, left no *lacuna* to be filled by reference to the sources listed in Article 21(1)(b) and (c) of the Statute.[11] Fourthly, the Chamber stated that:

> [...] by referring the Darfur situation to the Court, pursuant to article 13(b) of the Statute, the Security Council of the United Nations has also accepted that the investigation into the said situation, as well as any prosecution arising therefrom, will take place in accordance with the statutory framework provided for in the Statute, the Elements of Crimes and the Rules as a whole.

On 6 March 2009 and 21 July 2010, respectively, the Registry adhered to the Chamber's instruction to request all States Parties to arrest and surrender Al Bashir.[12]

In its decision of 12 December 2011, the same (but differently composed) Chamber found that the Republic of Malawi had failed to co-

---

[9] *Supra* note 6, para. 41.

[10] *Ibid.*, paras. 42–45.

[11] The formulation of the pertinent paragraph 44 of the decision is somewhat oracular so that its 'interpretation' involves a degree of speculation.

[12] International Criminal Court, *The Prosecutor v. Omar Hassan Ahmad Al Bashir ("Omar Al Bashir")*, ICC-02/05-01/09-7, Request to All States Parties to the Rome Statute for the Arrest and Surrender of Omar Al Bashir, 6 March 2009, available at http://www.legal-tools.org/doc/24341e/; Supplementary Request to All States Parties to the Rome Statute for the Arrest and Surrender of Omar Al Bashir, 21 July 2010, ICC-02/05-01/09-96, available at http://www.legal-tools.org/doc/66e485/.

operate with the Court by failing to arrest and surrender Al Bashir to the Court.[13] This finding is based on the convictions that: (1) there is no international law immunity of a State not party to the Statute in respect of proceedings before the ICC[14] and (2) the "unavailability of immunities with respect to prosecutions by international courts applies to any act of cooperation by States which forms an integral part of those prosecutions".[15] In support of the first conviction, the Chamber takes the view that there is a customary international law exception (even) to Head of State immunity when international courts seek a Head of State's arrest for the commission of crimes under international law and that therefore Article 98(1) of the Statute did not prevent the Court from proceeding with a request for surrender in the present case.[16] In support of the second conviction, the Chamber opines that:

> […] when cooperating with this Court and therefore acting on its behalf, States Parties are instruments for the enforcement of the *jus puniendi* of the international community whose exercise has been entrusted to this Court when States have failed to prosecute those responsible for the crimes within this jurisdiction.[17]

In its decision of 13 December 2011 pertaining to the Republic of Chad and presenting the same legal issues, the Chamber referred back to the decision it had rendered the day before[18] so that the legal analysis that follows in this chapter can focus on the latter decision.

The decisions of 12 and 13 December 2011 provoked a vigorous dissent by the African Union Commission. The press release dated 9 January 2012, by which this dissent was communicated to the world, contains the following passages:

---

[13] ICC, 2011, *supra* note 7, *in fine*.

[14] *Ibid.*, para. 18.

[15] *Ibid.*, para. 44.

[16] *Ibid.*, para. 43.

[17] *Ibid.*, para. 46.

[18] Cour Pénal Internationale, Le Procureur International Criminal Court, *Le Procureur c. Omar Hassan Ahmad Al Bashir*, Décision rendue en application de l'article 87-7 du Statut de Rome concernant le refus de la République du Tchad d'accéder aux demandes de coopération délivrées par la Cour concernant l'arrestation et la remise d'Omar Hassan Ahmad Al Bashir, 13 December 2011, ICC-02/05-01/09-140, para. 13, available at http://www.legal-tools.org/doc/c33d51/.

Following these Decisions of ICC Pre-Trial Chamber I, the
African Union Commission expresses its deep regret that the
decision has the effect of:

(i)   Purporting to change customary international law in re-
       lation to immunity ratione personae;

(ii)   Rendering Article 98 of the Rome Statute redundant,
       non-operational and meaningless;

(iii) Failing to address the critical issue of removal or non
       removal of immunities by the UN Security Council
       resolution 1593(2005), which referred the situation in
       Darfur to the ICC. [...]

As a general matter, the immunities provided for by international law apply not only to proceedings in foreign domestic
courts but also to international tribunals: states cannot con-
tract out of their international legal obligations vis-à-vis third
states by establishing an international tribunal. Indeed, contrary to the assertion of the ICC Pre-Trial Chamber I, article
98(1) was included in the Rome Statute establishing the ICC
out of recognition that the Statute is not capable of removing
an immunity which international law grants to the officials
of States that are not parties to the Rome Statute. This is because immunities of State officials are rights of the State
concerned and a treaty only binds parties to the treaty. [...]

The Security Council has not lifted President Bashir's immunity either; any such lifting should have been explicit,
mere referral of a "situation" by the UNSC to the ICC or requesting a state to cooperate with the ICC cannot be interpreted as lifting immunities granted under international law.
The consequence of the referral is that the Rome Statute, including article 98, is applicable to the situation in Darfur.[19]

The preceding summary demonstrates a sharp disagreement between Pre-Trial Chamber I and the African Union Commission. The latter's dissent does not clearly distinguish between the two legal questions I
have formulated in the introduction to my chapter and its precise legal
position leaves room for interpretation. My reading is that the Commission gives a negative answer already to my first question, although with
one qualification. The Commission appears to take the view that international law immunities of States not party to the Statute prevent the ICC

---

[19]   *Supra* note 8.

from exercising its jurisdiction over an incumbent Head of State, unless the Security Council has explicitly stipulated to the contrary in a resolution based on Chapter VII of the U.N. Charter. While Pre-Trial Chamber I has consistently given a negative answer to my first question, the above summary has revealed a remarkably different reasoning if the decision of 4 March 2009 is compared with the ones of 12 and 13 December 2011. While the latter postulate a special customary international law exception to international law immunities with respect to proceedings before international criminal courts, any reference to customary international law is conspicuously absent from the former decision. The former instead relies on the Statute itself and on the legal effect of a Security Council referral. The decisions of 4 March 2009 and of 12–13 December 2011 also differ in how they deal with my second introductory question. While this question has received an explicit treatment leading to a negative answer in the decisions of 12 and 13 December 2011, it was not specifically addressed in the decision of 4 March 2009. Yet, already in this decision the Chamber instructed the Registry to "proceed with a request for surrender" directed to all States Parties to borrow the words used in Article 98(1) of the Statute. In sum, the picture that results from the preceding summary is of considerable complexity.

10.3. Legal Analysis

In the following legal analysis, I shall make an attempt to disentangle the legal issues at stake.[20] In order to do so, I shall seek to clarify how Article 98(1) of the Statute relates to the international law of immunities outside the realm of the Statute, and how Article 98(1) of the Statute should be applied. I shall then separately explore the 'Security Council avenue' and the 'customary law avenue' to avoid the application of the prohibition contained in Article 98(1) of the Statute even in case of an incumbent Head of a State not party to the Statute. I shall begin, however, with a

---

[20] It builds on and develops Claus Kreß and Kimberly Prost, "Article 98", in Otto Triffterer (ed.), *Commentary on the Rome Statute of the International Criminal Court*, C.H. Beck/Hart/Nomos, second ed., 2008, pp. 1601–1614; and on Claus Kreß, "Commentary on the Decision on Immunity from Jurisdiction (Prosecutor v. Taylor)", in André Klip/Göran Sluiter (eds.), *Annotated Leading Cases of International Criminal Tribunls, Volume IX: The Special Court for Sierra Leone*, Intersentia, Antwerp-Oxford, 2006, p. 202.

brief comment on the first three considerations advanced in the Pre-Trial Chamber's decision of 4 March 2009.

10.3.1. An Initial Critique of the Decision of 4 March 2009

It is not clear from the wording of the pertinent passages of this decision whether the four considerations advanced in support of its conclusion on the immunity issue are to form one composite legal argument or whether they should provide for different legal bases to independently reach the same conclusion. While the latter reading of the decision is possible, it would not make for a convincing legal argument, because neither Article 27(2) of the Statute nor the Statute's Preamble can *per se* affect the (immunity) rights of those States which are not party to the Statute.[21] For this reason, it is also unhelpful in the specific context at stake to say that a Chamber of the ICC cannot resort to international law outside the realm of the Statute where the latter does not leave a *lacuna*. The Statute as such simply cannot give a comprehensive legal answer to a question that implies the rights of States not party to it. It follows that the persuasiveness of the decision of 4 March 2009 depends on the strength of the reference to the Security Council referral. Unfortunately, the Pre-Trial Chamber did not develop what I shall call the 'Security Council avenue'.

10.3.2. Negotiating Article 98(1) of the ICC Statute

As we have seen, the African Union Commission, in its protest against the decisions of 12 and 13 December 2011, relied heavily on Article 98(1) of the Statute and this provision is indeed relevant when it comes to the arrest of the Head of a State not party to the Statute for the purpose of the latter's surrender to the ICC. According to the African Union Commission,

> [A]rticle 98(1) was included in the Rome Statute establishing the ICC out of recognition that the Statute is not capable of

---

[21] The Pre-Trial Chamber's reference to the Preamble may have been influenced by a very similar reference made by Dapo Akande in his important and influential article Akande, 2004, *supra* note 5, pp. 423–424. Contrary to the Pre-Trial Chamber, however, Akande carefully confines the legal effect *per se* of both the Preamble and Article 27 of the ICC Statute to the legal relationship between the Court and States Parties and between States Parties.

> removing an immunity which international law grants to the
> officials of States that are not parties to the Rome Statute.[22]

This statement requires some qualification.

While it is true that the drafters of Article 98(1) of the Statute[23] were certain that a provision of the Statute could not take away a right under international law of a State not party to it, the inclusion of Article 98(1) of the Statute does not express the drafter's recognition of a customary international law immunity for the Head of such States that would prevent the Court from exercising its jurisdiction or at least prevent it from requesting such a person's surrender to a State Party. Instead, Article 98(1) of the Statute has been carefully worded so as to avoid any view on this question of general international law.[24]

Perhaps it is useful to recall the drafting history of Article 98(1) of the Statute. The issue of conflicting immunities was a rather late arrival in the negotiations on Part 9 and even the 1998 Draft Statute did not explicitly refer to the matter.[25] One group of delegations took the view that developments in general international law had substantively reduced, if not eliminated, immunities with respect to crimes under international law with respect to proceedings before the ICC. However, on the insistence of some other delegations a provision on possibly conflicting immunities was included. Yet, this inclusion did not occur, as consensus could not be reached on the existence of certain immunities under general international law. In Rome, there was simply no time for such a debate and so the obvious way out was to not take a purely procedural decision on the matter and instead to include an open-ended reference to general international law as it exists at the given moment in time.

It is perhaps also worth stating that those delegations which were sceptical about the inclusion of Article 98(1) of the Statute eventually saw merit in having this provision. They felt that there is little evidence in State practice that immunity rights pertaining to State or diplomatic prem-

---

[22] *Supra* note 8.

[23] Having been the member of the German delegation to the Rome Conference, who was in charge of the negotiations on Part 9 of the Statute, I was among those drafters.

[24] See Akande, 2004, supra note 5, p. 656.

[25] Article 87, Option 2(e) of the 1998 Draft Statute can be read as to contain an implicit reference to the matter; for the formulation, see Kreß and Prost, 2008, *supra* note 20, p. 1602, marginal note 1.

ises or property had suffered from an exception pertaining to investigative or other measures relating to proceedings for crimes under international law. They also recognised that Article 27(2) of the Statute does not cover those rights. This explains why, perhaps surprisingly for those not present in Rome, State or diplomatic immunities concerning property were the main driving force behind Article 98(1) of the Statute, and this explains why the term 'third State' in Article 98(1) of the Statute refers not just to States not party to the Statute, but to any State other than the requested State.[26]

One important first conclusion can be drawn from the drafting and negotiation history of Article 98(1) of the Statute. In and of itself, this provision provides no basis for a presumption that a certain international law immunity exists. This holds even truer with respect to an international law immunity covering a certain category of persons. In the same vein, it follows that the interpretative presumption that a treaty provision should retain an independent scope of application is inapplicable in the special case of Article 98(1) of the Statute because, at least with respect to the "State and diplomatic immunity of a person", there was a widespread expectation and hope among the drafters that the open-ended reference to international law in Article 98(1) of the Statute would leave the prohibition formulated herein "redundant, non-operational and meaningless" to borrow the words used by the African Union Commission.

10.3.3. The Purpose and the Operation of Article 98(1) of the ICC Statute and a Further Critique of the Decision of 4 March 2009

The purpose of Article 98(1) of the Statute is to prevent a State Party from being confronted by a conflict between the duties; on the one hand, to co-operate with the Court, and, on the other hand, to respect the international law immunities of other States. Yet, as the preceding summary of the drafting history was to demonstrate, there was uncertainty in Rome on the extent to which any such conflict could at all arise, and Article 98(1) of the Statute is no more than a procedural device to avoid a conflict of duties in case there should be one.

---

[26] *Ibid.*, p. 1602, marginal note 9.

The way this procedural device has been construed is remarkable, because it is the Court that has been entrusted by the drafters with the competence to determine, as the cases arise, whether or not a request to co-operate could place the State Party concerned in a situation of conflicting duties. This decision is reflected in the wording of Article 98(1) of the Statute because the prohibition contained therein is directed to the Court. The latter may proceed with a request for surrender or assistance only after it has determined that the requested State could not run into a conflict of duties as a result of the request. Rule 195, sub-Rule 1, of the Rules of Procedure and Evidence confirms that this is the way Article 98(1) is meant to operate because this sub-rule requires the State Party concerned to provide the Court with "any information relevant to assist the Court in the application of Article 98".[27]

It is noteworthy that the drafters of Article 98(1) of the Statute and of Rule 195, sub-Rule 1, of the Rules of Procedure and Evidence were fully aware that the Court would be able to make an authoritative determination only *vis-à-vis* States Parties, and that States not party would not be bound by any decision of the Court under Article 98(1) of the Statute. This provision therefore implies the remarkable decision by States Parties to entrust the Court with the power to make a decision about the existence or non-existence of "legal obligations [of those States] under international law with respect to the State or diplomatic immunity of a person or property". Article 98(1) of the Statute therefore provides a powerful piece of evidence for the determination of States Parties to establish a system of collective justice with a strong vertical component. It would seem that a good number of States Parties have accurately translated the procedural scheme in Article 98(1) of the Statute into their respective piece of implementing legislation. The fact that some other States Parties may have acted differently is no sufficient reason to consider the emergence of a subsequent practice deviating from the texts of Article 98(1) of the Statute and Rule 195, sub-Rule 1, of the Rules of Procedure and Evidence.[28]

---

[27] For the same view, see Akande, 2004, *supra* note 5, pp. 431–432, who, in addition, mentions Article 119(1) of the Statute in this context.

[28] For a collection of country reports on the implementation of the co-operation duties flowing from the Statute, see Claus Kreß, Bruce Broomhall, Flavia Lattanzi, and Valeria Santori (eds.), *The Rome Statute and Domestic Legal Orders. Volume II: Constitutional Issues, Cooperation and Enforcement*, Nomos/ilSirente, Baden-Baden/Ripa di Fagnano Alto, 2005; for States which have legislated in line with Arti-

In its decision of 12 December 2011, the Pre-Trial Chamber fully captures the way Article 98(1) of the Statute is meant to apply when it states that "[t]he Republic of Malawi did not respect the *sole* authority of this Court to decide whether immunities are applicable in a particular case [emphasis added]".[29] It is impossible to give similar praise to the decision of 4 March 2009 issued by the same but differently composed Pre-Trial Chamber. In the five paragraphs of the latter decision dealing with the immunity issue, there is no mentioning of Article 98(1). In defence of this silence, it cannot be said that those paragraphs only deal with my first introductory question as to whether the Court may exercise its jurisdiction over the Head of a State not party to the Statute and that those paragraphs do not concern the triangular legal relationship between the Court, the State Party to whom a request is made, and the non-State party that is the sole subject matter of Article 98(1) of the Statute. To the contrary, the decision of 4 March 2009 goes well beyond my first introductory question and squarely addresses the above-mentioned triangular relationship by directing the Registrar to prepare co-operation requests for States Parties to arrest and surrender Al Bashir. The decision of 4 March 2009 should therefore have addressed my second introductory question, and to not have even begun to do so constitutes a significant omission.[30] The 12 December 2011 decision must therefore be read as the subsequent and laudable attempt to fill a regrettable gap in the earlier decision of the same Chamber.

---

cle 98(1) of the Statute, see, by way of example, Canada (Kimberly Prost and Darryl Robinson, *ibid.*, pp. 61–62), Germany (Claus Kreß and Jan MacLean, *ibid.*, p. 140; New Zealand (Juliet Hay, *ibid.*, pp. 254–255); for States whose implementing legislation would seem to leave room for a national decision in conflict with that made by the Court, see again by way of example, Australia (Helen Brady, *ibid.*, pp. 18–19); Switzerland (Jürg Lindemann and Olivier Thormann, *ibid.*, p. 440); United Kingdom (Peter Lewis, *ibid.*, p. 463).

[29] ICC, 2011, *supra* note 7, para. 11.

[30] For the same critique, see Akande, 2009, *supra* note 5, p. 337; even irrespective of the missing analysis of Article 98(1) of the Statute, the five paragraphs of the 4 March 2009 decision dealing with the immunity issue are of a deplorably poor quality compared to the importance and sensitivity of the question.

10.3.4. The Immunities Covered by Article 98(1) of the Statute

As was stated before, Article 98(1) of the Statute deals with international law[31] of immunities with respect to persons or properties, and the concern for the latter category of immunities was the driving force behind its inclusion in the Statute. The example that figured most prominently in the negotiations was the customary inviolability of diplomatic premises as codified in Article 22 of the Vienna Convention on Diplomatic Relations.

As far as persons are concerned, the term 'State immunity' in Article 98(1) of the Statute requires some explanation. In the more recent scholarly debate, an argument has been made that, contrary to what was stated by the ICJ in the *Djibouti v. France* case[32], a clear conceptual distinction should be drawn between State immunity in civil proceedings and immunity of State officials *ratione materiae* in criminal proceedings.[33] The sophisticated considerations underlying this argument do certainly have merit and the ICJ has made it clear in its 3 February 2012 judgment on the *Jurisdictional Immunities of the State* case that the international law of immunities may recognise this distinction.[34] Yet, the postulated distinction cannot be made with respect to the term 'State immunity' in Article 98(1) of the Statute because this provision is part of the legal framework for criminal proceedings and because the latter term explicitly also refers to persons. The term 'State immunity' in Article 98(1) of the Statute therefore covers the international law immunity *ratione materiae* of a State official.

---

[31] The reference to "obligations under *international* law [emphasis added]" makes it plain that Article 98(1) of the Statute does not address domestic legal order immunities.

[32] ICJ, 2008, *supra* note 1, p. 242, para. 188.

[33] Gionato Piero Buzzini, "Lights and Shadows of Immunities and Inviolability of State Officials in International Law: Some Comments on the *Djibouti v. France* Case", in *Leiden Journal of International Law*, 2009, vol. 22, p. 463, drawing on Natalino Ronzitti, "L'immunità funzionale degli organi stranieri dalla giurisdizione penale: Il caso Calipari", in *Rivista di diritto internatzionale*, vol. XCI, 2008, p. 1039.

[34] International Court of Justice, *Jurisdictional Immunities of the State (Germany v. Italy: Greece Intervening)*, Judgment, 3 February 2012, para. 91, available at http://www.legal-tools.org/doc/674187/; for an excellent analysis of the limited importance of this judgment for the international legal situation in criminal proceedings, see Helmut Kreicker, "*Die Entscheidung des Internationalen Grichtshofs zur Staatenimmunität - Auswirkungen auf das (Völker-) Strafrecht?*", in *Zeitschrift für Internationale Strafrechtsdogmatik*, 2012, vol. 7, p. 116.

It must further be asked whether the term 'State immunity' also covers the international law immunity *ratione personae* of Heads of State, Heads of Government, Foreign Ministers and certain other holders of high-ranking office of such a State. This was at the heart of the ICJ's judgment in the *Arrest Warrant* case.[35] While the ICJ did not elaborate in this case on the distinction between the international law immunities *ratione materiae et personae* of State officials in criminal proceedings, it emphasised this distinction in the subsequent *Djibouti v. France* case.[36] The distinction between international immunities *ratione materiae et personae* would also seem to be generally accepted in State practice and in international legal scholarship.[37] Important and generally recognised as it thus is, the distinction between the international immunity of persons in criminal proceedings *ratione materiae et personae* does not require the interpreter of Article 98(1) of the Statute to confine this provision's concept of 'State immunity of a person' to international law immunities *ratione materiae*. While both the scope and the rationale of the two types of immunities are different, the Special Rapporteur of the ILC on the subject of "immunity of State officials from foreign criminal jurisdiction" is right to say that "[t]he State stands behind both the immunity *ratione personae* of its officials from foreign jurisdiction and their immunity *ratione materiae*".[38] It is therefore warranted to construe the term of 'State immunity of a person' in Article 98(1) of the Statute so as to cover both international law immunities *ratione materiae et personae*. To do otherwise would have the odd consequence that the most powerful international law immunity, and so the one most likely to give rise to the conflict of duties that Article 98(1) of the Statute seeks to avoid, would, except for the diplomatic immunity *ratione personae*, remain uncovered. The resulting *lacuna* would then have to be filled by applying either the concept of 'State

---

[35] I shall not in this essay explore the meaning to be given to the words "certain other holders of high-ranking office of such a State" which the ICJ used in ICJ, 2002, *supra* note 1, pp. 20–21, para. 51.

[36] ICJ, 2008, *supra* note 1, pp. 240–244, paras. 181–197.

[37] By way of example, see, for the practice of the United States of America, Harold Hongju Koh, "Foreign Official Immunity After *Samantar*: A United States Government Perspective", in *Vanderbilt Journal of Transnational Law*, 2011, vol. 44, pp. 1153–1154; for a useful exposition of the distinction, which he states is "usually drawn", see Roman Anatolevich Kolodkin, *Preliminary report on immunity of State officials from foreign criminal jurisdiction*, 29 May 2008, A/CN.4/601, paras. 78–83.

[38] Kolodkin, *ibid.*, para. 94.

immunity of a person' or that of 'diplomatic immunity of a person' by way of analogy to, for example, Heads of State.[39] Instead of resorting to this complicated and artificial solution, it is suggested to interpret the term 'State immunity of a person' in Article 98(1) of the Statute so that it covers both international law immunities *ratione materiae et personae*.

10.3.5. A Short Digression: Article 98(1) and the Immunity Rights of States Parties

It is perhaps useful to restate that the scope of application of Article 98(1) of the Statute is not confined to the triangular legal relationship between the Court, a State Party to whom a request is made, and a State not party to the Statute.[40] Rather, the provision also covers the situation where the request for arrest and surrender concerns an official of a 'third' State Party present on the territory of another State Party (to whom a request from the Court is directed) or where the request for co-operation other than surrender is directed to the State or diplomatic property of a 'third' State Party which is located on the territory of another State Party (to whom the Court has directed its request).[41]

In the first situation, the prohibition contained in Article 98(1) of the Statute will remain redundant, non-operational and meaningless because the 'third' State Party concerned has already waived its immunity right by virtue of his acceptance of Article 27(2) of the Statute. It is not convincing to interpret this provision more narrowly to the effect that it applies only to the legal relationship between the Court and States Parties.[42] If such an interpretation were accepted, Article 27(2) of the Statute would enable the Court to issue an arrest warrant against a national of a

---

[39] For an illuminating argument on the importance of the diplomatic immunity *ratione personae* for the international law immunity *ratione personae* in general, see Mark A. Summers, "Diplomatic Immunity Ratione Personae: Did the International Court of Justice Create a New Customary Rule in *Congo v. Belgium*?", in *Michigan State Journal of International Law*, 2007–2008, vol. 16, p. 459.

[40] For a different, albeit unconvincing view, see Paola Gaeta, "Official Capacity and Immunities", in Antonio Cassese, Paola Gaeta and John R.W.D. Jones (eds.), *The Rome Statute of the International Criminal Court: A Commentary*, Oxford University Press, Oxford, 2002, p. 991; Gaeta, 2009, *supra* note 5, p. 328.

[41] Akande, 2004, *supra* note 5, p. 423; Kreß and Prost, 2008, *supra* note 20, p. 1606, marginal note 9.

[42] For a different view, see Kreicker, 2007, *supra* note 4, p. 1391.

State Party otherwise protected by an international law immunity, but Article 98(1) of the Statute would still require the Court to obtain a waiver of immunity from this State Party before it could issue a request to arrest or surrender to another State Party on whose territory the person sought is present. In light of the fact that the Court has no enforcement powers and that the State Party whose official is sought by an ICC arrest warrant will typically be reluctant to co-operate with the Court when a higher ranking official is sought by it, the need to obtain a waiver of immunity from this State Party would often pose an insurmountable obstacle to the surrender of the person concerned to the Court. This means that the practical effect of Article 27(2) of the Statute would be largely nullified if this provision governed only the relationship between the Court and the national State Party of the suspect. To avoid such nullification in light with the Statute's overarching aim to end impunity, the waiver contained in Article 27(2) of Statute must extend to the triangular relationship between the Court, the requested State Party and the 'third' State Party.[43]

The situation is different with respect to, say, the diplomatic premises of a 'third' State Party because such property is not covered by the waiver contained in Article 27(2) of the Statute. Here, Article 98(1) of the Statute may require the Court, depending on its evaluation of the existing general international law, to first turn to the 'third' State Party in order to obtain its 'co-operation for the waiver of the immunity'.

10.3.6. Article 98(1) of the Statute and International Law Immunities of Persons of States Not Party to the Statute

Having clarified the legal ground so far, I shall now turn my attention to the burning question raised by the case against Al Bashir before the ICC. It concerns the international immunity right of a State not party to the Statute with respect to its incumbent Head of State. As the African Union Commission rightly states, the immunity at stake is that *ratione personae*.[44] In its judgment on the *Arrest Warrant* case, the ICJ recognised that

---

[43]   This argument has already been well made by Akande, 2004, *supra* note 5, pp. 423–425.

[44]   The case would in addition concern the immunity *ratione materiae* of the State of Sudan with respect to acts of its Head of State if *Al Bashir*'s conduct, which forms the subject matter of the proceedings before the Court, were to be qualified as official for the purposes of the international law on immunities. Despite its most significant practical importance, I shall not deal with this controversial question of qualification in

the international immunity protection *ratione personae* is subject to an exception for crimes under international law that are prosecuted in domestic criminal proceedings. On the basis of this decision, the non-application of the prohibition contained in Article 98(1) of the Statute requires an exception from the immunity right *ratione personae* of the State of Sudan, which is specifically designed to cover the proceedings before the ICC.

There are two conceptually distinct avenues to arrive at such an exception. The first one is to rely on the legal effect of the Security Council referral of the situation of Darfur (Sudan) to the Court. This avenue was alluded to, but not explained in any detail, by the Pre-Trial Chamber in its decision of 4 March 2009. The second one is to refer to a customary international law exception to otherwise existing international law immunities of persons for the specific purpose of criminal proceedings before an international criminal court. This avenue was chosen by the Pre-Trial Chamber in its decisions of 12 and 13 December 2011. The African Union Commission rejected both avenues.

In the analysis that follows, I shall explore both possible avenues. In doing so, I shall keep my two introductory questions in mind, and shall each time distinguish between the bipartite legal relationship between the Court and the State not party to the Statute, and the triangular legal relationship between the Court, the State Party to whom a request is made, and the third State not party to the Statute.

10.3.6.1. The 'Security Council Avenue' for Arriving at an Exception to the International Law Immunity *Ratione Personae*

The African Union Commission rightly accepts that the Security Council, based on its powers under Chapter VII of the U.N. Charter, may decide that otherwise existing international law immunity rights do not apply

---

this essay and I shall also not deal with the equally important related question, whether an international criminal law exception from the international immunity protection *ratione materiae* in cases of an alleged crime under international law exists under customary international law. Such an exception would cover both foreign domestic and international criminal proceedings and it could, within its reach, make the prohibition of Article 98(1) of the Statute "redundant, non-operational and meaningless". Suffice it to say that such an exception would not solve the issue in the case of *Al Bashir* that goes beyond the reach of the customary international exception in question.

with respect to certain proceedings before the ICC. The Commission, however, holds that such a decision must be taken explicitly. This view is unconvincing. Nothing in the U.N. Charter and more particularly in its Chapter VII makes the validity of such a decision by the Security Council dependent on the fact that is has been expressed explicitly. Nor is the ICC bound by its Statute and more particularly by Article 98(1) to accept a Security Council decision on the non-applicability of an immunity right only if this decision has been made explicitly. Whether or not the Security Council has decided that an otherwise existing international law immunity shall not apply with respect to certain proceedings before the ICC, is therefore a matter of construction of the relevant Security Council resolution.

Security Council Resolution 1593 of 31 March 2005[45], by which the Council referred the situation in Darfur to the ICC, does not contain a provision that deals explicitly with the international immunity rights of the State of Sudan. The second operative paragraph of the resolution, which is based on Chapter VII of the U.N. Charter, reads as follows:

> *Decides* that the Government of Sudan and all other parties to the conflict in Darfur, shall cooperate fully with and provide any necessary assistance to the Court and the Prosecutor pursuant to this resolution and, while recognizing that States not party to the Rome Statute have no obligation under the Statute, urges all States and concerned regional international organizations to cooperate fully.

As we have seen, the Pre-Trial Chamber, in its decision of 4 March 2009, took this to mean that:

> [...] the Security Council of the United Nations has also accepted that the investigation into the said situation, as well as any prosecution arising therefrom, will take place in accordance with the statutory framework provided for in the Statute, the Elements of Crimes and the Rules as a whole.

This is a sensible inference in light of the fact that the Security Council not only referred the situation in Darfur to the Court, but that it also required the State of Sudan to "cooperate fully" with the Court. By borrowing the terms used in Article 86 of the Statute, the Security Council expresses its intention to place the State of Sudan in a legal situation

---

[45] S/RES/1593 (2005), 31 March 2005.

analogous to that of a State Party for the purposes of the proceedings that result from the referral. It would go too far to demand that the Security Council goes one step further and specifies that the Court should proceed as if Article 27(2) of the Statute applied to the State of Sudan. Rather, this effect is implied in the resolution.[46] This holds all the more true as the Security Council could not be under any doubt that the Court would wish to focus its investigation on those allegedly most responsible for the crimes and that its investigation would thus likely concentrate on high ranking officials of the State of Sudan.[47]

The question remains whether the Security Council's implicit decision to render inapplicable any international law immunity of the State of Sudan for the proceedings resulting from the referral extends beyond the relationship between the Court and the State of Sudan to the triangular relationship between the Court, a State Party requested to co-operate with the Court, and the State of Sudan. According to one commentator, this is not the case.[48] Under this analysis, the Court was legally empowered to issue an arrest warrant against Al Bashir, but, in accordance with Article 98(1) of the Statute, it should have obtained a waiver of immunity from the State of Sudan before requesting a State Party to arrest and surrender this high level suspect. This position is unconvincing. The better view flows naturally from the above-explained interpretation of Article 27(2) of the Statute.[49] The same interpretation must hold true when the Security Council, acting under Chapter VII of the U.N. Charter, places a State not party to the Statute in a legal situation analogous to that of a State Party.[50]

---

[46] This argument has already been well put by Akande, 2009, *supra* note 5, pp. 340–342.

[47] Helmut Kreicker, "Der Präsident des Sudan vor dem Internationalen Strafgerichtshof – ein Verstoß gegen das Völkerrecht? Überlegungen zur völkerrechtlichen Immunität von Staatsoberhäuptern anlässlich des Haftbefehlsantrages gegen Omar al-Bashir", in *Humanitäres Völkerrecht – Informationsschriften*, 2008, vol. 21, pp. 161–162.

[48] Gaeta, 2009, *supra* note 5, p. 329.

[49] *Supra* Section 10.3.5.

[50] For the correct view, see again Akande, 2009, *supra* note 5, pp. 340–342; Kreicker, 2008, *supra* note 47, p. 163, argues that, whatever the correct interpretation of Article 27(2) of the Statute is, Resolution 1593 (2005) implies the decision to render any international law immunity of the State of Sudan inapplicable also for the purpose of an arrest executed by a requested State Party. For this reason alone, the prohibition contained in Article 98(1) of the Statute is irrelevant in the case of *Al Bashir*. It must be presumed, so the argument goes, that the Security Council wished to act consistently

To conclude, the Pre-Trial Chamber, in its 4 March 2009 decision, alluded to a possible avenue to overcome any immunity challenge by the State of Sudan both for the Court's arrest warrant against Al Bashir and any subsequent request by the Court to a State Party to arrest and surrender Al Bashir. It is thus particularly unfortunate that the Chamber presented its argument in such a superficial and incomplete fashion.

10.3.6.2. The 'Customary Law Avenue' for Arriving at an Exception to the International Law Immunity *Ratione Personae*

As we have seen, in its decisions of 12 and 13 December 2011, the Pre-Trial Chamber did not remedy the shortcomings of the 4 March 2009 decision issued by the same (but differently composed) bench by setting out the 'Security Council avenue' in a comprehensive manner. Instead, it followed the 'customary law avenue' to explain that Al Bashir does not enjoy immunity before the Court and that the latter could request Malawi and Chad to arrest and surrender the suspect without the need to first obtain a waiver of immunity from Sudan pursuant to Article 98(1) of the Statute. There is much more than a technical difference between the two explanations offered by the same Chamber. While the 'Security Council avenue' is open only in case of a Security Council referral, the 'customary law avenue' does not require Security Council action. It could be availed whenever the Court may exercise its jurisdiction over an incumbent Head of State not party to the Statute in accordance with Article 12(2) of the Statute. For this practical reason alone, it is important to give close attention to the 'customary law avenue' for setting aside any international law immunities of incumbent Heads of State, Heads of Government, Foreign Ministers and certain other holders of high-ranking office of States not party to the Statute. Such an exception would apply to proceedings before the ICC and enable authorities of a State Party to arrest and surrender a suspect falling into one of the aforementioned categories when trying to adhere to such a request made by the Court.

10.3.6.2.1. The Relationship between the ICC and the State of Sudan

Importantly, the Pre-Trial Chamber, when setting out the 'customary law avenue' in its decision of 12 December 2011, did not challenge the ICJ's

---

by not only activating the ICC's jurisdiction, but by also eliminating any potential key obstacle to an effective exercise of this jurisdiction over those most responsible.

decision in the *Arrest Warrant* case that incumbent Heads of States, Heads of Governments, Foreign Ministers and certain other holders of high-ranking office enjoy immunity *ratione personae* in criminal proceedings in a foreign State even in cases of an alleged crime under international law. Instead, the Pre-Trial Chamber set out a customary law exception from the immunity right *ratione personae* for the specific and limited purpose of proceedings before an international criminal court. The Pre-Trial Chamber could feel encouraged by the ICJ's decision in the *Arrest Warrant* case to draw such a distinction between national and international criminal proceedings for crimes under international law. In that case, the ICJ held that:

> [...] an incumbent or former Minister of Foreign Affairs may be subject to criminal proceedings before certain international criminal courts, where they have jurisdiction. Examples include the International Criminal Tribunal for the former Yugoslavia, and the International Criminal Tribunal for Rwanda, established pursuant to Security Council resolutions under Chapter VII of the United Nations Charter, and the future International Criminal Court created by the 1998 Rome Convention. The latter's Statute expressly provides, in Article 27, paragraph 2, that 'immunities or special procedural rules which may attach to the official capacity of a person, whether under national or international law, shall not bar the Court from exercising its jurisdiction over such a person.[51]

It is well known that this passage is an *obiter dictum* and that the Court included it in its judgment without adducing State practice based on *opinio juris* in support of it and without in any other way explaining and justifying its content. These facts, however, do not warrant the following suggestion:

> [T]he statement by the ICJ that international immunities may not be pleaded before certain international tribunals must be read subject to the condition (1) that the instruments creating those tribunals expressly or implicitly remove the relevant immunity, and (2) that the state of the official concerned is bound by the instrument removing the immunity.[52]

---

[51] ICJ, 2002, *supra* note 1, pp. 25–26 (Nr. 61).

[52] Akande, 2004, *supra* note 5, p. 418.

Whether or not correct as a description of the existing law, this is simply not what the ICJ has said. To the contrary, the ICJ's *dictum*, on the face of it, supports the distinction drawn by the Pre-Trial Chamber and only if one reads the ICJ's 'international criminal courts *dictum*' as it is worded, it substantially adds to the same Court's separate 'waiver *dictum*' that immunity *ratione personae* does not apply in a case of waiver of that immunity.[53]

The ICJ's 'international criminal courts *dictum*', in its literal form, had been followed and developed by the Special Court for Sierra Leone in its 2004 *Charles Taylor* jurisdiction decision. Therein, the Special Court held:

> [T]he principle seems now established that the sovereign equality of states does not prevent a Head of State from being prosecuted before an international criminal tribunal or court.[54]

Interestingly, even the Special Rapporteur of the ILC on the subject of "immunity of State officials from foreign criminal jurisdiction", who has otherwise formulated cautious views (to put it rather mildly), holds the opinion that:

> [i]mmunity from international criminal jurisdiction appears to be fundamentally different from immunity from national criminal jurisdiction.[55]

China has made a similar statement in the Sixth Committee of the United Nations General Assembly in 2008. The relevant sentence reads as follows:

> Immunity from criminal jurisdiction of a foreign State was not the same as immunity from international criminal jurisdiction such as that of the International Criminal Court, and the two should not be linked.[56]

---

[53] "[T]hey [the high-ranking State officials qualifying for immunity *ratione personae*] will cease to enjoy immunity from foreign jurisdiction if the State which they represent or have represented decides to waive that immunity"; ICJ, 2002, *supra* note 1, p. 25.

[54] Special Court for Sierra Leone, *Prosecutor v. Charles Ghankay Taylor*, Decision on Immunity from Jurisdiction, 31 May 2004, SCSL-2003-01-I, para. 52, http://www.legal-tools.org/doc/3128b2/, last accessed on 3 October 2012.

[55] Kolodkin, 2008, *supra* note 37, para. 103.

[56] A/C.6/63/SR.23, 21 November 2008, para. 35.

10.3.6.2.1.1. Principles

This, of course, provokes the question why international criminal proceedings should be seen as being "fundamentally different" from their national counterparts. In fact, there would be no real difference at all if international proceedings were simply the collective exercise of State rights to conduct national proceedings.[57] Such a delegation model, however, is not the most convincing manner to conceptualise international criminal justice *stricto sensu*. Instead, international criminal law in the true (and narrow) sense of the word is ultimately based on the idea of a *jus puniendi* of the international community as a whole and, as a matter of principle, the exercise of this *jus puniendi* is therefore primarily entrusted not to States, but to organs of the international community.[58] Those organs constitute the direct embodiment of the 'collective will' and offer the best guarantee that the enforcement of international community values does not lead to notably hegemonic-abuses. This does not rule out the power of States to exercise the *jus puniendi* of the international community in the case of crimes under international law, but it explains the possibility that an international criminal court, which acts as an organ of the international community in conducting proceedings for crimes under international law, has wider powers than a national criminal court, which acts as a mere fiduciary of the common good.

Yet, not every international criminal court qualifies as an organ of the international community. It is fairly clear, for example, that France and Germany cannot create an organ of the international community by setting up a joint criminal court on the basis of a bilateral treaty.[59] The ICJ is likely to have alluded to this fact by confining its "international tribunals *dictum*" to "*certain* international criminal courts" [emphasis added] and it is a shortcoming of the 12 December 2011 decision of the Pre-Trial Chamber not to have accordingly confined its 'customary law avenue'. This brings us to the question of which international criminal courts may

---

[57] For such a view, see Akande, 2004, *supra* note 5, p. 417.

[58] International criminal law *stricto sensu* must ultimately be rooted in customary international law of a general nature; for the full exposition of this view, see Claus Kreß, "International Criminal Law", in Rüdiger Wolfrum (ed.), *The Max Planck Encyclopedia of Public International Law*, vol. V, Oxford University Press, Oxford, 2012, paras. 10–14.

[59] Up to this point, I agree with Nouwen, 2005, *supra* note 4, p. 656.

qualify as organs of the international community.[60] On an abstract level, it can be said that only those courts should count, which can make a convincing claim to directly embody the 'collective will'. This is certainly the case with international criminal tribunals set up by the Security Council and the same should hold true for international criminal tribunals which, as is the case with the Special Court for Sierra Leone, act with that Council's blessing. The case of the ICC is more difficult whenever this Court's exercise of jurisdiction has not been triggered by a Security Council referral. The obvious argument not to treat the ICC as an organ of the international community is the lack of (quasi-)universal adherence to the ICC Statute. On the other hand, it is impossible to deny that the ICC Statute constitutes a legitimate attempt to establish an organ that directly exercises the international community's *jus puniendi*; the treaty has been negotiated on a universal level, it contains a standing invitation for universal adherence, and it does not display elements lending themselves to a (hegemonic) manipulation of the collective will. The fact that the ICC Statute has attracted a very significant number of ratifications, that the Security Council has referred two situations threatening international peace and security to the ICC for investigation, and that the United Nations have endorsed the vision behind Article 2 of the Statute through the conclusion of the Relationship Agreement between the International Criminal Court and the United Nations all add further weight to the view that the ICC in substance, and despite its formal creation by treaty, derives its mandate from the international community.

As a matter of principle, it is therefore possible to draw a distinction between national criminal proceedings and proceedings before the ICC with respect to international law of immunities.[61] It is important to add that the principles outlined so far are not merely scholarly speculations about 'natural' international law. Instead, the 'international community' is a point of reference, not only in the fourth preambular paragraph of the Statute, but also in Article 53 of the Vienna Convention on the Law of

---

[60] *Ibid.*, p. 657, does not believe a distinction between international criminal courts according to the criterion "international community involvement" possible. It is readily conceded that the elements listed in the following text do not amount to a watertight concept. Yet, they will yield sensible results in practice and, in addition, they may be refined in the future.

[61] For the contrary view, see Akande, 2004, *supra* note 5, p. 417; Nouwen, 2005, *supra* note 4, p. 657.

Treaties, in the famous ICJ's *dictum* on international obligations *erga omnes* in *Barcelona Traction* case[62], and in Article 48(1)(b) of the ILC's Articles on State Responsibility.[63] Furthermore, there does not appear to be disagreement with the concept that international criminal law *stricto sensu* protects values belonging to the international community as a whole.

Up to this point, I have demonstrated no more than the possibility that the ICC possesses wider powers than a national criminal court. It is now necessary to have a closer look at the issue of international law immunities, and here again I shall do so on the level of principles first. Almost by definition, international criminal law *stricto sensu* poses a fundamental challenge to traditional international law immunities. To criminalise what is typically state-related conduct tends to run counter to the old idea of shielding acts of States from foreign judicial scrutiny by means of a procedural bar. The difficulty of reconciling traditional international law immunities with the very idea of international criminal law *stricto sensu* becomes even more apparent once it is recognised that the use of the international criminal law instrument is most important in cases involving those persons who bear the greatest responsibility for what is typically macro-criminality. For, those persons will often be precisely the ones in respect of whom traditional immunity protection is strongest. It is therefore no surprise at all that the International Military Tribunal at Nuremberg addressed the challenge upfront and clearly articulated the idea that the acceptance of an international criminal law *stricto sensu* implies the retreat of traditional international law immunities:

> The principle of international law, which under certain circumstances, protects the representatives of a state, cannot be applied to acts which are condemned as criminal by international law. The authors of these acts cannot shelter themselves behind their official positions in order to be freed from punishment in appropriate proceedings. Article 7 of the Charter expressly declares:

---

[62] ICJ *(Belgium v. Spain: Barcelona Traction, Light and Power Company, Limited)*, Judgment, 5 February 1970, ICJ Reports 1970, p. 32, paras. 32–33, available at http://www.legal-tools.org/doc/75e8c5/.

[63] James Crawford (ed.), *The International Law Commission's Articles on State Responsibility. Introduction, Text and Commentaries*, Cambridge University Press, Cambridge, 2002, p. 276.

> "The official position of Defendants, whether as
> heads of State, or responsible officials in Government
> departments, shall not be considered as freeing them
> from responsibility, or mitigating punishment."

> On the other hand the very essence of the Charter is that in-
> dividuals have international duties which transcend the na-
> tional obligations of obedience imposed by the individual
> state. He who violates the laws of war cannot obtain immu-
> nity while acting in pursuance of the authority of the state if
> the state authorizing action moves outside its competence
> under international law.[64]

The Nuremberg precedent, therefore, clearly sent out the message
that international criminal law *stricto sensu* implies an important restriction on the traditional international law concept of State sovereignty.
While it has been, and continues to be, the key function of this concept to
allow scope for moral disagreement within a pluralist international legal
order, and while the international law concept of State sovereignty includes the protection of States against intrusions into their territory even
in cases of violations of international law[65], the rules of international
criminal law *stricto sensu* draw the red line beyond which State sovereignty no longer provides an impenetrable shield for those acting on behalf of the State.

The very idea of international criminal justice *stricto sensu*, which
is not simply a scholarly speculation about 'natural' international law, but
which has been accepted by States at Nuremberg, and which has been re-
vitalised by States since the 1990s, therefore poses a formidable challenge
to traditional international law immunities. Yet, the ICJ has authorita-
tively determined in the *Arrest Warrant* case that the traditional international law immunity *ratione personae* holds firm in national criminal proceedings for crimes under international law. It is oversimplified to explain
the *Arrest Warrant* case's qualification of the rigorously worded rejection
of immunities by the Nuremberg Tribunal on immunities by saying that,
in criminal proceedings in a foreign State, the right of the State of the of-

---

[64] International Military Tribunal (Nuremberg), Judgment and Sentences, 1 October
1946, in *The American Journal of International Law*, 1947, vol. 41, pp. 172 and 221.

[65] For a thoughtful exposition of this key function, see Brad R. Roth, *Sovereign Equality
and Moral Disagreement: Premises of a Pluralist International Legal Order*, Oxford
University Press, Oxford, 2011, pp. 3–130.

fender to sovereign equality trumps the *jus puniendi* of the international community. A more convincing explanation would refer to the sovereign right of States to be protected against an abusive (hegemonic) use of the criminal law instrument by another State in the name of the international community in those cases where such an abuse would have a seriously destabilising effect on international relations. The message underlying the *ratio decidendi* of the *Arrest Warrant* decision would seem to be that, when it comes to persons enjoying international law immunity *ratione personae*, the State sovereignty interest to be protected against an abusive use of the criminal law instrument by a foreign State carries more weight than the international community's interest in the fiduciary exercise of this community's *jus puniendi* by such a State. At this point, the balance may be struck differently in criminal proceedings before a judicial organ of the international community. Such an organ may, of course, also fail in its attempt to serve the interests of justice, but the institutional safeguards against an abuse of the criminal law instrument are such that the international community's interest weighs heavier. In light of the preceding observations, the truth would appear to lie between the two extremes of saying that the principle of sovereign equality has "no relevance to international criminal proceedings which are not organs of a state but derive their mandate from the international community"[66] and that "[i]t makes little difference whether foreign states seek to exercise this judicial jurisdiction unilaterally or through some collective body that the state concerned has not consented to".[67] The truth is that there is no 'fundamental' difference between proceedings for crimes under international law conducted by a State as the fiduciary of the international *jus puniendi* and by an international criminal court that qualifies as an organ of the international community. There is, however, an appreciable difference regarding the institutional framework for such proceedings that justifies treating the question of international law immunities differently in both *fora*.

10.3.6.2.1.2. Practice and *Opinio Juris* Up to the Pre-Trial Chamber's Decision

The considerations so far were situated at the level of general principles. Although those principles are not the result of scholarly speculation, but

---

[66] *Prosecutor v. Charles Ghankay Taylor*, 2004, *supra* note 54, para. 51.
[67] Akande, 2004, *supra* note 5, p. 417.

could be derived from international practice, they are not sufficient *per se* to demonstrate that the 'customary law avenue' is open under the *lex lata*. More specific practice based on *opinio juris* is needed to make the case. This does not mean, however, that the above highlighted principles are irrelevant to the question whether new customary international law has come into existence. The development of international criminal law since the 1990s provides clear evidence of the existence of what has been called 'modern custom'[68], the ascertainment of which usually involves a degree of deduction from broader principles such as those established above[69].[70] Where such principles clearly point in the direction of new customary law, the latter may crystallise without the need to identify a huge amount of more concrete State practice and verbal State practice (the latter being almost indistinguishable from *opinio juris*) and may largely take the place of hard State practice in the traditional sense. Modern custom may thus come into existence at a relatively high speed and without a voluminous body of hard practice confirming the respective rule. Importantly, such custom will, however, be relatively vulnerable to change if contrary hard practice occurs.[71]

---

[68] The literature on the topic is vast and I do not wish to reproduce a complete list of it here; for a very useful study with many further helpful references, see Anthea Elizabeth Roberts, "Traditional and Modern Approaches to Customary International Law: A Reconciliation", in *The American Journal of International Law*, 2001, vol. 95, p. 757; see also Anja Seibert-Fohr, "Unity and Diversity in the Formation and Relevance of Customary International Law: Modern Concepts of Customary International Law as a Manifestation of a Value-Based International Order", in Andreas Zimmermann and Rainer Hofmann (eds.), *Unity and Diversity in International Law*, Duncker and Humblot, Berlin, 2006, p. 257, 264–270.

[69] For some insightful reflections on the matter, see Matthias Herdegen, "Das 'konstruktive Völkerrecht' und seine Grenzen: die Dynamik des Völkerrechts als Methodenfrage", in Pierre-Marie Dupuy, Bardo Fassbender, Malcolm N. Shaw and Karl-Peter Sommermann (eds.), *Völkerrecht als Wertordnung* (*Common Values in International Law*); *Festschrift für* (*Essays in Honour of Christian Tomuschat*), N.P. Engel Verlag, Kehl, 2006, p. 899.

[70] On the crystallisation of war crimes committed in non-international armed conflicts, see Claus Kress, "War Crimes Committed in Non-International Armed Conflict and the Emerging System of International Criminal Justice", in *Israel Yearbook on Human Rights*, 2001, vol. 30, pp. 104–109.

[71] On "relative resistance to change" and customary international law, see Michael Byers, *Custom, Power and the Power of Rules*, Cambridge University Press, Cambridge, 1999, pp. 157–160.

In its analysis of State practice on this point, the Pre-Trial Chamber, like the Special Court for Sierra Leone before it[72], referred to Article 7 of the Charter for the Nuremberg Tribunal, Article 6 of the Charter for the Tokyo Tribunal, Principle III of the 1950 Nuremberg Principles, Article 7(2) of the ICTY Statute, Article 6(2) of the ICTR Statute and Article 7 of the 1996 ILC Draft Code of Crimes against the Peace and Security of Mankind.[73] One may wonder whether the Chamber was justified in relying on those documents despite the fact that they are all framed in terms of substantive law and thus do not directly address the immunity issue like Article 27(2) of the ICC Statute. While it is true that "[i]mmunity from criminal jurisdiction and individual criminal responsibility are quite separate concepts"[74] – so that the distinction drawn in the two paragraphs of Article 27 of the ICC Statute marks progress in the clarity of drafting, it is also true that the two concepts have not been neatly distinguished in the earlier practice of international criminal law. [75] Beginning with the Nuremberg judgment, as can be seen from the above citation[76], the immunity issue has been addressed in conjunction with the statutory provision that confirms the applicability of the substantive law. It is therefore in line with the historic development that the ILC states in its commentary on Article 7 of the 1996 Draft Code of Crimes against the Peace and Security of Mankind:

> [...] the absence of any procedural immunity with respect to prosecution or punishment in appropriate judicial proceedings is an essential corollary of the absence of any substantive immunity or defence [77]

---

[72] *Prosecutor v. Charles Ghankay Taylor*, 2004, *supra* note 54, paras. 45–47.

[73] ICC, 2011, *supra* note 7, paras. 24–32.

[74] Kolodkin, 2008, *supra* note 37, para. 66.

[75] This point has not received sufficient attention in Nouwen, 2005, *supra* note 4, pp. 660–668.

[76] *Cf.* the citation preceding fn. 64.

[77] Para. 6 of the Commentary on Article 7, in Gabrielle Kirk McDonald and Olivia Swaak-Goldman (eds.), *Substantive and Procedural Aspects of International Criminal Law*, vol. II, part 1, Kluwer Law International, The Hague/London/Boston, 2000, p. 354; in fn. 3, the ILC further notes:

> Judicial proceedings before an international criminal court would be the quintessential example of appropriate judicial proceedings in which an individual could not invoke any substantive or proce-

It is also true that the language of the texts cited by the Pre-Trial Chamber seems to extend to incumbent Heads of States *et cetera* without drawing a distinction as to whether the State concerned can be said to have waived its immunity rights in proceedings before the jurisdiction concerned. In light of this, the Pre-Trial Chamber was justified to refer to the aforementioned documents as relevant verbal State practice.

At the same time, it must be recognised that, until the *Charles Taylor* decision, this verbal State practice did not yield any hard practice as regards the international immunity *ratione personae* with the one single exception of the ICTY's arrest warrant against the then incumbent Head of State Slobodan Milošević and the ICTY Trial Chamber's decision confirming the jurisdiction of the Tribunal.[78] The precedential value of the latter decision is somewhat weakened, however, by the fact that the *Milošević* decision did not confront the legal issue of the immunity *ratione personae* of the Federal Republic of Yugoslavia[79] as a distinct legal problem. To the contrary, the ICTY Trial Chamber placed the pertinent paragraphs of their decision under the title "Lack of competence by reason of his status as *former* President" (emphasis added). As a result, the decision does not clearly recognise that the *Milošević* precedent exceeds the denial of immunity *ratione materiae* concerning the conduct of a former Head of State before a judicial organ of the international community.

The only judicial decision that explicitly acknowledges setting such a precedent before the 12 December 2011 decision of the Pre-Trial Chamber is the Special Court for Sierra Leone's Decision on Immunity from Jurisdiction in the *Charles Taylor* case.[80] Importantly, this precedent, to the best of this commentator's knowledge, has not provoked a protest from Member States of the African Union or from any other State.

It is, of course, possible to have different views on these materials depending on the approach to the ascertainment of customary interna-

---

dural immunity based on his official position to avoid prosecution and punishment.

[78] ICTY, *Prosecutor v. Milošević*, Decision on Preliminary Motion, 8 November 2001, IT-99-37-PT, paras. 26–34, available at http://www.legal-tools.org/doc/f15771/.

[79] Importantly, the Federal Republic of Yugoslavia was not a member State of the United Nations at the time of *Milošević*'s indictment. The case can thus not be explained on the basis of an (indirect) waiver of immunity of the State concerned.

[80] *Prosecutor v. Charles Ghankay Taylor*, 2004, *supra* note 54.

tional law one believes to be the preferable one.[81] Under the modern positivist approach to customary international law, which I have set out above for reasons of methodological transparency, a weighty case can be made for the crystallisation of a customary international criminal law exception from the international law immunity *ratione personae* in proceedings before a judicial organ of the international community. The case builds, as has been developed in the course of the preceding observations, on the combined effect of a set of guiding principles pertaining to the concepts of 'international community' and 'international criminal law *stricto sensu*' as accepted by States over the last decades, on a consistent line of verbal State practice beginning with the Charter for the Nuremberg Tribunal, on the *Milošević* precedent before the ICTY (though with a somewhat limited effect), on the literal formulation of the 'international criminal courts *dictum*' of the ICJ in the *Arrest Warrant* case and on the culmination of all this in the *Charles Taylor* decision by the Special Court for Sierra Leone and the absence of State protest against this decision in any significant manner. However, it must be added that, according to my approach to the ascertainment of customary international law, this new customary norm has come into existence with a relatively high vulnerability to change because the hard practice that contributed to its crystallisation is fairly scarce.

It is therefore necessary to inquire whether subsequent State practice challenged the new customary law exception to State immunity before the 12 and 13 December 2011 decisions of Pre-Trial Chamber I. Clearly, Malawi and Chad have, through their conduct and their legal ob-

---

[81] For a different approach on the subject, see Penrose, 2009–2010, *supra* note 4, pp. 85–144, who makes the general critique that "modern courts dogmatically overemphasize the hollow written words relating to head of state immunity and ignore the empty actions or actual practice". There is no explaining away of the methodological difference between (for example) Penrose's approach and the one preferred in this chapter. Two specific comments, however, would seem in place. First, however one evaluates the international practice in point, since the issuance of the indictment in the *Milošević* case it is no longer possible to speak on 'empty actions'. Second, Penrose much overemphasises the fact that the Tokyo precedent on immunity, other than that of Nuremberg, does not include the Head of State. While the latter is true, there is nothing in the subsequent practice to suggest that Tokyo instead of Nuremberg should be followed upon as far as Head of State immunity is concerned. After all, the General Assembly solemnly endorsed the Nuremberg principles soon after the judgment and did not add any Head of State *caveat* pertaining to Tokyo.

servations before the Pre-Trial Chamber[82], posed such a challenge and the same is probably true for the State of Sudan given the latter's rigorous opposition to the proceedings before the Court. The opposing practice of three States cannot, however, on its own, turn back the development of customary international law as analysed before. It would be different, though, if all Member States of the African Union and, in particular, those Member States which are not party to the ICC Statute, had endorsed this challenge. At its thirteenth Ordinary Session (1–3 July 2009), the Assembly of the African Union, in its Decision 245(XIII) formulated one request and issued one decision on the subject-matter in question. The Assembly requested:

> [T]he Commission to convene a preparatory meeting of African States Parties at expert and ministerial levels but open to other Member States at the end of 2009 to prepare fully for the Review Conference of States Parties scheduled for Kampala, Uganda in May 2010, to address among others, the following issues, […].
>
> v.) Comparative analysis of the implications of the practical application of Articles 27 and 98 of the Rome Statute; […].

The Assembly decided:

> […] that in view of the fact that the request by the African Union [to defer the proceedings initiated against President Bashir] has never been acted upon, the AU Member States shall not cooperate pursuant to the provisions of Article 98 of the Rome Statute of the ICC relating to immunities, for the arrest and surrender of President Omar El Bashir of The Sudan; […].[83]

It is submitted that these formulations do not amount to the rejection of the 'customary law avenue' by all Member States of the African Union in a manner that should have prevented Pre-Trial Chamber I to declare this avenue open on 12 and 13 December 2011. The Assembly's request to the Commission to prepare a legal analysis does not express a legal position on the issue, but the wish to form such a position at a later stage. It is not easy to harmonise this wish with the decision that Member States of African Union shall not co-operate with the Court. On close in-

---

[82] For these observations, see CPI, 2011, *supra* note 7, para. 7; ICC, 2011, *supra* note 7, para. 8.

[83] Assembly/AU/Dec.245(XIII) Rev.1, paras. 8 and 10, 3 July 2009.

spection, however, this decision cannot be read as the articulation of precisely that legal position which the request to the Commission was meant to prepare. Instead, the decision is explicitly made "in view of the fact that the request by the African Union [to defer the proceedings initiated against President Bashir] has never been acted upon". It is thus (and somewhat curiously so) drafted as a political reaction to a prior (political) decision by the Security Council. It is therefore not possible to read a sufficiently clear, let alone unambiguous position of the Member States of the African Union into Decision 245 (XIII). This assessment is confirmed by the Report of the Second Ministerial Meeting on the Rome Statute of the International Criminal Court ('ICC') held on 6 November 2009 the pertinent passage of which states that,

> Articles 27 and 98 of the Rome Statute should be discussed by the Assembly of States Parties under the agenda item "stock taking" in order to obtain clarification on the scope and application of these Articles particularly with regard to non States Parties. In this regard, there is need to clarify whether immunities enjoyed by officials of non states parties under international law have been removed by the Rome Statute or not.[84]

While perhaps not drafted with the utmost legal precision, this passage clearly does not contain a legal position on our subject matter. Instead, the Ministers once more emphasised the "need to clarify" the law. This may reflect the fact that there appeared to be a lively discussion among Member States of the A.U. about the right course of action on the matter.[85] In sum, the practice of the Member States of the African Union before 12 December 2011 has not been strong enough to change the new customary law exception to the international law immunity *ratione materiae* despite the latter's vulnerability to change.

---

[84] African Union, Min/ICC/Legal/Rpt. (II), p. 4 (R. 4), as annexed to EX.CL/568 (XVI).

[85] For an illuminating overview, see Elise Keppler, "Managing Setbacks for the International Criminal Court in Africa", in *Journal of African Law*, 2012, vol. 56, pp. 4–6.

10.3.6.2.2. The Triangular Relationship Between the ICC, the Requested State and the State not Party to the Statute

At this stage of the analysis again, there is a need to distinguish between my two introductory questions. Therefore the question remains whether the 'customary law avenue' was also open within the above triangular relationship between the ICC, the requested States of Malawi and Chad, and the State of Sudan with respect to the arrest and surrender of Al Bashir. Pre-Trial Chamber I held that this was the case and it argued that,

> [...] when cooperating with this Court and therefore acting on its behalf, States Parties are instruments for the enforcement of the *jus puniendi* of the international community whose exercise has been entrusted to this Court when States have failed to prosecute those responsible for the crimes within this jurisdiction.[86]

This argument is situated at the level of principles and at this level it is convincing. While the State of arrest and surrender is formally exercising its national authority, it is on substance acting for the Court to assist the latter in the direct enforcement of the *jus puniendi* of the international community. For this reason, there is an important difference between the *Arrest Warrant* case, where a State conducts national criminal proceedings against a person suspected of having committed a crime under international law, and the Al Bashir case, where a State party to the Statute has been requested by the ICC to arrest and surrender a person suspected of having committed a crime under international law for proceedings before the Court. Pre-Trial Chamber I was therefore justified to believe that the principles underlying the customary law exception to the international law immunity *ratione personae* cover the triangular relationship in question.

There is, however, no precedent in hard practice covering this extension of the 'customary law avenue'. This raises the methodological question whether such a precedent is needed to defend the approach chosen by the Pre-Trial Chamber. At this juncture once more, there is certainly room for disagreement between reasonable international lawyers depending on how they draw the line between the necessary judicial refinement of rules of customary international law and inappropriate 'judi-

---

[86] ICC, 2011, *supra* note 7, para. 46.

cial legislation'. In my view, the extension of the 'customary law avenue' from the bilateral relationship between the Court and a State not party to the Statute to the triangular relationship in question does not constitute the recognition of a different rule of customary international law, but the delimitation of the scope of application of the same customary law exception to the international law immunity *ratione personae*. It is therefore submitted that, in extending the 'customary law avenue' to the triangular relationship in question, Pre-Trial Chamber I did not overstep the confines of what constitutes legitimate international judicial activity.

10.3.6.2.3. The Practice within the African Union Subsequent to the 12 and 13 December 2011 Decisions of Pre-Trial Chamber I

Up to this point of the legal analysis, I have sought to demonstrate that, on 12 December 2011, Pre-Trial Chamber I had a good, although not compelling, case to open the 'customary law avenue'. At the same time, I have recognised that the customary law exception underlying this avenue is not yet firmly grounded in the international legal order, but retains a relatively high vulnerability to change and has been challenged by at least three States. In light of this latter fact, I shall now turn to the practice within the African Union after 13 December 2011 to see whether this practice has 'closed the customary law avenue' shortly after it had been declared open.

On 9 January 2012, the African Union Commission published its Press Release criticising the decisions of Pre-Trial Chamber I of 12 and 13 December 2011, the reference of which has repeatedly been made in the course of this chapter.[87] This Press Release contains a protest against the 'customary law avenue' because the Commission expresses its "deep regret that the decisions rendered by Pre-Trial Chamber I on 12 and 13 December 2011 have the effect of [...] [p]urporting to change *customary* international law in relation to immunity *ratione personae*" [first emphasis added]. The African Union has, therefore, through one of its organs, rejected the opening of the 'customary law avenue'. This legal position cannot, however, be attributed to the Member States of the African Union, because the African Union possesses an international legal personality which is distinct from that of its Member States, and because nothing in

---

[87] *Supra* note 18.

the African Union's Constitutive Act suggests that the Commission is empowered to formulate and express its legal position on the international law of immunities on behalf of the Union's Member States.[88] It is also not possible to attribute the conduct of the individual members of the Commission to their national States because the Commission constitutes an integrated (and not an intergovernmental organ) of the African Union.

Finally, there is no evidence that the African Union's Assembly has subsequently endorsed the Commission's legal view. Quite the contrary, there is evidence of some instances of an African State practice to the contrary. On 23 January 2012, the High Court of Kenya issued a provisional warrant of arrest against Al Bashir and the Court based its decision of the request to arrest and surrender by the ICC.[89] In June 2012, the new President of Malawi, Joyce Banda, announced that the State would not host Al Bashir during the summit of the African Union. The Republic of Botswana supported Malawi's change of position and stated:

> The Government of Botswana is deeply concerned about the pressure exerted by the African Union Commission on the Government of Malawi to commit to hosting President Al Bashir at the forthcoming AU summit in July this year. Unfortunately, this pressure has consequently led to the Summit being moved to Addis Ababa, thus depriving Malawi to host the meeting. Botswana therefore condemns this action as it is inconsistent with the very fundamental principles of democracy, human rights and good governance espoused by the AU, and which Malawi upholds. It is our considered view that Malawi as a sovereign state has the right to make decisions it may deem necessary in fulfilment of her obligations under both the Rome Statute and the AU. In this regard, Botswana will take the opportunity at the forthcoming AU Summit to put its case across on this important matter of principle.[90]

In its most recent Decision on the Implementation of the Decisions on the International Criminal Court, the Assembly:

---

[88] In fact, as Keppler, 2012, *supra* note 85, vol. 56, p. 4, has shown, the stand taken by the African Union Commission was not shared by all Member States of the Union.

[89] A copy of the arrest is on file with the author.

[90] A copy of the Press Release of Botswana's Ministry of Foreign Affairs and International Cooperation of 12 June 2012 is on file with the author.

> [e]ndorses the recommendation of the Meeting of Ministers of Justice/Attorneys General to approach the International Court of Justice (ICJ), through the United Nations General Assembly (UNAG), for seeking an advisory opinion on the question of immunities, under international law, of Heads of State and senior state officials from States that are not Parties to the Rome Statute of ICC [sic] and this regard [sic], [r]equests the Commission to undertake further study on the advisability and implications of seeking such advisory opinion from ICJ [sic] and to report thereon to the Executive Council.[91]

This decision does no more than to restate the view of the Member States of the African Union that the immunity issue is in need of clarification and to point to a possible way to achieve it. There is thus clearly no unanimity within the African Union on the matter and it is likely that the debate in Africa will continue. Members of the civil societies are taking an active part in this debate and it remains to be seen whether their arguments may influence their governments. In Malawi, representatives of national civil society organisations issued a noteworthy statement on 9 June 2012 that contains the following passages:

> Informed that the Malawi government decided to not to host the African Union summit this July following AU's insistence that our government must accept the attendance of the Sudanese President, Omar Al Bashir in the face of a warrant of arrest from the International Criminal Court for war crimes charges in Darfur where thousands of people have been killed and displaced;

> Noting that earlier Sudan had already requested the AU to shift the summit to Ethiopia after President Joyce Banda indicated that Malawi would arrest al-Bashir if he came for the summit. This also followed equal sentiments by other Principled African countries such as South Africa, Botswana, Zambia and Tanzania against Omar Al Bashir's attendance of the Summit.

> Observing that while we have obligations to abide by decisions of the AU, we are also under obligation to other international agreements including the Rome Statutes;

---

[91] Assembly/AU/Dec.419(XIX), p. 1 (para. 3), 15/16.7.2012.

> Recognizing that the government arrived at the decision with
> the primary consideration of what is in the best interests of
> Malawians as part of its effort to reposition the country's im-
> age to the international community and in fulfilment of the
> international obligations placed on itself under the various
> international instruments our government has accented to or
> ratified.
>
> [...]
>
> Although it may be understood that the invested resources
> into the hosting of the 19th Summit of the AU has gone down
> the drain, we are still of the view that the decision is timely
> and beyond our government's control. More so, we believe
> that this painful decision demonstrates our government's
> commitment to defending its human rights record and the in-
> terests of Malawi against the potential economic gains asso-
> ciated with hosting the Summit.[92]

To summarise, the decisions of 12 and 13 December 2011 issued by
Pre-Trial Chamber I on the 'customary law avenue' have met with the
opposition of the African Union. In view of this practice, it cannot be said
that the two decisions have, as of yet, decisively contributed to consolidate the 'customary law avenue'. Quite to the contrary, the 'customary
law avenue' has come under quite severe stress soon after its opening.
Yet, this avenue has not been closed as a result of the African Union
Commission's protest because the latter has not been endorsed by the
Member States of the African Union. Instead, a number of those Member
States have recently made it clear that they are willing to execute the international arrest warrant against Al Bashir. For the time being, the 'customary law avenue' remains open without providing for an altogether safe
walking ground.

10.3.6.2.4. Another Short Digression: Some Remarks on the Practice of States Parties on the 'Customary Law Avenue'

In the foregoing sections, no distinction has been made between the practice of States Parties to the Statute and other States. There is an important

---

[92] The *Civil Society Statement on Malawi's Decision's to Withdraw from Hosting the 19th Summit of the African Union* of 9 June 2012 is on file with the author. The above citation does not correct a couple of typos in the text.

qualification to be added to this analysis. As explained above[93], Article 98(1) of the Statute operates in a remarkably vertical manner and Pre-Trial Chamber I rightly referred to the Court's "sole authority to decide whether immunities are applicable in a particular case".[94] In light of this verticality of the Statute's scheme, it may well be asked whether States Parties have agreed that the Court acts on their behalf when it comes to the formation or identification of a customary law exception to the international law immunity *ratione personae* for proceedings before the Court. Irrespective of the answer to this question, the Statute's vertical scheme at least implies a duty of States Parties to be loyal to the Court when the latter has made an attempt to clarify the relevant customary international law in a way that is not manifestly mistaken. Indeed, it would amount to a self-contradictory behaviour by States Parties to entrust the Court, by virtue of Article 98(1) of the Statute, with the duty to clarify the relevant customary international law and to then let the Court down once it has fulfilled this duty in a manner that is not manifestly erroneous. In light of the fact that the decisions of 12 and 13 December 2011 constitute an attempt to clarify the law which is not manifestly mistaken, the duty of loyalty which States Party owe to the Court with respect to its application of Article 98(1) of the Statute includes the reasoning underpinning these decisions.

10.4. Concluding Remarks

This chapter has set out and analysed two avenues to explain why the international law immunity *ratione personae* of States not party to the Statute is inapplicable before the ICC, and why this immunity does also not prevent the Court from requesting a State party to arrest and surrender a suspect, who is otherwise enjoying such an immunity. While the 'Security Council avenue' constitutes solid legal ground, the same cannot, as of yet, be said of the 'customary law avenue'. According to the view set out in this chapter, this avenue is now open, but it does not yet offer a solid walking ground due to the relative scarcity of hard practice in support of it and because of the African Union Commission's protest against its opening.

---

[93] *Supra* Section 10.3.3.

[94] ICC, 2011, *supra* note 7, para. 11.

I will not pretend that my defence of Pre-Trial Chamber I's opening of the 'customary law avenue' is a compelling one, and I seriously doubt that a compelling defence is possible at this stage of the development of the law. To the contrary, I believe that the current state of customary international law leaves room for disagreement between reasonable international lawyers. My modest ambition has been to show that the African Commission went much too far when it criticised the opening of the 'customary law avenue' by Pre-Trial Chamber I as "ill-considered".

At this final juncture, I wish to also add that the African Union Commission's portrayal of the decisions of 12 and 13 December 2011 as "self-serving" constitutes an unhappy formulation at best. In fact, it would have been the easier way out for Pre-Trial Chamber I to confine its reasoning to the 'Security Council avenue' in order to minimise the risk of any serious controversy with States not party of the Statute. For this reason alone it is hard to see why Pre-Trial Chamber I should have been misguided by institutional interests when it entered into the thorny terrain of customary international law. Very much to the contrary, the 'customary law avenue' is in full harmony with principles which have been solemnly referred to by States time and again since Nuremberg and which have been directing the development of international criminal law since then. Furthermore, the 'customary law avenue' makes the ICC less dependent on the Security Council in order to effectively exercise its jurisdiction over incumbent Heads of State not party to the Statute. Compared to the 'Security Council avenue', the 'customary law avenue' thus enables the Court to exercise its jurisdiction less asymmetrically and such an advance in the equal application of international criminal law is not "self-serving", but serves the legitimacy of the emerging system of international criminal justice. While this is, of course, a matter of speculation, the said advance in the equal application of international criminal law may well have been the most important motivation for Pre-Trial Chamber I on 12 December 2011 not to confine its reasoning to the confirmation of the 'Security Council avenue', but to also open the 'customary law avenue' and to even place it in the foreground.

Whether or not one agrees with the position taken by Pre-Trial Chamber I on the 'customary law avenue', this Chamber's decisions of 12 and 13 December 2011 have certainly moved the development to a law-crystallising point. At this important moment in time, the suggestion submitted by the Member States of the African Union to request the ICJ to render an advisory decision on the matter deserves the closest attention. This suggestion does not imply any disloyalty towards the ICC, but duly recognises the fact that the Court's "sole authority" under Article 98(1) of the Statute does not extend to States not party to the Statute. Of course, an advisory opinion of the ICJ would, by definition, not carry any binding legal force. The authority of the ICJ, however, is such that it would be difficult to criticise the ICC if it followed the advice rendered by the ICJ whatever its content. At the same time, the proceedings before the ICJ would provide all States with the opportunity to set out their *opinio juris* on the matter and the ICJ would be given the chance to clarify its somewhat oracular 'international criminal courts *dictum*' in the *Arrest Warrant* judgment.[95] This is not the place to enter into a debate about the technical details and the best timing for a request for an advisory opinion. It suffices to conclude that the Member States of the African Union are to be commended for having submitted a most constructive proposal to clarify the difficult legal question under scrutiny in this chapter.

In November 2008, China stated in the Sixth Committee of the United Nations General Assembly that the ILC's topic "Immunity of State officials from foreign criminal jurisdiction" is "an important one, in view of the need to maintain the international legal order and the stability of inter-State relations".[96] I believe that this statement holds true also with respect to the topic under consideration in this chapter. To conclude this chapter, I wish to add that the particular difficulty of the topic of immunities and international criminal law resides in the fact that, at times, the maintenance of the international legal order, on the one hand, and the stability of inter-State relations, on the other hand, may prove to be conflicting goals. Clearly, the international criminal proceedings against Al Bashir adversely affect the stability of the relations of all those States which support those proceedings, with the State of Sudan, as long as Al Bashir stays in power. At the same time, however, those criminal proceedings aim at the maintenance and at the strengthening of the *noyau dur* of the international legal order. The difficult policy question is therefore where to strike the balance. In its *Arrest Warrant* case, the ICJ gave preference to the stability of inter-State relations as far as national criminal proceedings and the international law immunity *ratione personae* are con-

---

[95] For this *dictum*, see ICJ, 2002, *supra* note 1.
[96] A/C.6/63/SR.23, 21 November 2008, para. 32.

cerned. I accept the wisdom of this judgment, not only on legal, but also on legal policy grounds. In its decisions of 12 and 13 December 2011, the Pre-Trial Chamber I of the ICC has followed the precedent set by the Special Court for Sierra Leone and has struck the balance differently as far as criminal proceedings before a direct judicial embodiment of the international community are concerned. I have attempted to show that this way of 'striking the balance' is defensible on legal grounds. I now wish to add that it seems convincing to so strike the balance on legal policy grounds. This legal policy view is, however, premised on the expectation that the scope of substantive international criminal law *stricto sensu* will remain strictly and narrowly confined, and that the ICC will refrain from 'progressively' developing this body of law without giving due consideration to the consequences in sensitive adjacent fields such as the law of immunities. The need for such caution is imperative, in particular, with respect to the interpretation of crimes against humanity.

Taken seriously, international criminal law *stricto sensu* comes at a price with respect to the stability of inter-State relations. I believe this price is worth paying, provided that the scope of application of substantive international criminal law *stricto sensu* will not be diluted, but remains confined to the conduct that constitutes a fundamental assault to the *noyau dur* of the international legal order.

INDEX

A

A.U.. *See* African Union
A.U.-E.U. Expert Report
  African concerns, 134
  concerns, 143
  recommendations, 135
  view of European states, 134
A.U.-E.U. Ministerial Troika, 197
Act concerning the Punishment of Grave
  Breaches of International
  Humanitarian Law, 158
act jure gestionis, 47
act jure imperii, 47
act of aggression
  actus reus, 110
  criminalisation, 107, *See*
    criminalisation of aggression
  criticism, 103
  definition, 101
  key issue, 101
  mens rea, 111
  purpose of criminalisation, 108
  purpose of defining, 104
action popularis, 143
Acts of Nuclear Terrorism, 171
Addis Ababa, 197, 198
African Union Commission, 233
aggression, 171
aircraft hijacking and unlawful acts
  against international air safety, 172
Akande, Dapo, 64
Al Bashir, Omar, 52, 260
Al-Adsani v. U.K., 89
Algeria, 200, 202
Alien Tort Statute, 82
Al-Qaida, 106
apartheid, 172
Argentina, 200, 202, 203, 210
Armenia, 201
Arrest Warrant case, 41
  absence of customary rule denying
    immunity, 80

absolute immunity for heads of state,
  61
difference with Al Bashir case, 257
immunities, 144
immunity from criminal jurisdiction of
  foreign nations, 50
legality of the exercise of universal
  jurisdiction, 195
sovereign immunity, principle of, 56
subsidiarity principle, 141
treaty-based crime, 88
Assembly of State Parties, 100
Assembly of the African Union
  Decision 245 (XIII), 256
  Ordinary Session (1–3 July 2009), 255
attacks with explosives, 172
Audencia Nacional, 141
Australia, 200, 201, 209
  War Crimes Act (1945), 165
Austria, 200, 201
aut dedere aut judicare, 81, 131, 168, 208
aut dedere aut punire, 151
Azerbaijan, 201, 203

B

BAI Guimei, 174
Banda, Joyce, 259
Barcelona Traction case, 42
  international obligation *erga omnes*,
    248
Bassiouni, M. Cherif, 171
  28 international crimes, 171
Beccaria, 176
Belarus, 201
Belgian Act on Punishment of Grave
  Breaches of International
  Humanitarian Law, 195
Belgium, 200, 201, 202
Belgium v. Senegal, 38
Bergsmo, Morten, 18
BIN Cheng, 79
Blair, Tony, 36
Bolivia, 201

OTHER VOLUMES IN THE
FICHL PUBLICATION SERIES

Morten Bergsmo, Mads Harlem and Nobuo Hayashi (editors):
Importing Core International Crimes into National Law
Torkel Opsahl Academic EPublisher
Oslo, 2010
FICHL Publication Series No. 1 (Second Edition, 2010)
ISBN 978-82-93081-00-5

Nobuo Hayashi (editor):
National Military Manuals on the Law of Armed Conflict
Torkel Opsahl Academic EPublisher
Oslo, 2010
FICHL Publication Series No. 2 (Second Edition, 2010)
ISBN 978-82-93081-02-9

Morten Bergsmo, Kjetil Helvig, Ilia Utmelidze and Gorana Žagovec:
The Backlog of Core International Crimes Case Files in Bosnia and Herzegovina
Torkel Opsahl Academic EPublisher
Oslo, 2010
FICHL Publication Series No. 3 (Second Edition, 2010)
ISBN 978-82-93081-04-3

Morten Bergsmo (editor):
Criteria for Prioritizing and Selecting Core International Crimes Cases
Torkel Opsahl Academic EPublisher
Oslo, 2010
FICHL Publication Series No. 4 (Second Edition, 2010)
ISBN 978-82-93081-06-7

Morten Bergsmo and Pablo Kalmanovitz (editors):
Law in Peace Negotiations
Torkel Opsahl Academic EPublisher
Oslo, 2010
FICHL Publication Series No. 5 (Second Edition, 2010)
ISBN 978-82-93081-08-1

Morten Bergsmo, César Rodríguez Garavito, Pablo Kalmanovitz and Maria Paula Saffon (editors):
Distributive Justice in Transitions
Torkel Opsahl Academic EPublisher
Oslo, 2010
FICHL Publication Series No. 6 (2010)
ISBN 978-82-93081-12-8

Morten Bergsmo (editor):
Complementarity and the Exercise of Universal Jurisdiction for Core International Crimes
Torkel Opsahl Academic EPublisher
Oslo, 2010
FICHL Publication Series No. 7 (2010)
ISBN 978-82-93081-14-2

Sam Muller, Stavros Zouridis, Morly Frishman and Laura Kistemaker (editors):
The Law of the Future and the Future of Law
Torkel Opsahl Academic EPublisher
Oslo, 2010
FICHL Publication Series No. 11 (2011)
ISBN 978-82-93081-27-2

Morten Bergsmo, Alf Butenschøn Skre and Elisabeth J. Wood (editors):
Understanding and Proving International Sex Crimes
Torkel Opsahl Academic EPublisher
Beijing, 2012
FICHL Publication Series No. 12 (2012)
ISBN 978-82-93081-29-6

Morten Bergsmo (editor):
Thematic Prosecution of International Sex Crimes
Torkel Opsahl Academic EPublisher
Beijing, 2012
FICHL Publication Series No. 13 (2012)
ISBN 978-82-93081-31-9

Terje Einarsen:
The Concept of Universal Crimes in International Law
Torkel Opsahl Academic EPublisher
Oslo, 2012
FICHL Publication Series No. 14 (2012)
ISBN 978-82-93081-33-3

All volumes are freely available as e-books on the FICHL homepage www.fichl.org. Printed copies may be ordered online at www.amazon.co.uk.

www.ingramcontent.com/pod-product-compliance
Lightning Source LLC
Chambersburg PA
CBHW071031200526
45161CB00005BA/274/J